Managing Complex Networks

Managing Complex Networks

Strategies for the Public Sector

edited by
Walter J.M. Kickert, Erik-Hans Klijn
and Joop F.M. Koppenjan

SAGE Publications
London • Thousand Oaks • New Delhi

SAGE Publications Ltd
6 Bonhill Street
London EC2A 4PU

SAGE Publications Inc
2455 Teller Road
Thousand Oaks, California 91320

SAGE Publications India Pvt Ltd
32, M-Block Market
Greater Kailash – I
New Delhi 110 048

British Library Cataloguing in Publication data

A catalogue record for this book is
available from the British Library

    ISBN 0 7619 5547 X
    ISBN 0 7619 5548 8 (pbk)

Library of Congress catalog card number 97-066130

Typeset by M Rules
Printed in Great Britain by The Cromwell Press Ltd,
Broughton Gifford, Melksham, Wiltshire

Contents

Part II Network Dynamics and Management

Contributors' Notes

Dr J.A. de Bruijn studied Dutch law and political science at Leiden University. From 1986 to 1992 he worked at the Department of Public Administration at Erasmus University Rotterdam. He received his PhD on a dissertation about economic subsidization 'The Ministry of Economic Affairs: an Instrumental and Organizational Analysis of the Use of Economic Subsidies' (VUGA, Den Haag, 1991). Now he works as a senior lecturer at the Faculty of Systems Engineering, Policy Analysis and Management of the Delft University of Technology. He publishes in the field of public administration and the internal management of public organizations.

Professor K.I. Hanf is a faculty member of the Department of Public Administration at the Erasmus University Rotterdam. He received his PhD in 1968. The title of his thesis was 'The Higher Civil Service in West Germany' (University Microfilm International, London). He is co-author and editor of *Interorganizational Policy Making* (with F.W. Scharpf, Sage, London, 1978). In early 1993 he was named part-time professor in the field of environmental management at Nijenrode University.

Professor E.F. ten Heuvelhof is Professor of Public Administration at the Delft University of Technology and the Department of Public Administration at the Erasmus University Rotterdam. He received his PhD in 1982. His thesis was entitled 'Towards an Empirical Policy Theory: Local Municipal/Council Policy-making with regard to New Local Neighbourhood Shopping Centres' (in Dutch, Amsterdam, 1982). His publications include works on the administrative aspects of physical planning and environmental policy.

Dr P.L. Hupe has been a lecturer in the Department of Public Administration at the Erasmus University Rotterdam. For several years he worked as a policy adviser in the Dutch civil service since 1986. He has published on issues of the welfare state, institutional analysis, and policy implementation, in particular in the field of socio-economics. His thesis, 'The Quality of Power: Minister De Uyl's Employment Plan in a Fivefold Perspective', was published in October 1992.

Professor W.J.M. Kickert studied experimental physics at Utrecht University and received his PhD in organization science from the Department of Business Administration at the Technical University Eindhoven with his thesis 'Organization of Decision-Making' (North Holland Elsevier, Amsterdam, 1980). He then joined the Department of Public Administration at the University of Nijmegen and subsequently worked at the Ministry of Education and Sciences, most recently as an adviser. In 1990 he was appointed Professor of Public Administration, specializing in public management, at Erasmus University Rotterdam.

Dr E.-H. Klijn studied public administration at the University of Twente and was employed as a researcher from 1984 to 1989 on the Faculty of Architecture at the Technical University Delft. He has been a lecturer since 1989 in the Department of Public Administration at Erasmus University Rotterdam. In 1996 he received his doctorate from Rotterdam with his thesis 'Rules and Governance in Networks: the Influence of Network Rules on the Restructuring of Post-war Housing'. His research interests and publications focus on policy networks, housing policy and public–private partnerships.

Dr J.F.M. Koppenjan worked until recently at the Department of Public Administration at Erasmus University Rotterdam. In 1993 he received his doctorate from Rotterdam with his thesis 'Managing the Policy-Making Process: A Study of Public Policy Formation in the Field of Home Administration' (in Dutch, VUGA, Den Haag). Since September 1996 he has worked as a lecturer at the Faculty of Systems Engineering, Policy Analysis and Management of the Technical University of Delft. His publications focus on policy processes, governance of policy projects and network management. His research interests lie in the field of intergovernmental relations, safety policy and the environment.

Professor L.J. O'Toole Jr. is Professor of Political Science and Senior Research Associate in the Institute of Community and Area Development at the University of Georgia (USA). He has published widely on the subjects of policy implementation, administrative theory and intergovernmental relations. Previously he served in the faculties of the University of Virginia and Auburn University.

Professor A.B. Ringeling studied political science at the Free University Amsterdam. In 1969 he joined the staff of Nijmegen University, initially as a member of the law faculty and later with the Institute for Political Science. He received his PhD in 1978 with his dissertation 'Policy Discretion of Civil Servants' (in Dutch, Samsom Uitgeverij, Alphen a/d Rijn). In 1981 he became a professor at Erasmus University Rotterdam where he teaches public administration, specializing in the study of public policy.

Dr L. Schaap studied public sciences at the University of Groningen. In 1989 he was appointed as a research assistant at Erasmus University's Department of Public Administration. Since 1993 he has worked there as a lecturer. He publishes in the field of the formation of regions and the history of Dutch public administration. He is currently working on his PhD thesis on the contribution of the theory of autopoetic social systems to problems with societal steering.

Dr G.R. Teisman is a senior lecturer at the Erasmus University Rotterdam in the Department of Public Administration. He has been Professor of Physical Planning at the Catholic University of Nijmegen since spring 1997. He received his PhD in September 1992. The title of his thesis was 'Complex Decision Making. A Pluricentric Perspective on Decision Making about Investments in Infrastructure.' He specializes in interorganizational management, policy making, physical planning, infrastructures and public works.

Dr C.J.A.M. Termeer studied agricultural engineering at the Agricultural University in Wageningen. From 1988 to 1993 she worked at Erasmus University's Department of Public Administration in Rotterdam. In 1993 she received her PhD with her thesis 'Dynamics and Inertia in the Dutch Manure Policies: a Study of Change Processes in the Pig Farming Network' (VUGA, Den Haag). In 1993 she was appointed as a lecturer at the Technical University Delft. Since June 1996 she has worked at the Ministry of Agriculture and Fisheries. She publishes on change processes, the agricultural network and environmental policy.

Dr M.J.W. van Twist studied the sciences of public and business administration at Erasmus University Rotterdam. Since 1989 he has been working at the Department of Public Administration as a research assistant and lecturer. In 1995 he received his PhD from Rotterdam with his thesis 'Verbal Renewal: Notes on the Art of Administrative Science.' At present he is a lecturer at the Faculty of Systems Engineering, Policy Analysis and Management of the Technical University Delft, where he teaches public management and policy science.

Foreword by Professor R.A.W. Rhodes

Britain and the Netherlands are both unitary states. Not for them the messy intergovernmental games of federal states. They have coherent policy making and effective central control. Unfortunately, the simplicities of formal-legal categories mislead as often as not. Britain and the Netherlands may be unitary states but they are also differentiated polities, operating through a multi-form maze of institutions which central government can steer only imperfectly and indirectly. 'Governance' is a defining characteristic of such differentiated polities.

Finer (1970: 3–4) treats government and governance as synonyms but in current use governance stands for a change in the meaning of government, referring to: a *new* process of governing; or a *changed* condition of ordered rule; or the *new* method by which society is governed. Inevitably, there are several contending meanings for the term. It refers to, for example, the minimal state; corporate governance; the new public management; and 'good governance' (see Rhodes, 1997: ch. 3). Here, *governance refers to self-organizing, interorganizational networks,* with the following characteristics.

1   Interdependence between organizations. Governance is broader than government, covering non-state actors. Changing the boundaries of the state means the boundaries between public, private and voluntary sectors become shifting and opaque.
2   Continuing interactions between network members, caused by the need to exchange resources and negotiate shared purposes.
3   Game-like interactions, rooted in trust and regulated by rules of the game negotiated and agreed by network participants.
4   No sovereign authority, so networks have a significant degree of autonomy from the state and are not accountable to it. They are self-organizing. Although the state does not occupy a sovereign position, it can indirectly and imperfectly steer networks.

R.A.W. Rhodes is Professor of Politics (Research) at the University of Newcastle upon Tyne and Director of the Economic and Social Research Council's Whitehall Research Programme. He is the author or editor of several books including recently (with Patrick Dunleavy, eds), *Prime Minister, Cabinet and Core Executive* (Macmillan, 1995); (with P. Weller and H. Bakvis, eds), *The Hollow Crown* (Macmillan, 1997); and *Understanding Governance* (Open University Press, 1997). He has published chapters in a great number of books and articles in such major journals as *British Journal of Political Science, European Journal of Political Research, Parliamentary Affairs, Political Studies, Public Administration, Public Administration Review* and *West European Politics*. He has been editor of *Public Administration* since 1986.

Interorganizational linkages are a defining characteristic of service delivery. The term 'network' describes the several interdependent actors involved in delivering services. These networks are made up of organizations which need to exchange resources (for example, money, authority, information, expertise) to achieve their objectives, to maximize their influence over outcomes, and to avoid becoming dependent on other players in the game. As British government creates agencies, bypasses local government, uses special-purpose bodies to deliver services, and encourages public–private partnerships, so networks become increasingly prominent among British governing structures. Governance is about managing such networks:

> Instead of relying on the state or the market, socio-political governance is directed at the creation of patterns of interaction in which political and traditional hierarchical governing and social self-organization are complementary, in which responsibility and accountability for interventions is spread over public and private actors. (Kooiman, 1993: 252)

Crucially, networks are *self-organizing*. At its simplest, self-organizing means a network is autonomous and self-governing:

> The control capacity of government is limited for a number of reasons: lack of legitimacy, complexity of policy processes, complexity and multitude of institutions concerned etc. Government is only one of many actors that influence the course of events in a societal system. Government does not have enough power to exert its will on other actors. Other social institutions are, to a great extent, autonomous. They are not controlled by any single superordinated actor, not even the government. They largely control themselves. Autonomy not only implies freedom, it also implies self-responsibility. Autonomous systems have a much larger degree of freedom of self-governance. Deregulation, government withdrawal and steering at a distance . . . are all notions of less direct government regulation and control, which lead to more autonomy and self-governance for social institutions. (Kickert, 1993c: 275)

In short, integrated networks resist government steering, develop their own policies and mould their environments. Central government is no longer supreme. The political system is increasingly differentiated. We don't live in unitary states but in 'the centreless society' (Luhmann, 1982: xv); in the polycentric state characterized by multiple centres. The task of government is to enable socio-political interactions; to encourage many and varied arrangements for coping with problems and to distribute services among the several actors. Such new patterns of interaction abound: for example, self- and co-regulation, public–private partnerships, cooperative management, and joint entrepreneurial ventures.

Governments can choose between governing structures. To markets and hierarchies, we can now add networks. None of these structures for authoritatively allocating resources and exercising control and co-ordination is intrinsically 'good' or 'bad'. The choice is a matter of practicality; that is, under what conditions does each governing structure work effectively? Bureaucracy remains the prime example of hierarchy or coordination by administrative order and, for all the recent changes, it is still a major way of delivering services. Privatization, marketing testing and the purchaser–provider split are examples of government using markets or quasi-markets to deliver services. Price competition is the key to efficient and better quality services. Competition and markets are now a fixed part of the governmental landscape. It is less widely recognized, especially in Britain, that government now works through networks characterized by trust and mutual adjustment. Governance is one such structure and this book addresses the key issue in governance: 'How do we manage networks?'

The governance approach and network management remain a minority interest in Britain and too few are aware of the pioneering work carried out by Walter Kickert, Jan Kooiman and their colleagues at the Erasmus University, Rotterdam. The 'governance club' research programme was set up in 1990, building on earlier work on administrative decision making. It focuses on policy making and governance in and of networks. Specifically, the group's theoretical work focuses on: policy instruments for governance, polycentric decision making, managing the policy process, the role of rules and perceptions in games and networks, network management and evaluating networks and their outcomes. Their empirical work covers technology policy, employment policy, agriculture, and intergovernmental relations. In collaboration with the publisher VUGA Uitgeverij BV in The Hague, the group edits a series on 'Networks, complexity and dynamics'. Unfortunately, few of these works are available for the English reader. This volume is invaluable, because it provides the first conspectus of their work in English (see also Kickert, 1993b; Kooiman, 1993; Klijn, Koppenjan and Termeer, 1995).

Normally, the literature on socio-cybernetics and governance contents itself with redescribing government and policy making. It provides insights, not tools. This book takes the argument a stage further by showing how governments can manage networks. It itemizes and illustrates a toolkit for managing networks. Table 10.1 summarizes the available tools and Chapters 6–8 explain the several strategies of intervention. Recently, I discussed the work of the Erasmus school at a conference. I was told their work was too abstract; 'they live in the clouds'. In this book, they come down to earth with a bang. They would be the first to admit that a lot remains to be done to expand and refine the toolkit of network management, but they have taken important early steps.

There is one important gap in their work. They focus on steering networks, adopting a managerial perspective, and discuss only briefly the topic of the accountability of networks in representative democracies. There is even less discussion of how to open networks to citizens. There is a need to adopt a political perspective on policy networks; to explore ways of democratizing functional domains.

Markets and capitalism may have triumphed but we have some new ideologies voiced by the new tribes: vocal minorities with a taste for direct action over representation in 'normal politics'. The new tribes include the environmentalists, the anti-roads lobby, the anti-smoking campaign, the campaign against blood sports, and the claims of religious and racial minorities. There are many new ideologies; outside 'normal politics', possibly from choice but definitely by exclusion. Governments will have to cope with them and this challenge raises the problem of how to sustain the legitimacy of government. The answer does not lie with managerial fixes.

There is also an accountability deficit. Hirst (1990: 2) comments that representative democracy delivers 'low levels of governmental accountability and public influence on decision making'. He notes that 'big government is now so big' that it defeats effective coordination by the centre and grows 'undirected' and by 'accretion' (1990: 31–2). So, both the new tribes and the accountability deficit mean we need to reinvent representative democracy; to experiment with new forms of democracy.

There is no shortage of proposals for new forms of democracy. Hirst (1990: 8) argues for a pluralist state 'in which distinct functionally and territorially specific domains of authority enjoy the autonomy necessary to perform their tasks'. Such 'pluralizing of the state' reduces 'the scope of central state power'. The ways of so containing the central state vary. Hirst favours both functional representation in the guise of corporatism (1990: 12–15) and 'associational democracy' based on 'voluntary self-governing associations' (1994). Both schemes take domains of functional authority as the basic building block and are, therefore, consistent with a policy network interpretation of government.

The conventional account of policy networks treats them as an instance of private government, arguing that networks are political oligarchies that shut out the public (Marsh and Rhodes, 1992: 265). Fox and Miller (1995: 118–27) suggest a way of challenging this world of private governments and developing accountability in policy networks by arguing for a pluralism of discourse. They stipulate four 'warrants for discourse' which are necessary conditions for authentic communication: sincerity, situation-regarding intentionality, willing attention, and substantive contribution. They argue that: 'insincerity destroys trust' which is essential to authentic discourse; situation-regarding intentionality ensures that discourse is about something and considers the context of the problem; willing attention will bring about passionate engagement; and participants should offer a distinct view or specific expertise. These norms 'police the discourse' and Fox and Miller (1995: 149) argue that citizens could be regaining control of government through their participation in networks as users and governors, creating a 'post-modern public administration'. Policy networks are 'nascent forms' of 'publicly interested discourse' in which all the affected parties participate 'together to work out possibilities for what to do next'.

Representative democracy in differentiated polities requires, therefore, explicit accountability; in multiple forms and in many forums; with openness of information and access to sustain warrants of discourse; and flexible institutions willing to encourage experiments with multiple and new forms of accountability. The task has scarcely begun, in either theory or practice.

Perhaps the most common criticism of the governance approach stems from its roots in socio-cybernetic theory with its baffling neologisms. The specialized language gets in the way of the message, which seems arcane and unrelated to the everyday problems of government. A book is doomed among practitioners when written in social science-ese, extensively using jargon. Also, it is folk wisdom that the social sciences restate the obvious in an abstruse way. All too often academics make maps of complexity, insisting that complex problems require complex solutions. This stance contrasts sharply with the snappy 'ten commandments' of the latest management bestseller. The study of governance needs its bestseller with snappy aphorisms and vivid stories.

The task should not be beyond us. There are two aphorisms for which this book provides plenty of illustrations. 'For every complex problem there is a simple solution, and it is always wrong'; and, 'Messy problems demand messy solutions.' And if resorting to vernacular language upsets our academic colleagues we can always rephrase these insights more formally as 'reducing complexity through institutional differentiation' (Luhmann, 1982).

Equally, the vivid story should not escape our attention. I live in North Yorkshire, where one of my master's students did his thesis on the local-level implementation structure for AIDS in one district. It is a quiet rural area with a few small towns; it is not the cosmopolitan capital of the western world. There is night-life, but it shuts at 11 p.m. The government requires health and local authorities to provide for AIDS sufferers. To plan the service, 19 organizations have come together to form the planning team. An unbelievable 39 organizations are involved in delivering the service. There is no hierarchy among the organizations: no one organization can plan and command the others. And yet there are only 24 people who are HIV positive in the area. A tinge of black humour is unavoidable: there is only one clear policy choice – find a patient for each organization! Or if we forswear irony, we can always return to the safe haven of our jargon; we have here a clear case of 'multi-organizational sub-optimization'. But ironic humour, or at least telling a good story, must become part of the social scientist's toolkit, if we are to be accessible. We must do so to persuade governments to change their operating codes; to choose between governing structures and recognize governance and the skills of network management.

Managing institutional differentiation and pluralization is a task confronting all advanced industrial democracies because they all reduce complexity by differentiation; that is, fracturing problems into their component parts and designing legal-institutional 'solutions' for each part. This book provides some telling lessons on how to manage such organizational complexity and introduces a toolkit for managing the networks of differentiated polities.

Preface

In public administration the concept 'policy network' has become quite popular. It refers to the relatively stable relations between (different) governmental and (semi-) private organizations, in which processes of policy making take place. Until recently the concept 'policy network' had often been negatively evaluated. It was seen as one of the main reasons for policy failure: non-transparent and impenetrable forms of interest representations which prevent policy innovations and threaten the effectiveness, efficiency and democratic legitimacy of the public sector.

We do not support this view. Networks are a fundamental characteristic of modern societies and it should be the task of policy scientists to explore the potentials of public policy making and governance in networks. With this in mind, the idea of network management is elaborated and examined in this book.

Many of the ideas expressed in this book are inspired by the work of members of a group of researchers in the Departments of Public Administration of Erasmus University Rotterdam and Leiden University and the Faculty of Systems Engineering, Policy Analysis and Management of the Delft University of Technology. Since 1989, this group has met regularly in order to discuss theoretical issues, research designs and findings. Among their publications are a series of PhD theses in which the consequences of policy networks for public policy and governance in specific policy areas have been empirically analysed. Although there is diversity in the work of the researchers, a more or less coherent body of theoretical knowledge has been developed which forms the basis of this book.

This book makes two major contributions to the field, in addition to the ideas developed in the research group. First, although within the group the concept of policy networks has guided much of the research and analysis, the idea of network management has never before been elaborated as systematically and profoundly as it is here. Second, although members of the group have published in international journals, our ideas are presented here for the first time in a comprehensive way for an international audience. We hope this will contribute to the international debate on topics such as governance and new public management and we look forward to the discussions we hope it will encourage.

It was the ambition of the editors to make the book more than just a compilation of contributions of several individuals. We did this not only by investing our time, energy and knowledge in several 'editorial chapters' (Chapters 1, 2, 3, and 10), but also by inviting the authors to read and comment on each other's contributions. So this book is the joint product of all the authors, and we would like to thank them for their efforts.

We would also like to thank the other members of the research group 'Policy and governance in complex networks', who were likewise involved in reading and commenting on the concept texts. Our special thanks go to Kathy Owen, who, with the help of Vicky Wightman, transformed our Dutch and – probably worse – our attempts to write in English into readable text. We also wish to express our gratitude to Ankie Assink, Edith Aalbers, Steven de Waal, and Karin Feteris, who assisted us on various occasions with the processing of the manuscript.

1

Introduction: A Management Perspective on Policy Networks

W.J.M. Kickert, E.-H. Klijn and J.F.M. Koppenjan

1.1 Introduction

After the post-war establishment of the welfare state with its high expectations of governmental policy making and planning, in the late 1970s and 1980s following the oil crisis, disillusionment with government performance resulted in a lowering of ambitions. High expectations were replaced by suspicion of government intervention. Currently, however, we are witnessing a worldwide departure of the dark days of complete lack of trust and confidence in the public sector. Even in the United States, the period of an outright anti-government sentiment is seemingly coming to an end (Wamsley, 1990). New policy problems such as environmental pollution, the growth of organized crime and the need for a competitive infrastructure in order to keep pace with international economic developments, and old problems like the revision of the welfare state, call for government involvement. It is, however, also clear that government cannot reclaim its post-war welfare state position as the central governing authority in society. The experiences of the 1960s and 1970s have shown that the steering potentials of government are limited and that it must deal with many other important actors in the policy fields in which it operates. These observations necessitate reflection upon the relation between government and society. In social science this reflection has contributed to the rise of a new idea which is becoming increasingly popular: the concept of policy networks.

Policy Networks as a Perspective on Governance

The concept 'policy network' connects public policies with their strategic and institutionalized context: the network of public, semi-public, and private actors participating in certain policy fields. The concept is new in the sense that it combines insights from policy science, which focuses on the analysis of public policy processes, with ideas from political science and organization theory about the distribution of power and dependencies, organizational features, and interorganizational relations. As an empirical phenomenon policy networks can be found in almost every policy area. Some well-known policy networks are those of agriculture, the military-industrial complex, and networks in such areas as social security, national health, and housing.

Until recently the idea of policy networks was mainly used to explain why policies fail. It has contributed to the exposure of the rational central rule approach which many governmental agencies use in practice, as a major cause of policy failure. This approach neglects the fundamental dependencies of government upon individuals, groups and organizations in its policy environment. In many early network studies, policy networks were considered synonymous with the resistance of vested interests standing in the way of effective and democratically legitimized problem solving and policy innovation. The concept of policy networks seemed to confirm that government policies often fail and offered an explanatory framework for that deception. After the understandable reaction to the disillusionment with government planning in the form of over-emphasized interest in the failures and limitations of governmental steering, more attention has recently been given to the potentials of the concept of policy networks for public problem solving and societal governance. Used in such a way, the network approach provides an alternative to the reaction of many governments to the limits of governance by proclaiming a strategic retreat from the public domain by promoting privatization, deregulation and decentralization. This idea of policy networks as an opportunity for public policy making and governance forms the subject of this study. The central question we will deal with is:

What are the potentials of a network perspective on governance and public management for managing policy networks?

Governance, Public Management and the Central Argument of This Book

It is clear that a network perspective differs in a number of ways from more conventional views on governance and public management. Before we can elaborate on this we have to clarify the difference between governance and public management. Governance can roughly be described as 'directed influence of social processes'. It covers all kinds of guidance mechanisms which are connected with public policy processes. This means that these forms of guidance are not restricted to conscious or deliberate forms of guidance. In society, self-steering mechanisms exist which ensure that policy processes proceed smoothly. Nor is governance restricted to public actors. All kinds of actors are involved in governance, if only because government does not perform all the governing itself. A wide variety of actions from different actors has consequences for governance.

Public management differs from governance in that it focuses on the consciously and deliberately undertaken actions of public actors to influence societal processes (or policy processes). Therefore, public management is governance, but not all governance is public management.

The main argument in this book is that public policy of any significance is the result of interactions between public and private actors. Public policy is made and implemented in networks of interdependent actors. This observation has far-reaching consequences for our view on governance and public management. One of the major challenges with which public management as a form of governance is confronted, is to deal with network-like situations, that is, situations of interdependencies. Public management should therefore be seen as network management. This book addresses the question of what 'network management' is and what kinds of strategy exist to govern complex policy processes in networks. As such, the book provides the first steps towards a theory of network management.

With this idea of public management as network management, we disagree with the ideas of the new public management which has become dominant in the last ten years. These ideas stress a businesslike approach to government focusing on performance indicators, deregulation and privatization, and making goverment 'function like a firm'. Some of the ideas on the new public management will be elaborated in Chapter 3; they are set against our view on managing networks.

The aim of this introductory chapter is to illuminate the debate on governance and how ideas on policy networks and network management fit in this discussion. It also offers a preview to the other chapters. In the next section, the problem of the disappointing results of public policies and governmental steering, which underlies the early interest in the network perspective, will be elaborated. The political discourse concerning the limits of government has triggered a scientific debate about governmental steering in Europe and the United States. The network approach can, in fact, be considered one of the outcomes of this debate. After a more precise definition of the concept of policy network, the policy network approach will be presented as an alternative to both the conventional central rule approach and to the multi-actor approach put forward by critics of the former model. Subsequently the idea of network management will be introduced. This introductory chapter ends with an overview of the topics which will be dealt with in the next chapters and considers how they relate to the central issue of this book.

1.2   Governance: The Debate on the Limits of Government

The concept of policy networks did not just suddenly emerge in the theoretical discussions on public policy and governance. It is the result of an ongoing debate on governance and a reaction to other approaches. In this section a brief review of the background of this debate is presented.

From Planning Euphoria to Aversion to Government

The development of ideas and theories on public policy and governance has long been based on an image of government as standing above society and being able to 'steer' it. Policy was approached from a strongly rational-technical point of view with a strict division between politics and policy. Emphasis was placed on the neutral implementation of the policy formulated by the political system.

However, the administrative reality appeared to be different. Although governmental interventions in a wide variety of policy areas dramatically changed the outlook of modern societies, a substantial number of governmental policies in the 1960s and 1970s failed to meet their original targets. Despite the fact that large-scale policy programmes consumed enormous sums of money, they often failed to meet expectations, and the results were disappointing. Problems such as crime, pollution, unemployment, traffic and transport have remained impervious to governmental measures. In some cases the aspirations were simply too high. Problems like unemployment and drug-related crime turned out to be difficult to solve. The implementation of policy seemed to recognize its own dynamics whereupon numerous policy plans broke down, as happened with the attempts at decentralization and the setting of objectives for cutbacks in government expenditure. Other policy issues such as pollution and abortion were debated for decades, but decisions were either not forthcoming, or taken only after long delays. Sometimes the government's failures even took the form of policy disasters, affairs or scandals.

The results fell far short of the high expectations. At the end of the 1970s and in the 1980s this led to a pessimistic view of the government's abilities to achieve its goals and to influence social development. Due to severe budget cuts many Western governments began a strategic retreat. Supposedly the government had been setting its targets too high. Less public sector, more private sector, deregulation and decentralization became the new catchwords. As the government's aspirations dwindled, its legitimacy also went into a decline. The status of the public sector as a whole has undergone considerable damage as a result of these developments.

The most negative anti-government developments took place during the Reagan administration in the United States and the Thatcher regime in the United Kingdom, both inspired by a fierce 'new right' ideology which clearly proclaimed a retreat of the public sector in favour of the private sector and the introduction of a more businesslike 'managerialism' in government in order to lower costs and function more effectively. The governments in continental Western Europe did not suffer from such a negative trend, probably due to their long state traditions and higher public legitimacy. Public distrust and political aversion to government did not reach such dramatic depths as in America and England. Nevertheless privatization, deregulation, cutbacks and government withdrawal did play a major role in all Western European countries.

The collapse of the centrally planned economies of Eastern Europe at the end of the 1980s formed the most obvious proof of the deficit of central government steering. Central rule in modern industrialized societies has become an anachronism. Central government is unable unilaterally to control the complexities and pluralistic diversity which are fundamental characteristics of modern societies.

The Social Science Debate on Governance

The public and political debate on governmental steering has not been restricted to practice alone. During the last 15 years it has also been one of the main topics in the social sciences all over the world. The abundance of social scientific publications about the 'end', the 'afterdays', or the 'future' of the welfare state, bears witness to the apparent importance of the issue. Within the broad debate concerning the future of the welfare state, the issue of government steering has been given varying degrees of attention in different countries.

In the United States and the United Kingdom there is no evidence of a major scientific debate on governance. The focus of the debate there seems limited to budget retrenchments and a new public 'managerialism'. In traditionally statist France, the 1980s witnessed a social science debate on a more modern, more modest state that should serve its citizens rather than rule them. The French elitist administrative state seems to be undergoing a change. The dirigist central control of the Paris-based elite of high-ranking civil servants seems to be in crisis. A scientific debate was also held in Germany over *Steuerung*. The 1980s witnessed a de-bureaucratization, a withdrawal of the state from many societal sectors, the reinforcement of the role and importance of the non-profit 'third sector' of social organizations in public policy making. In the Netherlands a debate on the 'limitations of government steering' was conducted not only in the scientific community, but also in administrative and political circles as well. It was recognized that government is not able to steer society as a *deus ex machina* from a position above and detached from society; government itself is part of the social system and is only one of the many social actors influential in public policy processes.

A reflection of this general debate on governance was observed in many scientific subfields at that time, such as the international project on 'guidance control and evaluation in the public sector' (Kaufmann et al., 1986), the discussion on the limits of rational planning (Van Gunsteren, 1976), the difficulties of implementation (Pressman and Wildavsky, 1983), the problems of interorganizational coordination (Warren et al., 1975; Scharpf et al., 1976; Hanf and Schapf, 1978; Rogers and Whetten, 1982). Many of these debates were a reaction to the 'conventional steering perspective' in which the government is seen as society's central ruler, and citizens, private organizations and lower tiers of government are considered more or less passive objects of these steering efforts. This paradigm was considered one of the major reasons for the disappointing results of governmental steering since it does not take into account the dependencies of government on its social environment, its interdependencies with many other social actors. This idea of interdependencies was elaborated from various scientific perspectives, leading to the introduction of the concept of 'policy networks' (Hanf and Scharpf, 1978; Rogers and Whetten, 1982; Gage and Mandell, 1990; Hufen and Ringeling, 1990; Marin and Mayntz, 1991; Thompson et al., 1991; Marsh and Rhodes, 1992).

1.3   The Concept of the 'Policy Network'

The literature contains a rich variety of definitions and descriptions of networks and policy networks. This is a consequence of the fact that the policy network perspective finds its source in many different theories. The most prominent theoretical backgrounds are interorganizational theory (e.g. Benson, 1978; Aldrich, 1979; Rogers and Whetten, 1982) and the literature on concepts such as subsystems, policy communities, and issue networks (e.g. Heclo, 1978; Rhodes, 1981; Jordan, 1990a). The policy network approach does, however, also build on the tradition in policy science of analysing policy processes as complex interactions in which many actors participate and processes are ambiguous as a result of the multiple goals and strategies of actors and of uncertainty about information and outcomes (Allison, 1971; Cohen et al., 1972; Lindblom and Cohen, 1979).

An extensive discussion of the theoretical roots of the policy network perspective is presented in Chapter 2. In this introductory chapter we mention only the main characteristics to give an impression of the network approach to public policy and to determine the important consequences of this approach for the question of governance.

The concept 'policy network' is used to indicate patterns of relations between interdependent actors, involved in processes of public policy making. Interdependency is the key word in the network approach. Actors in networks are interdependent because they cannot attain their goals by themselves, but need the resources of other actors to do so. Dealing with public problems involves interactions between governmental agencies, quasi-governmental bodies and private organizations. Interdependency is based on the distribution of resources over various actors, the goals they pursue and their perceptions of their resource dependencies. Information, goals and resources are exchanged in interactions. Because these interactions are frequently repeated, processes of institutionalization occur: shared perceptions, participation patterns and interaction rules develop and are formalized. The structural and cultural features of policy networks which come about in this way influence future policy processes.

In this book we define policy networks as *(more or less) stable patterns of social relations between interdependent actors, which take shape around policy problems and/or policy programmes.* We speak of policy networks because our attention focuses on the way networks influence the making and implementation of public policy. It focuses on the collective action of corporate actors. The concept refers to interorganizational policy making and most studies which have been done apply the concept at the meso level of specific policy fields.

Policy networks develop around policy problems and resources which are needed or are generated to deal with policy problems. An example of this is the development of the housing network in the Netherlands after the Second World War. The source of this network can be traced to the housing shortages and lack of building capacities after the war. This resulted in governmental intervention which led to price regulations and the generation of resources to build new and relatively cheap housing. Each of the actors participating in this programme had its own agenda. Building companies were interested in continuity of projects, housing associations focused on growth and continuity and investors had, as their priority, profit-making projects. Because of the resources and the necessity for actors to cooperate, a rather tight network evolved in which all housing problems were formulated and 'processed'. The problem of housing shortage offered each of the actors an opportunity to realize its goals and interests. Organizational institutions were developing and rules of conduct and policy orientations were created in interactions involving policy programmes (Klijn and Van der Pennen, 1992).

The concept 'policy network' provides an alternative to the rational central rule approach. The network approach is also a reaction to critics of the conventional steering perspective, who from a bottom-up or market orientation advocate a multi-actor perspective.

1.4   The Network Approach to Governance

In this section the conventional steering model, the multi-actor model and the network model are presented. These models are lenses through which reality can be observed (compare Allison, 1971). They magnify some aspects of the world and disregard or leave out others. It may be that these three models coincide with the theories in use (Argyris and Schön, 1978) and steering conceptions of actors in the real world. In this book, however, we refer to them as theoretical frameworks which social scientists use in order to reflect on policy making and governance in the public sector.

The Rational Central Rule Model

The conventional steering model focuses on the relation between the agent and objects of steering. The model takes the ambitions and goals of the steering agent as a point of departure for analysis and evaluation. It can be qualified as a mono-actor model. When the central actor is the government, this bias is often justified by pointing out the democratic legitimacy of governments in Western democracies. According to this perspective, processes of public policy making and governance are characterized by the division between politics and administration. In the policy formulation phase consensus between the parties involved is reached regarding problem formulation. Scientific knowledge is used to design policy measures and an implementation programme. After authoritative decision making the implementation phase is considered a non-political, technical and potentially programmable activity. The criterion for success or failure is the attainment of the formal policy goals. The model suggests the following reasons for failure: incorrect assumptions about the causal relations between goals and means and the effectiveness of steering instruments, resistance from implementing bodies or target groups, lack of information about the goals of the policy, and lack of control. According to this model public policy making and governance can be improved by rationalization of policies, clarification of policy goals, reduction of the number of participants in the implementation phase, better information concerning the intentions of the policy, and increased monitoring and control of activities. Generally, in situations involving a number of actors, this model suggests strengthening coordination and if necessary proposes reorganization in order to bring previously autonomous actors within the jurisdiction of one central coordinating authority.

Criticism of the Central Rule Model: The Multi-actor Model

The disadvantages of the conventional steering model are expressed by many authors. The model presupposes that the central steering agent has at his disposal the necessary information about existing public problems, preferences and the available solutions, which is impossible given its limited capacity and the uncertainties involved. The model neglects the values and interests of implementing bodies and target groups and disregards their strategies by labelling them as 'uninformed' and as 'conservative reactions to innovation'. The rational central rule approach denies the political nature of governance and fails to utilize the resources and capacities of local actors. The assumptions about the reasons for failures and the prescriptions based on these assumptions reinforce the shortcomings of the model. The promotion of central coordination and central control gives way to further bureaucratization of the public sector and therefore to diminished effectiveness and efficiency (Van Gunsteren, 1976; Hanf and Toonen, 1985).

This criticism is quite convincing. The question is which alternative the critics present to the conventional steering approach. For instance, the bottom-up approach does not choose the perspective of the central ruler, but that of the implementing bodies and target groups, regardless of whether they are governmental, quasi-governmental or private. In the analysis and evaluation of public policies and governance the interests of these local actors are taken as the point of departure. The central focus in the analysis is the extent to which central policies provide local actors with sufficient resources and policy discretion to tackle the problems they encounter. Public policy making and governance is seen as an essentially political process in which local actors assess their interests and purposes. The introduction of knowledge, skills and goals of local actors in the policy design phase is considered important: policy formation and implementation are interrelated processes. Public policies and governance are judged successful if they leave room for local decision making and provide local actors with sufficient resources. According to the bottom-up approach policies fail because there is too little local policy discretion, local actors are excluded from policy formation, and resources are lacking. Public policies and governance can be improved by increasing the discretion of local actors, providing more resources and strengthening the autonomy of these actors (compare Teisman, 1992).

The model is a radical plea for decentralization, self-governance, and privatization, which in fact means the retreat of central government from the public domain. At the same time the central government is urged to give more attention to the problems of local actors and to provide them with more resources. The alternative that this approach offers to the conventional steering model is therefore disappointing: it is inconsistent and one-sided. It offers little more than a plea for the radical retreat of government (in which case the baby is thrown out with the bath water) or an argument for central rule for the benefit of local actors.

The Network Model as an Alternative Approach to Governance

The network approach builds on the bottom-up criticism, but offers a more realistic alternative for the rational central rule model. The network approach considers public policy making and governance to take place in networks consisting of various actors (individuals, coalitions, bureau, organizations) none of which possesses the power to determine the strategies of the other actors. The government is no longer seen as occupying a superior position to other parties, but as being on equal footing with them. Public policy making within networks is about cooperation or non-cooperation between interdependent parties with different and often conflicting rationalities, interests and strategies. Policy processes are not viewed as the implementation of ex ante formulated goals, but as an interaction process in which actors exchange information about problems, preferences and means, and trade off goals and resources. A success criterion for policy is the realization of collective action in order to establish a common purpose or avert common threats. This model assumes the following causes of failure: the lack of incentives to cooperate and the existence of blockades to collective action. Proposed goals may be vague or not provocative. Important actors may be absent, while the presence of other actors may discourage the participation of necessary actors. Crucial information about goals, means and actors may be lacking. Discretionary power may be absent. The absence of commitment of actors to the common purpose may also be a reason for failure. Prescriptions are aimed at the improvement of the conditions for collective action. This can be done by network management: the management of the interaction processes within networks or the changing of the structural and cultural characteristics of the network. Table 1.1 shows the three elaborated perspectives on public policy making and governance.

Although the concept of policy networks is quite new, it has already provoked a lot of criticism. Policy networks are said to refer to non-transparent and impenetrable structures of interest representation which prevent necessary innovations in public policy and form a threat to the effectiveness, efficiency and democratic legitimization of the public sector (for example Marsh and Rhodes, 1992: 249–68). Note that this criticism is mainly aimed at the existence of policy networks in the real world, and not at the network approach as a theoretical framework. We believe that many of the shortcomings are not intrinsic to policy networks and can be avoided through adequate management. Applying the approach to questions of public policy making and governance opens new perspectives to governmental steering.

Table 1.1   *Three perspectives on public policy making and governance*

Perspectives: Dimensions:	The rational central rule perspective	The multi-actor perspective	The network perspective
Object of analyses	Relation between central ruler and target groups	Relation between central ruler and local actors	Network of actors
Perspective	Central ruler	Local actors	Interactions between actors
Characterization of relations	Authoritative	Centralized versus autonomous	Interdependent
Characterization of policy processes	Neutral implementation of ex ante formulated policy	Political processes of interest representation and informal use of guidelines and resources	Interaction process in which information, goals and resources are exchanged
Criterion of success	Attainment of the goals of the formal policy	Local discretionary power and obtaining resources in favour of local actors	Realization of collective action
Causes of failure	Ambiguous goals; too many actors; lack of information and control	Rigid policies; lack of resources, non-participation of local actors	Lack of incentives for collective action or existing blockages
Recommendations for governance	Coordination and centralization	Retreat of central rule in favour of local actors	Management of policy networks: improving conditions under which actors interact

1.5   Managing Policy Networks: A Preliminary Exploration

Until recently policy network approaches mostly emphasized the limits and restrictions of governmental steering. Often, the very existence of policy networks was taken as proof of the incompetence of government. This negative assessment explains the direction of the research on this phenomenon until now. With a few exceptions (Hanf and Scharpf, 1978; Rogers and Whetten, 1982; Gage and Mandell, 1990) the potentials of policy networks for problem resolution and governmental steering have received little attention. In this book we will examine these potentials by elaborating the idea of network management. Network management is an example of governance and public management in situations of interdependencies. It is aimed at *coordinating strategies of actors with different goals and preferences with regard to a certain problem or policy measure within an existing network of interorganizational relations.*

Before going on, it is important to point out the distinction between the traditional intraorganizational approach and the network approach to (public) management. The 'classical', mostly intraorganizationally inspired management perspective cannot be used in a network situation. In this classical perspective the manager is a 'system controller concerned (depending on his position in the organization) with the total system called the organization or more frequently with a part of the organization' (Hunt, 1972: 25). In the classical vision management consists of three main activities: setting the goals of the organization (planning), structuring and designing the organization (organizing) and 'getting the job done' (leading). Management is a top-down activity based on a clear authority structure (Chandler, 1962, 1977; Robbins, 1980).

Managing networks, however, should not be confused with the 'classical management approach'. In a network situation a single central authority, a hierarchical ordering and a single organizational goal do not exist. None of the actors has enough steering capacity to unilaterally control other actors. Network management is, in essence, an interorganizational activity (Lynn, 1981; Mandell, 1990). A top-down or holistic perspective of management is not likely to be very productive. If a central actor is missing there can be no clear 'system controller'. There is no clear authority structure from which the manager can draw his (or her) steering resources (Mandell, 1990). This means that the manager has to handle complex interaction settings and work out strategies to deal with the different perceptions, preferences and strategies of the various actors involved. Network management aims at initiating and facilitating interaction processes between actors (Friend et al., 1974), creating and changing network arrangements for better coordination (Scharpf, 1978; Rogers and Whetten, 1982). Table 1.2 shows the main characteristics of the 'classical' and network perspectives of management.

As is illustrated by the table, there are many differences between the two approaches to management. The difference in assumptions has consequences for the possible role of the manager and the types of activity. In Chapter 3 a more detailed overview of governance and the consequences of the network perspective for (public) management is given.

1.6   The Focus of the Book

This book goes beyond most of the existing policy network studies. The aim is *to explore the possibilities and strategies of network management.* In order to do this we try to answer the following questions: What is network management? What activities does it comprise? What instruments can be used to manage networks? What are the main network properties on which the phenomenon depends? When is network management considered successful? What conditions determine its success or failure? The book consists of three parts. The first part contains an overview of the literature on networks and network management which not only serves to clarify the central concepts and their theoretical developments, but also provides a 'common ground' on which the rest of this book is built. In the second part, drawing on a variety of theoretical backgrounds and empirical observations, several important topics of network management are explored. Part III contains the conclusions of this book. The individual chapters are described in more detail below.

Table 1.2   *Two perspectives on management*

Perspectives: Dimensions:	'Classical' perspective	Network perspective
Organizational setting	Single authority structure	Divided authority structure
Goal structure	Activities are guided by clear goals and well-defined problems	Various and changing definitions of problems and goals
Role of manager	System controller	Mediator, process manager, network builder
Management tasks	Planning and guiding organizational processes	Guiding interactions and providing opportunities
Management activities	Planning, design and leading	Selecting actors and resources, influencing network conditions, and handling strategic complexity

Part I: Policy Networks and Network Management: A State of the Art

Chapter 2 examines the theoretical roots of the network approach. It presents the basic assumptions and concepts which underlie the approach and that establish the common frame of reference for the other articles in the book. Chapter 3 offers an exploration of the concept of network management starting with an overview of some recent developments in the field of public management and governance. The concept is defined and an overview of the various forms of network management mentioned in the literature is given.

Part II: Network Dynamics and Management

Drawing on a variety of theoretical backgrounds and empirical observations, several important themes are elaborated.

One topic in the network literature is the closed character of networks. Policy processes tend to take place in relatively closed communities with fixed actors and perceptions (Rhodes, 1988). This causes problems for steering. In Chapter 4, Schaap and Van Twist discuss this problem of closedness and its consequences for network management more thoroughly. Building on theoretical insights of the autopoiesis theory and especially on the work of the German sociologist Luhmann, they analyse closedness as the result of the (re)construction of meaning and draw conclusions for strategies of network management.

Koppenjan and Termeer (Chapter 5) take the different perceptions of actors in networks as a starting point for their analysis of network management strategies. From a theoretical framework which stresses the relation between cognitive and social processes, they discuss how and why perceptions in networks change and what network management strategies are suited to influence these perceptions.

If a network consists of many actors, each with their own perceptions and strategies how can collective action be achieved in a network? Building on earlier theoretical notions of games and strategies, Klijn and Teisman show, in Chapter 6, how policy processes can be analysed in terms of strategies and games and which management strategies are available for a network manager to guide complex strategic policy processes in networks.

In Chapter 7, De Bruijn and Ten Heuvelhof examine the question of what a network perspective means for the role of policy instruments in complex networks. They focus particularly on the instruments available for network management.

Hanf, Hupe and O'Toole focus, in Chapter 8, on the specific character of network management at the level of implementation structures. They relate the idea of network management to theoretical notions of implementation and street level bureaucracy.

In Chapter 9, De Bruijn and Ringeling elaborate on normative aspects of network management. If a network consists of different actors with different values and goals, whose goals should be used as criteria for effectiveness and efficiency? What are the consequences of a network perspective for criteria such as legitimacy? And, last but not least, what is the position of governmental actors in a network?

Part III: Conclusion: Strategies for Network Management

The concluding chapter (Chapter 10) summarizes the findings of the previous chapters, presents a critical reflection on these findings, and explores directions for further research.

PART I
POLICY NETWORKS AND NETWORK MANAGEMENT: A STATE OF THE ART

2

Policy Networks: An Overview

E.-H. Klijn

2.1 Introduction

In Chapter 1 policy networks were defined as more or less stable patterns of social relations between interdependent actors, which take shape around policy problems and/or policy programmes. Policy networks form the context in which policy processes take place. They thus represent an attempt within policy science to analyse the relationship between context and process in policy making. In this chapter, the theoretical background to this concept is explored in order to enhance our knowledge of the characteristics of the policy network approach and its influences.

From a theoretical perspective, the policy network approach builds on earlier theoretical concepts in policy science using insights from other social sciences. As far as the policy network approach is concerned, interorganizational theory and the literature on the concepts of subsystems and policy communities are particularly important. The literature on interorganizational theory is firmly embedded in the organizational sociology of the 1960s and 1970s, whereas the literature on subsystems and policy communities belongs mainly in the field of political science, and developed as a result of the power discussions between elitists and pluralists in the 1950s and 1960s.

The following section presents an overview of the theoretical background to the policy network approach in policy science, followed by a brief discussion of the first authors (mainly in the 1970s) to use a network approach to analyse policy processes. Most of these authors wrote on public policy implementation or intergovernmental relations. The interorganizational approach and the 'subsystem and policy community' approach are discussed in sections 2.3 and 2.4. In each section the various approaches are summarized in tables. This is done in each table by splitting them into five categories: actors/

organizations; processes; decisions; power; and information/values. Section 2.5 deals with the main characteristics of the policy network approach and traces the most important influences on its theoretical roots.

2.2   Policy Analysis: From Rational Actor to Network

Using the concept of policy networks to analyse complex policy processes fits within the history of policy science in which concepts are developed to analyse complex decision processes. A historical trend can be seen in the development of policy science where scholars attempted to incorporate the environment of the policy process in their theories.

From Rational Actor to Process Model

Policy science grew out of 'decision theory' which was concerned with optimizing the effects of decisions and calculating the costs and benefits connected with those decisions. Policy science focused on the behaviour of a (rational) actor who would reach a decision within a situation of being fully informed and of complete and clear preference ranking (Braybrooke and Lindblom, 1963). This model, of course, originated from economics. It is not surprising that Lindblom includes welfare economics in his criticism of the rational actor approach or, as he labels it, the 'synoptical model'. In the rational actor approach, the decision maker aims at 'a systematic canvassing of all possible politics, for a similar systematic analysis of the consequences of each possible alternative, and for a policy choice to serve goals or objectives somehow separately established' (Braybrooke and Lindblom, 1963: 38). The rational actor model assumes that policy processes proceed in stages (policy formulation, decision and implementation) based on a view in which the decision maker first analyses the problem and the alternatives and then makes a rational decision about which option he or she should choose.

The rational approach was vigorously attacked in the 1940s and 1950s by eminent scholars such as Simon and Lindblom who favoured an approach that can be labelled as a 'bounded rationality' approach. They stressed the impossibility of a full information situation. Complete analysis of problems was not possible and not desirable given the costs of information and the limited opportunities available to decision makers to process all this information (Lindblom, 1979: 518). Policy processes are unpredictable due to incomplete information and unclear values (Braybrooke and Lindblom: 1963: 23–31). Although the criticism of analysts like Simon and Lindblom is strong and convincing it does not get to the crux of the classical rational actor model, that is, the assumption that policy processes can be steered by or at least be analysed from the perspective of a single actor. Some of the implementation literature (Pressman and Wildavsky, 1983, first edition, 1973) and most of the literature on policy instruments (Hood, 1983; De Bruijn and Hufen, 1992) is included in this bounded rationality approach.

A newly emerging process approach to policy, however, represented a break with the traditional decision approach.[1] In the 1970s, various theoretical approaches conceptualized the first features of a process approach towards public policy: for example Allison's governmental politics model (1971), the agenda building theories of authors like Cobb and Elder (1983), Lindblom's interaction approach (Lindblom and Cohen, 1979), and the garbage can model of Cohen, March and Olsen (1972). In all these theories, public policy is the result of interaction between various actors trying to influence the policy process in a direction favourable to themselves. Lindblom, whose work shows a shift from a bounded rationality approach (see Braybrooke and Lindblom, 1963) towards a process approach (see Lindblom and Cohen, 1979) writes that 'an outcome will emerge from interaction among decision makers, each of whom is in pursuit of solutions to his own problems rather than the ostensible problem' (Lindblom and Cohen, 1979: 34). The garbage can model of Cohen, March and Olsen (1972) shows a similar interest in the process of policy making and the uncertainties which accompany it. They state that 'in a garbage can situation, a decision is an outcome or an interpretation of several relatively independent "streams" within the organization' (Cohen et al., 1972). They restrict themselves to four streams: problems, solutions, participants and choice opportunities. These streams are affected by the organizational and societal structure in which they take place. But the theory was not explored in any depth at that time. Recently, March and Olsen have attempted a more detailed discussion of the institutional context of decision processes (March and Olsen, 1989).

   In the process approach to public policy the focus is on the complexity of public policy processes. This complexity is due to a number of factors, i.e. that different actors try to influence the process, that actors do not have fixed preferences, that policy processes are the result of complex interactions of different forms of strategic action and that perceptions of problems and solutions change over time (e.g. March and Olsen, 1976; Lindblom and Cohen, 1979; Kingdon, 1984). Table 2.1 shows the three approaches in policy science with their main characteristics.

Policy Networks: The Contextualization of the Policy Process

When compared to decision-oriented approaches, process approaches to policy making tend to emphasize the dynamics of policy making. The recent interest in the concept of policy networks can be seen as an attempt to 'contextualize' the process approach. Not only does policy making take place in settings where there are many actors and there is ambiguity regarding preferences, information and strategies chosen, but it also occurs within certain interorganizational networks of a more lasting nature. The policy network approach thus takes up where the process approach leaves off. Problems, actors and perceptions are not chance elements of policy processes but are connected with the interorganizational network within which these processes occur.

   The concept of networks in the analysis of public policy processes first emerged in the mid-1970s and early 1980s. Scharpf (1978) criticized the

Table 2.1   *Approaches in policy science*

Approach: Dimensions:	Rational actor (Tinbergen)	Bounded rationality (1950–; Simon; Lindblom; Elmore; Wildavsky)	Process model (1970–; Allison; Lindblom; Cohen, March and Olsen; Kingdon)
Actors	Central actor/decision maker	Central decision maker in environment of uncertainty	Variety of actors
Processes	Phases (policy formulation, decision, implementation) Guided by a priori formulated goals	Incremental Coping with uncertainty	Conflicting interests and problem definitions Highly dynamic and unpredictable
Decisions	Choosing the best alternative (minimizing costs, maximizing benefits)	Choosing alternatives which are feasible and seem to diminish problems	Choosing alternatives which generate support and which can be linked to problems
Power	Centralized (central actor)	Centralized but bounded by uncertainty	Divided (many actors)
Information/ values	Information obtainable values given (goals of a central actor	Information incomplete and ambiguous Values not always clear	Information dispersed and ambiguous Values conflicting and unclear

instrumental logic of goals and means which dominated policy analysis. Referring to the earlier work of Thompson (1967) he cast doubts on the usefulness of the fiction of a unitary decision maker. He concluded that 'it is unlikely, if not impossible, that public policy of any significance could result from the choice process of any single unified actor. Policy formation and policy implementation are inevitably the result of interactions among a plurality of separate actors with separate interests, goals, and strategies' (Scharpf, 1978: 346). Instead, he argued that policy analysis should be geared towards the interorganizational network within which policy is made. Research should be directed not only towards specific interactions between organizations but also to the more stable, structural relations between organizations (Scharpf, 1978). Scharpf's efforts were aimed at first identifying the 'objective' problem situation, after which prescriptions were to be directed to the question of how the existing interorganizational network was equipped to deal with this problem. Scharpf's analytical framework was strongly influenced by the literature on interorganizational relations, as were those of other writers on intergovernmental relations (Friend et al., 1974; Hanf and Scharpf, 1978; Rhodes, 1981; Wright, 1983; Agranoff, 1990a) and on implementation (e.g. Barret and Fudge, 1981; Hjern and Porter, 1981). Because Scharpf also tried to find a contingent relationship between types of networks and types of problems or problem solving capacities of the network, he is sometimes labelled a structuralist (Rhodes, 1981). His approach is then contrasted with the games approach of authors like Crozier (see Crozier and Friedberg, 1980 and

Chapter 6 of this book).

Implementation studies, inspired by interorganization theory, emerged as a reaction to what was termed the 'top-down' approach to implementation in which the implementation process was viewed from the perspective of goals formulated by a central actor (e.g. Pressman and Wildavsky, 1983). Instead, the 'bottom-uppers', as they labelled themselves, began their analysis by focusing on the actors who interact on a particular problem at the local operational level. They looked at the problem solving strategies and interactions of a number of public and private actors within a specific policy field (e.g. Hjern and Porter, 1981; Sabatier and Hanf, 1985; Wamsley, 1985). In general, this bottom-up approach within implementation studies has been effective in providing insights into how local actors utilize programmes from higher levels of government for their own purposes and thus underline the unanticipated effects of the implementation of policy programmes (Sabatier and Hanf, 1985).

Intergovernmental studies focused on the relation and communication networks between the different levels of governmental agencies, on the strategic perspectives of these actors and on their problem solving capacities (Wright, 1983; Agranoff, 1990a). Governmental actors operated in complex settings where they were involved in more than one programme at the same time and where they found themselves involved in complex interaction networks (Agranoff, 1990a). Some scholars argued that a new approach to public management was called for in which more emphasis was placed on managing interorganizational relations (Lynn, 1981; Mandell, 1990).

The network approach to public policy was at first strongly influenced by interorganizational theory. At the same time, a virtually independent development occurred in political science which had an impact on policy analysis. The process model in policy science had already been influenced by the agenda theories which developed in political science in the 1970s. Partly as a result of these agenda studies and partly as a result of the original discussion between pluralists and elitists and the evolution of agenda theories (Cobb and Elder, 1983) in the United States as well as in Europe, a theoretical framework developed on policy making in relatively closed communities. The discussions on this framework evolved into discussions on policy communities and policy networks (Rhodes, 1988). Both the theoretical concepts and the empirical research which has been done in this field have affected the conceptualization of policy networks. The work which has been done in political science underlines, to a greater extent than that done in the interorganizational context, the relatively closed nature of networks and the (at times professional) norms and values within those networks. Due to their importance to the policy network approach, the interorganizational approach and the policy communities approach are discussed in the next two sections, each preceded by a concise overview of its predecessors in organizational and political science.

2.3   Interorganizational Relations and Networks

In the 1960s and 1970s, a new approach in organization sociology evolved: interorganization theory. This theory focused on the relations between organizations, their interdependencies and their strategies. In this section, the main features of interorganizational theory will be developed. Interorganization theory built on theories in organizational science. These earlier theories, especially contingency theory, are outlined in a brief introduction.

From Rational Organization to Interorganization Theory

Morgan states that our view of organizations has been shaped by an image of organizations as machines. If we talk about organizations, Morgan argues, we think of orderly, organized parts in some determinate order. The organization is 'a pattern of precisely defined jobs organized in a hierarchical manner through precisely defined lines of command and communication' (Morgan, 1986: 27). In this image of organizations as machines (in this chapter, this approach is termed 'the rational organization'), organizations are seen as units with clear purposes and with a clear authority structure which dominates all the work processes and decisions. This approach suggests that organizations should be or could be rational systems organized to operate as efficiently as possible. In order to effect this, the manager needs to ensure a very strict line of command and organized procedures of communication, control and coordination. These principles can be traced to the classical view of bureaucracy and divisionalized organizations. They can, however, still be found in many modern organization theories.[2]

The rational organization approach chiefly sees organizations as entities without relations with their environment. In the 1950s and 1960s, organization sociology showed a growing interest in the environment of organizations. One dominant approach to organization theory was the systems approach, in which the organization was seen as an open system having connections with its environment. Organization theory focused on the question of how the environment determined the internal organization processes.

Out of this open system concept a contingency approach evolved. An organization is dependent on its environment for its survival. It needs resources and clients to sustain itself. Only by adapting to its environment can an organization survive. This meant that organizations had to change their internal organization in response to the characteristics of their relevant environment. Theorists tried to relate environmental characteristics to types of organization (Emery and Trist, 1965; Lawrence and Lorsch, 1967). This meant that there was 'no one best way to organize' but that a contingency relationship exists between characteristics of the environment and of the organization. Several classifications for types of environments and the organizational forms connected with them were constructed. Some of the best known are those of Emery and Trist (1965) and the Tavistock group.[3] The organization is no longer a unity but consists of subsystems which need to be coordinated. The organization responds strategically to its environment and varies the internal coordination between and within parts of the organization according to its need to adapt to the environment (Mintzberg, 1979).

In an early phase of the contingency approach, environment was conceptualized as a factor. An environment could have a certain value (turbulent, quiet, etc.). Interorganization theory conceptualized the environment as a set of organizations that have a relationship with the focal organization. Interorganizational analysis focused on the relations between organizations, the exchanges of resources between them and the organizational arrangements that are developed to secure coordination between organizations (Levine and White, 1961; Litwak and Hylton, 1962; Negandhi, 1975). These relation patterns exist and develop as a result of interdependency relations between organizations. Table 2.2 shows the three approaches in organizational science which have been discussed: the rational organization approach, the contingency approach and the interorganizational approach.

Table 2.2   *Approaches in organizational science*

Approach: Dimensions:	Rational organization (1900–; Fayol; Taylor; Weber)	Contingency theory (1960–; Burns and Stalker; Lawrence and Lorsch, Mintzberg)	Interorganization theory (1970–; Levine and White; Aldrich; Pfeffer; Benson: Crozier)
Actors	Organizations as coherent units with clear purposes	Organizations as open systems that consist of interrelated subsystems	Organizations as part of a network of organizations

Processes	Rational, structured from top, directed towards goals and highest possible output
	  Planning, organizing and controlling
		Strategic anticipation of developments in environment
		  Adjustment of subsystems and their interactions
			Interorganizational interaction in which resources are exchanged
			  Guided by organizational arrangements (links) between organizations

Decisions	Result of strategic actions of central authority
	  Aimed at reaching formulated goals
		Result of interaction between subsystems
		  Aimed at 'best fit' of organization structure and environment
			Result of negotiations between organizations
			  Aimed at sustaining necessary resource flow for survival

Power	Clear, centralized authority structure (top of the organization)	Ambiguous authority structure (depends on configuration of subsystems)	No central authority structure Power depends on (need for) resources

Information/
values
	Scientific way of gathering information available
	  Clear goals and values
		Strategic information gathering (tuned to environmental characteristics)
		  Value ambiguity
			Information is a power resource possessed by different actors
			  Values are conflicting

Resource Dependency: The Core of Interorganization Theory

A good deal of influence on the development of interorganization theory can be attributed to the ideas of Levine and White (1961). They stressed the exchange processes between organizations, whereby organizations acquire resources from other organizations.

Building on Levine and White's theories, most scholars focused on the division and exchange of resources between organizations. The theoretical ideas which developed into a kind of resource dependency model form the core of interorganization theory (see Thompson, 1967; Cook, 1977; Benson, 1978; Scharpf, 1978; Aldrich, 1979). In this resource dependency model, the environment of an organization is made up of a set of other organizations. Each of these controls resources such as capital, personnel, knowledge, etc. Each organization has to interact with others in order to acquire the necessary resources for goal achievement and survival since no organization can generate all the necessary resources on its own. The resources an organization needs depend on which goals it has set itself. These interdependencies create networks of organizations which interact (with each other) (Benson, 1978; Aldrich, 1979). Organizations can be linked by direct or indirect ties of relations, i.e. they can carry out direct resource exchanges or have these carried out by a third party (Pfeffer and Novak, 1976; Scharpf, 1978). Empirical research using the resource dependency model attempted to 'map' the interaction patterns between organizations and described these relations using concepts such as frequency, intensity and centrality (e.g. Mitchell, 1969; Aldrich and Whetten, 1981).

In addition to mapping relation patterns, analysis using the resource dependency approach focused on the strategies used by organizations to cope with interdependency and to control the necessary resource flow (Benson, 1978; Aldrich, 1979). Organizations can try to avoid or influence interdependency by acquiring crucial resources, by finding alternative resources, by acquiring authoritative powers to coerce other actors or by changing ambitions and goals (Aldrich, 1979). Power is a central concept in the resource dependency model and is connected with the possession of resources (Aldrich, 1979) or with the asymmetry of the dependency relations between actors (Emerson, 1962; Cook, 1977; Scharpf, 1978; Crozier and Friedberg, 1980).

Although differences in conceptualization exist between researchers, it is clear that dependency and exchange are the central aspects of relations between organizations in interorganization theory. Interorganizational analysis involves analysing dependency and resource exchange relations between organizations and the conditions which influence these processes. As a result of this strong emphasis on resources, interorganization theory took little account of the existence of actors' norms and meaning structures. Aldrich stated that 'Values and sentiments are treated as either resulting from a pattern of resource flows already established or created to justify such a pattern' (Aldrich, 1979: 269). With a few exceptions (e.g. Crozier and Friedberg, 1980),[4] researchers using the interorganizational approach took little account of the norms or rules which figure in interactions between organizations.

Implementation and Coordination in Interorganizational Networks

In interorganizational analysis, the problem of cooperation and coordination and that of implementation have constituted important theoretical and empirical research issues. This explains the influence of interorganization theory on writers on implementation and intergovernmental relations within policy science.

If the performance of an organization and its survival are dependent on the way it is connected with other organizations, it would seem logical to carry out research into how the relations of an organization affect its performance and how this performance can be improved. Several research projects were conducted on the way organizations cooperate with each other and the way they form organizational arrangements to secure cooperation. These research projects revealed that large, complex organizations, employing large numbers of professionals, participated more often in joint projects (Aiken and Hage, 1968), that the opportunity to enter into links between organizations constitutes an important factor for new initiatives (Turk, 1970), but that many domain conflicts existed between organizations which blocked effective interorganizational coordination (Warren et al., 1975). It is not apparent in the research projects whether the quality of services improved as a result of interorganizational coordination. Although the continuity of services was improved, the effect on efficiency is not clear (Rogers and Mulford, 1982). This is probably related to the fact that criteria for measurement are difficult to find in a situation in which different actors have different goals and thus different ways of measuring effectiveness and efficiency.

Interorganization theory did, however, devote a good deal of attention to the formal structures or organizational arrangements which were designed to secure cooperation. In accordance with the tradition of the contingency approach, research focused on the relationship between the nature of dependency and the nature of coordination. Thompson (1967) assumed that for pooled interdependency, in which each part makes its own contribution to the network, coordination on the basis of standardization is the most appropriate. If the dependency relation is one of sequential interdependency, that is, units are dependent for their inputs on outputs from other actors and so on, coordination 'by plan' is the most appropriate. If a mutual dependency relationship exists between units, i.e. when each party's outputs constitute inputs for the other, coordination by mutual adjustment is the most suitable form of coordination.

These three types of coordination share strong similarities with the classifications made by other writers (Rogers and Whetten, 1982) who made a distinction, according to the degree of autonomy of the separate organizations, between three forms of coordination: mutual adjustment, alliance and corporate. With mutual adjustment, parties retain their autonomy: coordination is achieved by voluntary, more or less spontaneous interaction and is based on informal rules. The second type of strategy, that of alliance, is indicative of a situation in which no authority exists and where coordination is achieved by negotiated rules. Coordination strategies are labelled 'corporate' when organizations develop a joint authority structure to which they hand over some of their autonomy.

It is debatable whether the analysis of interorganizational relations is greatly enriched by such typologies. They can serve as a means of comparing different coordination situations. The chief importance of the research on interorganization theory is that it makes it clear that if organizations want to reach their goals, many of them will have to adjust their strategies in some way to those of other organizations. They can achieve this by means of various organizational arrangements.

2.4   Policy Communities, Subsystems and Networks

In political science there is an abundance of literature dealing with the relations between governmental agencies and private or semi-private organizations and the way these relations influence policy making. Widely differing traditions are reflected in this literature. These traditions use different concepts and focus on different research issues. The next section summarizes the main features of the literature on policy communities, subsystems and networks, starting with a brief outline of the roots of this literature in political science. Four main research traditions are briefly presented: pluralism, agenda research, neo-corporatism and subsystems/policy communities, followed by a more detailed exploration of the concepts of subsystems and policy communities.

From Pluralism to Subsystems and Policy Communities

Does power tend to be distributed equally in society, with active groups shifting a great deal between one decision and the next or is it concentrated in a relatively small group of actors who dominate most of the decision processes? This was the central theme of the debate between pluralists and elitists in the 1950s and early 1960s. The pluralists stated that the important actors varied with each decision process and that the political arena was relatively open: any organized group could gain entrance. Since each group had the opportunity to organize itself and organizations represent the interests of their members, one could say that the pluralists visualized the political process as a 'market-place': actors are relatively free to enter the arena in which the bargaining between different actors with different interests takes place.

As a result of the discussion between elitists and pluralists, a type of research evolved which focused on the relation between governmental agencies and pressure groups and the way policy was made (Jordan, 1990a: 297). In this research concepts are found such as subsystems, iron triangles, policy communities, issue networks, subgovernments, meso corporatism and policy networks (for a review, see Jordan, 1990b; Rhodes, 1990; Van Waarden, 1992). All these concepts indicate in some way the connections between governmental agencies and pressure groups. They also all underline the fact that policy is made in a complex setting in which many actors interact to ensure that the outcome suits their interests. The concept of policy networks is the most recent one and is rapidly replacing all the others. Broadly speaking, the concepts of iron triangles and subsystems or subgovernments were most popular in the United States and the concepts of neo-corporatism and policy communities (and, recently, policy networks) were more popular in Europe, especially in England.

The American research on the relation between pressure groups and governmental agencies was strongly influenced by the research on agenda setting and agenda forming which evolved out of the elitist–pluralist discussion of the 1950s and early 1960s. Research within this tradition focused on the questions of which policy issues would appear on the policy agenda, how this process takes shape and which actors and factors influence the process (Cobb and Elder, 1983). The agenda approach focused in particular on barriers to policy processes and the resulting 'non-decision' (Bachrach and Baratz, 1962). It also underlined the fact that issues which gained a place on the policy agenda had to overcome several barriers (formulating the issue, generating support, etc.) and that issues were subjected to a transformation process in which they were (re)formulated (Van der Eijk and Kok, 1975; Cobb and Elder, 1983). During this transformation, different groups tried to oppose or encourage the issue of formulation. Some of this research tried to classify the type of policy arenas in which agenda forming took place. Lowi's first attempt to classify these into distributive, redistributive and regulative policy arenas (Lowi, 1963) has been incorporated and adopted into the research on the relation between pressure groups and governmental agencies (e.g. Ripley and Franklin, 1987).

The European/English research was influenced by the discussion between pluralism and corporatism which emerged in the mid-1970s (Schmitter and Lehmbruch, 1979; Lehmbruch and Schmitter, 1982). In contrast to pluralism, corporatism stressed the fact that political processes were not open but relatively closed. Only well organized and state-licensed interest groups played a prominent role in policy formation (Williamson, 1989). Again in contrast to pluralism, corporatism emphasized the fact that not all interests had the opportunity to organize. The arena is often closed to less well-organized groups. Corporatism also placed more emphasis on the role of the state (Cawson, 1986). Owing to the expansion of its policy task, government is dependent on societal groups for information and implementation. Granting interest groups a special position in the political process is a way of enhancing the steering capacity of governmental agents and creating consensus between government and interest groups (Streeck and Schmitter, 1985). The research on policy communities was also influenced by interorganization theory (Rhodes, 1990).

In the final part of this section, the concepts of subsystems and policy communities are explored in more detail. An outline of the literature on the terms 'subsystem' and 'subgovernment' will be followed by a review of the literature on policy communities and networks. The section will conclude with an overview of the four approaches in political science: pluralism; agenda research; corporatism; and subsystems/policy communities.

Subsystems and Subgovernments

The concept of subsystems is not a new one. It emerged in the 1960s and stressed the fact that most routine decisions were taken within a cluster of individuals in a certain policy area (e.g. Freeman and Parris Steevens, 1987; Jordan, 1990a). The concept of subsystems was introduced by Freeman and referred to 'the pattern of interactions, or actors, involved in making decisions in a special area of public policy' (Freeman, 1965). Freeman was especially interested in actors connected with the US Congress: congress committees, executive agencies and special pressure groups.

The idea of subsystems was further developed by Ripley and Franklin (1987). Instead of subsystems they used the term 'subgovernments' which, according to them, are 'clusters of individuals that effectively make the most of the routine decisions in a given substantive area of politics' (Ripley and Franklin, 1987: 8). A typical subgovernment consists of members of Congress and/or the Senate, members of the congress staff, a number of civil servants and representatives of special interest groups. Ripley and Franklin emphasized the fact that subgovernments are involved in routine decisions. These decisions change only marginally over time and the participants involved are well informed about the content of those decisions and the procedures involved. Because subgovernments are involved in routine decision making they can often function undisturbed for long periods. According to Ripley and Franklin, subgovernments can be opened to outsiders if:

- subgovernment participants themselves disagree fundamentally on some points;
- the president or other high administrative officials and members of Congress intervene and mobilize resources to achieve changes;
- new policy issues attract the attention of outsiders, and these issues are placed within the subgovernment by outsiders or by members of the subgovernment themselves.

The concepts of subsystem and subgovernment are used to indicate interaction patterns in policy areas or, more specifically, parts of policy areas (Jordan, 1990a). In Ripley and Franklin's conceptualization, the concept of subsystems or subgovernments has a meaning very similar to the far more controversial concept of iron triangles.[5] In general, it is the search for stable interaction patterns, together with the question of which actors are responsible for decisions, that characterizes the empirical research which has been undertaken on the concepts of subsystems, subgovernments or iron triangles.[6] The research has focused on the question of which relationships can be found between actors and which of them are important for the decisions that are being made.

In more recent publications, attempts have been made to give the concept of subsystems a wider and more dynamic meaning. Wamsley described a subsystem as being 'comprised of actors seeking to influence the authoritative allocation of values. They are heterogeneous, have variable cohesion and they exhibit internal complexity. These functionally specialized policy subsystems span both the public and the private sectors as well as the branches and different levels of our government' (Wamsley, 1985: 77–8). According to Wamsley, a subsystem consists of a network of actors, a normative structure and a political economy, that is, the costs and benefits that are connected to participation in the subsystem. In addition to a horizontal structure which consists of representatives of pressure groups, civil servants from various departments and specialized politicians, the subsystem displays a vertical structure. This vertical structure is of major importance for the implementation of policy programmes. 'Government programs bind the program professionals and their professional associates together through all layers of government into vertical functional autocracies' (Milward and Wamsley, 1985: 106). In this view, the concept of subsystems is connected to the concept of networks. The latter refers to the pattern of relationships between actors and the former to the interaction system as a whole. In this way a correlation can be established between the 'classical' literature on interorganizational relations and networks and the literature on subsystems and iron triangles.

A similar approach was chosen by Laumann and Knoke (1987) who studied the interaction patterns and events taking place between actors in the two policy areas of health and energy[7]. After an intensive empirical study of these two policy domains, they concluded that national policy domains consisted of a group of core participants, made up of public as well as private organizations. At the end of their study they noted that

> Despite their lack of formal decision-making authority, many private participants possess sufficient political clout to secure that their interests will be taken into account. This mutual recognition creates and sustains the legitimacy of core actors' involvement in domain issues and events. . . . In explaining most decisions, the peripheral organizations may be ignored. . . . Within the group of core participants, however, there exists a relatively dense system of knowledge on interorganizational interaction. (Lauman and Knoke, 1987: 375)

Policy Communities and Networks

The concept of policy communities evolved from empirical research begun in the 1970s and 1980s. The research was mainly carried out in the United Kingdom (e.g. Heclo and Wildavsky, 1974; Richardson and Jordan, 1979; Grant et al., 1988; Rhodes, 1988) although some interesting, but often less well-known research was also done in other countries (Heisler, 1974; Koppenjan et al., 1987). In nearly all of the research the importance of the sectorization of policy making was underlined. This literature emphasized that policy making took place increasingly within closed communities of actors. According to Richardson and Jordan, 'the policy making map is in reality a series of vertical compartments or segments – each segment inhabited by a different set of organized groups and generally impenetrable by "unrecognized groups" or by the general public' (Richardson and Jordan, 1979: 73–4). Richardson and Jordan also argue that policy areas can contain several different policy communities. This same idea can be found in a study on government and the chemical industry by Grant, Paterson and Whitston

(1988). In addition to a core 'policy community' which deals with major issues affecting the chemical industry as a whole and which contains the most important public and private actors, they discovered four sectoral policy communities dealing with particular subsections of the industry (pharmaceuticals, agricultural chemicals, the paint industry and the soap and detergents industry).

The description of the concept of policy communities used by Grant et al., originally came from Rhodes. He described policy communities as

> Networks characterized by stability of relationships, continuity of a highly restrictive membership, vertical interdependence based on shared service delivery responsibility and insulation from other networks and invariably from the general public (including parliament). They have a high degree of vertical interdependence and limited horizontal articulation. They are highly integrated. (Rhodes, 1988: 78)

In other words, policy communities are a special type of policy network. Policy network, then, refers mainly to a complex of organizations connected to each other by resource dependencies and distinguished from each other by breaks in the structure of resource dependencies (Benson, 1982: 148). In analysing policy communities, Rhodes suggested that attention should be paid to the resources that actors have at their disposal, the value systems which are applied in a particular policy community and the rules of the game and strategies that are used (Grant et al., 1988; Rhodes, 1988; Wright, 1988; for an empirical application see Marsh and Rhodes, 1992). Broadly speaking, if the literature is compared to the US literature on subsystems, the English policy community approach and related concepts in the European literature tend to concentrate more on the analysis of value systems and perceptions of actors within communities.

The concept of policy communities thus usually refers (though not always: for an exception see Wilks and Wright, 1987) to a tightly integrated network with dense interactions between actors. Most authors emphasize the relatively closed nature of policy communities or subsystems. New actors can only enter this kind of network at a high cost to themselves. These costs are related to the investments that have to be made in learning the language and rules, establishing patterns of relationships and offering advantages for one or more actors in the network. It is this emphasis on the relatively closed nature of policy arenas which distinguishes the policy community approach from earlier pluralist theories. In general, the issue of their closedness plays a more important role in the discussion than in the US literature on subsystems.

An important theme in the policy community literature concerns the degree to which the network is closed and opinions are shared within it. Most authors agree that there is no need for substantial agreement but that at least some agreement on the rules of the game is necessary. Authors sometimes stress the fact that members of policy communities also share a policy paradigm, that is, a view of the world which consists of the most urgent problems that need to be dealt with, the actors who are part of the community and the main instruments which can be or need to be used to tackle the perceived problems (Benson, 1982). Nearly all authors underline the fact that actors within a policy community have certain interests in common which separate them from the actors of other policy communities (e.g. the housing policy community versus the health policy community) and from actors not included in their particular policy community.

An Overview of the Approaches in Political Science

As has already been argued above, the literature on subsystems and policy communities is heavily influenced by other approaches in the political science tradition. Table 2.3 shows the four approaches described with their main characteristics.

Table 2.3   *Approaches in political science*

Approach: Dimensions:	Pluralism (1950–1970; Dahl, Truman)	Agenda research (1960–; Bachrach and Baratz; Cobb and Elder; Lowi)	Neo-corporatism (1975–; Schmitter; Lehmbruch; Cawson)	Subsystems/policy communities (1965–; Freeman; Ripley and Franklin; Jordan; Rhodes)
Actors	Variety of actors	Variety of actors	Limited number of functional, well-organized actors	Limited number of sectoral-oriented actors
(Policy) Processes	Political market-places (free association, admission and exit)	Struggle between actors over issues Issues have to overcome several barriers before they arrive on the policy agenda	Bargaining between governmental actors and powerful semi-private actors Integrated and institutionalized	Bargaining/mutual adjustment between actors Integrated and institutionalized
Decisions	Result of group struggle and dominant coalitions Government ratifies compromises	Depends on support for issue	Governmental actors try to reach agreement with major interest groups	Compromise between important actors Routine decisions (sectoral-oriented)
Power	Dispersed widely Shifting coalitions on different decisions	Unequally divided Institutional power affects (non) decisions	Unequally divided Depends on scale and integration of interest groups	Depends on position and resources within policy sector
Information/ values	Different information is possessed by different actors (Conflicting) values weighted in market-like processes	Information scarce and a basis of power Issues involve conflicting values	Information mono-polized by powerful organizations Actors have different values	Information of specialized/sectoral nature Different and shared (sectoral/professional) values

2.5   Characteristics of Policy Networks

The concept of networks has been used with quite different meanings. This section will attempt to sum up some of the main characteristics of the concept of networks as it appears in the contemporary literature. After a brief recapitulation of the theoretical roots of policy networks and a discussion of some of the existing definitions, three main characteristics of networks are selected from the literature: dependency, variety of actors and goals, and relations. The section will then explore each of these characteristics in more depth.

Theoretical Roots of Policy Networks

The theoretical roots of policy networks can be found in policy science, organizational science and political science. The concept, derived from policy science, of policy processes as complex interactions involving many actors has been incorporated in theories on policy networks. The concept, derived from political science, of policy making taking place in relatively closed communities has influenced theories on policy networks. The policy network approach, derived from organizational science, was strongly influenced by the resource dependency approach and the central idea that organizational networks can be analysed in terms of organizational problems or resources.

These theoretical roots are shown in Figure 2.1.

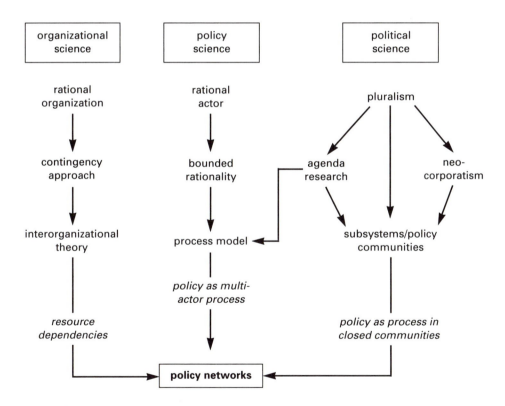

Figure 2.1   *Theoretical roots of policy networks*

What's in a Name?

It will have become clear that most descriptions and definitions of the concept of networks have defined them as clusters of organizations or sets of inter-organizational relations. There are currently many different definitions of networks.

Based on the literature in interorganizational analysis, Aldrich and Whetten (1981) made a distinction between networks, organization sets and action sets. A network, according to them, was the 'totality of all the units connected by a certain type of relationship', and was constructed by finding the ties between all the organizations in a population under study (Aldrich and Whetten, 1981: 387). Networks both constrain and facilitate the actions of organizations. A distinction was further drawn between organization sets and action sets. Organization sets consist of those organizations with which a focal organization has direct links. Action sets are groups of organizations that have formed a temporary alliance for a special purpose and who try to coordinate their strategic actions on specific topics.

The concept of action sets displays some similarities with Scharpf's selective activation. He argues that a network consists of numerous relations between actors and has defined networks as 'the ensemble of direct and indirect linkages defined by mutual relationships of dependency' (Scharpf, 1978: 362). For specific policy initiatives only some of these relationships have to be activated to achieve a priori formulated goals. Scharpf's description is more accurate than that of Aldrich and Whetten. Theirs could also be used to describe the concept of social systems and does not clarify what is so special about policy networks. Scharpf's description specifies the nature of the relationship: one of mutual dependency.

Another description which specifies the nature of the relationship is Benson's, which is often cited in network studies. He refers to policy networks as 'a complex of organizations connected to each other by resource dependencies and distinguished from each other by breaks in the structure of resource dependencies' (Benson, 1982: 148). Although Benson's definition adds two pieces of information on networks to Scharpf's definition (i.e. that they are relations between organizations and, specifying the nature of the dependency relations, that these are the result of dependency of resources between organizations), the second point is mentioned by Scharpf elsewhere, in his conceptualization discussing the various kinds of dependency relations.

It may be concluded that analysing policy processes from a network perspective means that the analyst focuses on the relation patterns between actors, their interdependencies and the way these patterns and interdependencies influence the policy process. The definition of policy networks used in this book is consistent with contemporary descriptions. *Policy networks are more or less stable patterns of social relations between interdependent actors, which take shape around policy problems and/or policy programmes.*

Comparing the preceding descriptions of networks with each other and with other literature on networks (Negandhi, 1975; Godfroy, 1981; Rhodes, 1981), three important characteristics of networks can be observed:

- networks exist because of interdependencies between actors;
- networks consist of a variety of actors each with their own goals;
- networks consist of relations of a more or less lasting nature between actors.

Dependency as a Precondition for Networks

Networks develop and exist because of the interdependency between actors. Interorganization theory stresses the fact that actors are dependent on each other because they need each other's resources to achieve their goals. This central idea lies at the core of most theories on networks. Interorganization theory has thus had a major influence on the development of network theories. The dependency relationship is elaborated in the bottom-up research on implementation and in many intergovernmental studies. In these studies the analysis focuses on the set of actors involved in policy making and implementation and the relations and resource exchanges in which they are involved. Rhodes, building on the European contribution to Crozier's interorganization theory, sees central–local relations as a complex game in which various levels of government are interdependent and in which they exchange resources (Rhodes, 1981; Marsh and Rhodes, 1992). Interdependencies cause interactions between actors, which create and sustain relation patterns. The term 'interdependencies' also implies that there is something to be gained by the actors involved. This can be the result of a more or less joint interest in a specific policy sector, as has frequently been pointed out in the studies on subsystems and policy communities. In such a situation, financial and legal resources are available to several actors in a policy field. Actors in these networks have a joint interest in securing the financial and legal resources of the political system.

A number of conceptualizations of types of interdependencies have been proposed by various authors. In addition to Thompson's typology mentioned above (pooled, sequential and mutual interdependency), there is also Scharpf's well-known typology. Based on Emerson's ideas on dependency and power (Emerson, 1962) he distinguished between two dimensions of dependency: the importance of the resource and the substitutability of the resource (Scharpf, 1978). One actor is dependent on another if his relation to that actor is characterized by low substitutability and a high level of importance.

One problem with applying such typologies is that interdependence is not static. It is something actors discover in interaction and which is changed in interaction (Crozier and Friedberg, 1980).

Variety of Actors and Goals

Policy networks consist of a wide variety of actors who all have their own goals and strategies. Policy is the result of interaction between a number of actors. There is no single actor who has enough power to determine the strategic actions of the other actors. There is no central actor and there are no a priori given goals of one central actor which can be used as a method of measuring effective policy (Scharpf, 1978; Gage and Mandell, 1990). In interorganizational studies this characteristic of networks is more strongly present. This is a logical result of the fact that this literature deals with the relations between organizations and does not have a special interest in the role of governmental organizations. In policy community and subsystem studies as well as in the implementation literature, more attention is devoted to the role of governmental organizations. However, an important shift in the analysis is made here. Governmental organizations are no longer analysed as the central actor but as one of the actors in the policy process (Scharpf, 1978; Hjern and Porter, 1981; Benson, 1982; Gage and Mandell, 1990).

This means that in the literature on policy networks the strategic interaction between actors is emphasized. Actors need each other because of the interdependencies that exist but at the same time try to steer towards their own preferences. This results in complex interaction and bargaining processes (Benson, 1978, 1982; Rhodes, 1988; Gage and Mandell, 1990). Policy processes in networks are unpredictable and complex. Not only are many actors involved but actors' preferences change in the course of the interaction. As a result of a situation where there are many actors with different strategies and a wide variety of goals, actors cannot know in advance which outcomes are likely to occur and which targets they can meet in the process. They have to learn this partly during the process itself. This means that strategic interaction is an important feature of processes in networks. Many authors have tried to define these processes in typologies of strategies (e.g. Warren et al., 1975; Benson, 1978; Godfroy, 1981).

Relation Patterns between Actors

Interdependencies between actors and the interactions which result from them create patterns of relations. All the literature on policy networks stresses the fact that more or less lasting relation patterns between actors develop which influence the interaction patterns taking place within networks.

The network literature which derives its inspiration from interorganization theory tends to describe this relation pattern in terms of the regularity of communication and interactions. Mathematical network analysis concepts such as frequency, directness and centrality (see Aldrich and Whetten, 1981) are used to characterize the positions of actors in a network. It is assumed, for instance, that actors who occupy a central position in the network (i.e. the relation pattern of the actor reveals a large number of direct contacts with other actors) are in a better position to reach their goals. They have more information, are better able to activate other actors and can mobilize better resources. The literature which derives its inspiration from the policy community approach has a tendency to emphasize the role of more or less formalized organizational arrangements (advisory bodies, consultation procedures, permission by the state to enter the policy process or to undertake the implementation of policy). Research also focuses on the interactions which take place within those arrangements and the positions of the various actors.

Focusing on the relation pattern between actors also entails focusing on the question of institutionalization. If actors interact with each other over a long period they create rules which regulate their behaviour and resource divisions which influence their strategic options (e.g. Warren et al., 1975; Rhodes, 1981; Benson, 1982). This means that relation patterns are characterized by regularities in behaviour caused by the existence of rules and resource divisions. The question is under what conditions these rules and resource divisions change.[8]

Conclusion: An Approach to Governance

As an approach to governance, the policy network approach underlines the highly interactive nature of policy processes while at the same time highlighting the institutional context in which these processes takes place. Institutional contexts are characterized by relatively stable relations between organizations which are sustained by ongoing resource flows between those organizations.

This leads to a different view of governance. Governmental organizations are no longer the central steering actor in policy processes and management activities assume a different role. This does not imply that all actors have equal power. Most network theories assume that the power of an actor is linked to the resources he or she possesses. In contrast to 'traditional' approaches, in the policy network approach the management role of governmental actors is no longer self-evident. In principle, every actor involved can perform a management role. But the management role itself also differs from that of more traditional approaches. Management activities are directed to a greater extent at improving and sustaining interaction between the different actors involved and uniting the goals and approaches of the various actors. Thus, not only do governmental organizations occupy a different position but they are also engaged in different activities.

In addition, the policy network approach draws attention to the importance of the institutional context for the issue of governance. If policy processes take place within a certain institutionalized context, (i.e. a stable relation pattern between organizations), it becomes important to understand this context and, where necessary and if possible, to change it. Understanding the institutional context is important because, from a policy network perspective, organizational arrangements are necessary for coordinating complex interaction between the various actors involved in policy processes. If organizational arrangements are not available it becomes difficult to link the various actors' viewpoints and interactions. The next chapter will address these issues of governance in policy networks.

Notes

1 Although a process perspective on policy can be found in the political science literature of the 1950s and early 1960s (Dahl, 1961; Truman, 1964) this literature does not focus to any great extent on the role of public policy, its processes and effects. It is more concerned with the relations between interest groups and the way these affect public policy.

2 The principles of the rational organization perspective can be found in the work of the scientific management school (Fayol, Taylor) but also in that of theorists like Weber in his model of bureaucracy (for a more extensive overview, see Morgan, 1986: 20–35).

3 The theoretical and empirical research of the contingency approach suggested that turbulent environments create a need for flexible, adaptive organization structures (e.g. Emery and Trist, 1965; Lorsch, 1975), for a more differentiated orientation on the part of managers (e.g. Lawrence and Lorsch, 1967) and cause more internal problems of coordination and control (e.g. Thompson, 1967; Aiken and Hage, 1968).

4 Crozier and Friedberg, commenting on the role of organizational rules and structures, express the view that 'Structures and rules have two contradictory aspects. In one sense, at any given moment they are constraints upon all the members of an organization, including the leaders who created them, while in another sense they are themselves a product of relations of force and of prior bargaining. They are provisional, always contingent institutionalizations of the solution to the problem of cooperation among relatively free actors' (Crozier and Friedberg, 1980: 53). Crozier's game analysis sums up the conduct of actors as the expression of 'a rational strategy associated with a game to be discovered'.

5 The term 'iron triangle' first emerged in the late 1950s to indicate a strong cooperation between specific interest groups, civil servants working on specific policy areas and parliamentary specialists. The concept of iron triangles, in common with that of subgovernments, emphasizes the intimate relations between congressional committees, representatives of pressure groups and parts of the civil service. Again, in common with the other two concepts, that of iron triangles underlines the tightly organized and stable nature of the relations between actors. The term 'iron triangle', however, has acquired a more rigid connotation. It is doubtful whether this connotation is entirely correct (Freeman and Parris Steevens, 1987).

6 A concept which is very different from this idea of 'closedness' is Heclo's concept of issue networks. In it he emphasizes the openness and unpredictability of policy making processes (Heclo, 1978). Heclo suggests that policy processes take shape in situations in which participants are constantly moving in and out. He is, however, alone in taking this stand, and has often been criticized for contributing 'nothing new' in comparison with the classical ideas of pluralism (Jordan, 1990a).

7 In their study they made use of the network techniques which have been developed in network research over the last 20 years. They used the concept of 'policy domains' which, according to them, is a subsystem 'identified by specifying a substantial defined criterion of mutual relevance or common orientation among a set of consequential actors concerned with formulating, advocating, and selecting courses of action (i.e. policy options) that are intended to resolve the delimited substantive problems in question' (Lauman and Knoke, 1987: 10). Lauman and Knoke also looked at the involvement of actors in certain issues. They labelled sets of actors who were interested in the same issues as 'issue publics'.

8 This question has not been addressed extensively in the literature on networks. The literature focuses on mapping networks (Marsden and Lin, 1982; Lauman and Knoke, 1987) but does not address the question of how networks evolve and are sustained. The question of how rules in networks are formed and what their function is has generally been neglected (Ostrom, 1986, represents an exception).

3

Public Management and Network Management: An Overview

W.J.M. Kickert and J.F.M. Koppenjan

3.1 Introduction

Governance and public management frequently take place in network-like situations. This is the case where sustainable patterns of interaction between actors have formed in the policy area in question and public problems are dealt with in highly interactive processes (see Chapter 2). It is remarkable that in a number of studies on policy networks such as those of Marin and Mayntz (1991), Marsh and Rhodes (1992) and recently that of Bressers, O'Toole and Richardson on water policies (1994), consideration is given to networks, their characteristics, factors which affect their formation and – to a lesser extent – their effects on policy outcome, whereas the impact of the existence of networks on governance and public management hardly receives attention. Yet an analysis of network management is precisely the vehicle for providing a perception of how networks can be utilized in endeavouring to developing policy and tackling problems in complex policy fields.

This chapter provides an inventory of the ideas and perceptions from the public administration literature which have been advanced on governance and public management in networks. The purpose of this 'state of the art' is to examine how governance and public management can take shape in situations in which central steering is not possible. In particular, the issue of what network management involves, and the forms network management can take, will be examined.

In section 3.2 we examine recent developments in the field of public management and governance in general and the implications of these for forms of governance which are based on a network approach. Section 3.3 examines the issue of governance and public management in policy networks. In section 3.4, the concept of network management is further defined and explored. Section 3.5 deals with forms of network management. The factors relevant to the success or failure of network management are explored in section 3.6. The position of public organizations as network managers is discussed in section 3.7. Section 3.8 offers a summary and conclusions.

3.2   Public Management and Governance: Some General Trends

The international developments and trends in Western public administration seem to have led to a new kind of 'public management'. In a survey of the developments in public management in 22 OECD countries (OECD, 1990, 1993), a number of common trends were described. Public management was found to be more results and cost conscious, with more provision of services and customer orientedness, performance budgeting, human resource management, computerization, performance control and evaluation of results. In a description of administrative reform in Great Britain, Australia and New Zealand – a smaller, less divergent and better comparable group of countries – Auctoin (1990) also came to the conclusion that two trends are apparent in public management: the wish to increase the primacy of politics over bureaucracy; and the tendency to introduce more businesslike management into government. Auctoin pointed out the possible contradiction between the two trends. Reasoning from the perspective of the primacy of politics, central control over bureaucracy should be increased. Reasoning from a business management perspective, one should decentralize, deregulate and delegate.

In his inaugural lecture at the London School of Economics, Hood (1991) examined the development of a new public management. Though well aware of the differences between Western countries, he concluded that the following common characteristics figure in all the discussions on 'new public management': clearer responsibilities for top management, performance indicators, output- and results-oriented behaviour, disaggregation of large bureaucracies into smaller, more autonomous units, market orientation and competition, emphasis on businesslike management, parsimony and discipline. Hood further concluded that these trends are not founded on one single common body of ideas, but on different and sometimes conflicting basic thoughts. The impression which Hood had gained during his stay in New Zealand was confirmed by a recent review of public sector reforms in Australia, New Zealand and Great Britain (Mascarenhas and Sienkiewicz, 1993): an 'enterprise culture' is arising there, a new public management.

In the Anglo-American world the new trend in public management is apparently to emphasize business and market orientation. The United States underwent a period in which the Reagan administration explicitly aimed at a reduction in government. The political and public debate at that time was highly anti-government. Following on from these rough times for the public sector the United States now seems to be pursuing a 'third way'. If taxes cannot be further increased and expenditure cannot be cut back, it will be necessary to produce better and more at less cost. Such 'third way' ideas about 'entrepreneurial government' proposed in *Reinventing Government* (Osborne and Gaebler, 1992) are intended as a defence of the public sector, and were fully embraced in the Al Gore report in the National Performance Review in September 1993. This new form of public management stresses increasing productivity, efficiency and flexibility, wants government to perform in a more businesslike way, to 'work better and cost less' and to produce 'results, not red tape'.

In the United Kingdom, the period of the Thatcher administration and that of her successor Major have also evinced an increasing emphasis on businesslike managerialism and market orientation in government management. The Rayner 'scrutinies' and his 'efficiency unit' resulted in substantial efficiency cutbacks. The 'Financial Management Initiative' of the mid-1980s, was followed at the end of the decade by a vast reorganization of the British civil service, initiated by the 'Next Steps' report (Jenkins et al., 1987). The idea underlying 'next steps agencies' was that autonomy would lead to better management of the implementation of public services, which in turn would lead to greater efficiency and better 'value for money' from those services. In 1991, Prime Minister Major introduced the idea of 'citizen's charters', a kind of public announcement by public organizations of the qualitative and quantitative standard of service delivery the client-citizens could count on. Major's next measure, forcing public agencies to 'compete for quality' in a regular open tender called 'market testing', was intended to force the public service delivery organizations to adopt a strong client and market orientation. Thus, British public management has moved from a Whitehall policy making orientation in the civil service towards businesslike management and client and market orientation in public agencies.

In his study of the rise of 'managerialism' in the public sectors in the United States and the United Kingdom, Pollitt (1993) showed that the idea of 'working better with less costs' has led government to introduce models and techniques from a more classical style of business management. His conclusion is that ideological and political 'new right doctrines' seem to play a larger part than scientific 'reason'. The introduction of methods and techniques from the private sector should correspond to the confidence in government and the extent to which it is valued. Pollitt concluded that this new managerialism, which emphasizes the need for better productiveness for lower costs, is 'the acceptable face of new-right-thinking about the state'. As to its meaning and content, Pollitt concludes that it is the kind of generic model of management which ignores the public–private distinction and which in fact boils down to classical neo-Tayloristic 'managerialism'.

Public and Private Management

The difference between public and private management has been extensively discussed in the management and organization sciences. Allison (1980) has categorized the differences into three groups. First, the differences in environmental characteristics – market exposure, legal, formal constraints and political influence; second, those in the relationship between environment and organization – coerciveness, scope of impact, public scrutiny and expectations; and third, the differences in organizational factors – goal complexity, authority relations, performance, incentive structures and personal characteristics. Perry and Rainey (1988) have created a three-dimensional typology of organizations: is the organizational ownership public or private, is the funding public or private and is the mode of social control market or 'polyarchy'?

The environment of government, especially the interaction between government and its context, differs fundamentally from that of the private sector. Generally speaking, the 'environment' of government can be characterized by basic notions such as 'political democracy' and 'legal state'. The societal, political and legal environment of government is distinctive. The administrative relations between societal sectors and government, the relationship between politics and the administrative part of government, the meaning of law and legislation, all differ fundamentally from the private sector. In business administration, no equivalent exists for the many theories about the relations between politicians and bureaucrats. Assuming that the environment and the nature of an organization are important to its management and structure – the fundamental assumption of contingency theories – then public management would have to differ from private management. Public management certainly cannot blindly imitate business management. The specificity of the object – management in the public sector – leads to the need for a methodological and theoretical specificity – public management (Bozeman, 1987, 1993; Kooiman and Eliassen, 1987; Pollitt, 1990; Rainey, 1991).

Norms and Values in Public Management

Public management is not only about increasing effectiveness and efficiency, but is also a matter of legality and legitimacy, of more than strictly businesslike values. When the organization of government is considered, one has to bear in mind the basic starting points of democracy and the legal state. According to Dahl (1970), the three criteria which a democratic state has to meet are democracy, efficiency and rationality. These criteria can be conflicting. In order to achieve a high degree of democracy, a price may have to be paid *vis-à-vis* the degree of rationality and effectiveness of government. Without denying the importance of the effective and efficient functioning of government, other values also play a role in government steering.

Hood (1991; Hood and Jackson, 1991) identified three different value patterns. In the first pattern government is supposed to be lean and purposeful. Effectiveness and efficiency, parsimony and performance orientation play pivotal roles. In the second, honesty and fairness are the central values. In government, social justice, equality, legitimacy and the proper discharge of duties are central principles. In the third pattern robustness and resilience dominate. Government must be reliable, robust, adaptive, secure and confident and must be able to survive catastrophes. Harmon and Mayer (1986) also identified other norm and value patterns for government besides effectiveness and efficiency. According to these authors, the norms and values which play a part in government can be divided into three groups: first of all, efficiency and effectiveness, regarding the functioning of government itself and the production and distribution of goods and services; second, rights and the adequacy of the governmental process, concerning the relation between government and its citizens; third, representation and power checks, concerning public scrutiny of the functioning of government. These last values are also reflected in the 12 commandments of the 'ethical code' which the American Association for Public Administration (ASPA) drew up founded on the basic notions of honesty, justice and equality.

Complex Networks

In modern society, an approach to public management not only has to deal with norms and values that go far beyond the criteria of effectiveness and efficiency which dominate the debate about new public management. The approach to management that we seek also has to encompass the complexity of government's environment. Public management is the 'governance' of complex networks, consisting of many different actors, such as parts of national, provincial and local government, political and societal groups, pressure, action and interest groups, societal institutions, private and business organizations, etc. The management of such public networks is a form of external government 'steering', steering having a broader meaning than strict administrative control, being more adequately defined as 'directed influencing'. Public 'governance' is the directed influencing of societal processes in a network of many other co-governing actors. These actors have different and sometimes conflicting objectives and interests. Government is not the single dominant actor that can unilaterally impose its will. Hierarchical, central top-down steering does not work in networks, which have no 'top'. The monocentric and monorational style of coordination and management cannot be applied in a network.

In the perspectives on new public management, the internal functioning of public organizations is the central focus. In so far as new public management is limited to transferring management insights from business administration to the public sector it is not really new at all. In fact, it is concerned with the micro-economic issues of the public sector. This means that the discussion has a limited application for the issue of governance in a complex environment.

Governance in networks requires a different perception of public management which is more geared to the external functioning of the public sector and its legitimacy. Network management might constitute one form of this type of public management. This book is an attempt to work out in detail this variation on 'new public management'. The next section will examine the consequences of the existence of policy networks for governance and public management. In Table 3.1 the differences between new public management and governance in policy networks are summarized.

Table 3.1   *New public management and governance in policy networks*

	New public management	Governance in policy networks
Problem	(Cost-)effectiveness	Interdependence
Main orientation	Intraorganizational	Interorganizational
Main concern	Administrative control	(Facilitating) co-governance
Public–private dimension	Businesslike	Specific role government

3.3   Public Management and Governance in Policy Networks

Co-governance and Negotiating Government

In order to achieve their goals, actors in networks need to participate in games: interactions between actors which develop around issues in which they have an interest (Allison, 1971; Crozier and Friedberg, 1980). This means that they have to exchange their 'go alone strategies' for 'contingent strategies': courses of action tailored to the behaviour of others (Ostrom, 1990). Thus, according to Lynn, successful public management is also 'effective gamesmanship'. One element of this is to answer the questions of which games should be participated in and what form this participation should take (Lynn, 1981: 154–5). Kooiman (1993), in his book *Modern Governance*, points out the importance of 'co-governance', a new form of steering which he describes as 'doing things together instead of doing them alone, either by "state" or "market"' (1993: 1).

'Doing things together' assumes that actors see some advantage in joint action. This advantage lies in the surplus value of the solution achieved jointly compared to outcomes pursued in isolation. In many cases, by seeking joint interests instead of adhering to one's own goals, situations may be achieved which represent an improvement for all parties either *vis-à-vis* the existing ones, or as regards those which can be achieved on the basis of go alone strategies. In this context, Agranoff (1986: 9) mentions integrative 'mutually beneficial solutions' (and cf. Dery, 1984). He points out that these are more than just a compromise between the various parties' go alone strategies. It is precisely because actors are prepared to modify their perceptions of problems and interests that it becomes possible to find new solutions which have a surplus value compared to solutions which actors pursue independently. In game theory, this process is described as converting zero-sum into zero-plus games. In a zero-plus game it is possible to achieve 'win-win situations'.

In the renowned negotiation theory of Fisher and Ury (1981), described in their book *Getting to Yes*, they argue that win-win situations are to be reached through integrative negotiation. In integrative negotiation, parties do not cling to their previously held positions, but go in search of joint interests during the negotiating process. 'Exploration' plays an important role in this: the creative searching for new solutions which take account of the problem and interest definitions of all parties concerned. Co-governance may be defined as negotiating government whereby opportunities for creating win-win situations by means of integrative strategies are explored and pursued.

From Go Alone Strategies to Cooperation

Actors will not always decide on such a course of action, however. Joint action does have its downside. First there are decision making costs: invest-ments in terms of money, time and energy which participation in games demands. Second, there are external political costs: the compromises which actors in a game will have to accept. Depending on these social interaction costs, actors will have to decide whether or not to participate (cf. Hirschman, 1970). The way in which this process of consideration develops is examined in the transaction costs approach (Williamson, 1985).

Elster (1986) demonstrates that this decision is not always a question of cal-culation but may be linked to the rationale according to which actors operate. He identifies a parametric and a strategic rationality. Actors who allow their behaviour to be guided by a parametric rationality see themselves as the sole steering entity, surrounded by static objects. This leads to attempts to coor-dinate behaviour unilaterally, and to go alone strategies aimed at devising in advance the best possible solution, taking into account as many parameters as possible. Actors who allow themselves to be guided by a strategic ratio-nality, on the other hand, perceive the interactive aspect of policy processes. They see their environment as consisting of other actors, all with their own objectives, on whom they are dependent for achieving their goals (cf. Scharpf, 1978: 350–2; Mandell, 1990: 33).

In order to achieve joint action on problems within existing networks, bar-riers which hamper this action need to be removed. Actors must be prepared to exchange their 'go alone strategies' for contingent or cooperative strategies. In order to achieve this they must recognize that cooperation is to their advantage. However, that is not enough. Theories about collective action and game theories demonstrate that even though actors have an interest in coop-eration, the structure of interaction situations results in actors nevertheless clinging to non-cooperative strategies.

Barriers to Joint Action: The Collective Action Problem

The public choice approach links this problem to the external costs and ben-efits of interaction between actors. External benefits occur when actors who are not involved in the interaction are nevertheless able to reap the rewards. A classic example is the tendency shown by employees not to join a union because they are able to benefit from that organization's efforts anyway. This problem of free-riders, described in particular by M. Olson (1965), may lead to a collective good not coming about because actors either choose free-riders' behaviour or refuse to accept the costs for these free-riders. In other words: positive externalities result in an underinvestment in cooperation. In the case of negative externalities of cooperation, the decision makers do not bear all the costs of their activities and will therefore 'overinvest'. This leads to activities proceeding despite their socially undesirable consequences (Scharpf et al., 1978). Industrial activities with environmental consequences provide an example of this. Since environmental costs are not 'included' in the calculations for the production costs, they do not constitute a relevant factor in entrepreneurs' strategic decision making. In short, the structure of inter-action situations can result in social interests being inadequately served.

Hardin's 'tragedy of the commons' illustrates this issue (Hardin and Baden, 1977). In his analysis he argues that the decline of the 'commons' in pre-industrial England was due to the fact that individual shepherds benefited from the use of the commons, while the costs had to be paid by the commu-nity. This resulted in overgrazing, which finally led to the destruction of the commons.

The example of the prisoner's dilemma taken from game theory illustrates how the actions of two players who are out to achieve optimum results for themselves, but are unable to communicate with each other, result in less favourable outcomes for both players. Thus, game theory demonstrates that problems of cooperation may damage not only 'collective interests' but also self-interest. Based on these considerations, the hypothesis advanced in pub-lic choice theory and game theory is that cooperation aimed at achieving collective goals will only be established under duress.

The Problem of Collective Action Challenged

Seeking solutions to the problem of collective action has caused this hypoth-esis to come under attack. In game theory, it is challenged on the grounds that games are not discrete entities but form part of a series of games. Axelrod (1984) and Taylor (1987) argue that through the repetition of games (the so-called 'supergames') actors are made aware that they will meet their adversaries again in the future. This provides a rationale for the players to choose cooperative strategies. Thus, these authors demonstrate that although assumptions concerning actors' individual rationalities are maintained, coop-eration can nevertheless be accounted for.

However, the question is whether it is not precisely this assumption of indi-vidual rationality as the basic principle for action that is in need of adjustment. First of all, the prisoner's dilemma game is criticized because of the assumption of absence of communication between actors. This is fre-quently not the case in policy practice. Those concerned, therefore, are in a position to exchange information with each other and reach a consensus on solutions which are favourable for all parties. Second, March and Olsen, in their book *Rediscovering Institutions* (1989), point out that much behaviour is of a routine nature. Many complex patterns of behaviour are not based on cost–benefit considerations, but on the use of 'standard operating proce-dures': rules concerning appropriate behaviour (pp. 21–38), and rules, incidentally, which are not 'blindly' applied. Usually, in concrete situations, the question of which rules are applicable should first be answered. Moreover, rules may be vague or even intrinsically contradictory. This means that their use is accompanied by considerable policy freedom. It is also conceivable that rules might be broken. In short, behaviour may be determined by a varying mix of calculation and routine.

Based on these considerations, Ostrom (1990) challenges the assumption that actors are not able to achieve cooperation voluntarily. Owing to actors being allowed to communicate, in contrast to the prisoner's dilemma, they are able to build consensus and agree on the mutual adoption of rules. By committing themselves to collective action, the strategic uncertainty preventing them from investing in collective action is reduced. Actors commit themselves to agreements in which they promise to abandon opportunistic strategies, such as premature withdrawal, free-riders' behaviour and so forth. This commitment may be laid down by actors in various arrangements or 'sets of rules', such as cooperative agreements, contracts, joint ventures, and so forth.

The Need for Network Management

The question, however, is whether Ostrom is not over-optimistic about the capacity of actors to achieve cooperation independently. In administrative practice, actors will undoubtedly succeed in many cases in achieving successful cooperation and co-governance. However, that does not alter the fact that there are a good many situations where it does not happen. Attention has been drawn in this context to the existence of 'second order collective action problems'. If actors do not succeed in achieving cooperation with regard to a concrete problem, how then is it conceivable that they could succeed in building consensus on how they are going to organize that cooperation? We take the position that in certain situations, given the attitudes of the actors concerned, the current game rules and the social capital available, actors might independently reach a consensus on collective action, whereas in other situations an outside impetus is needed. As alternatives to self-regulation, Ostrom sees only Leviathan or the market. In our opinion, there are a number of options between these two extremes. Network management provides a way for actors to cooperate without solutions being forcibly imposed or cooperation becoming redundant as a result of decentralization or privatization. Nevertheless, our viewpoint does not differ wholly from that of Ostrom. She mentions the presence of public sector backing as one of the success factors for self-governance. Network management is one of the forms which this backing may take.

3.4 Network Management

Network Management: Furthering Interaction

Network management is a form of steering aimed at promoting joint problem solving or policy development. It should be distinguished from usual strategies which actors, including public organizations, implement within policy games. In order to achieve goals in situations of mutual dependency, actors need to employ a versatile approach in their attempts to influence policy games, that is, to incorporate the effects of their dependence on other actors into their own strategies and to see and make use of opportunities for co-governance. Network management is an activity which takes place at the meta level: it involves steering efforts aimed at promoting these cooperative strategies within policy games in networks. Thus, network management may also be seen as *promoting the mutual adjustment of the behaviour of actors with diverse objectives and ambitions with regard to tackling problems within a given framework of interorganizational relationships.*

This mutual adjustment contrasts with other forms of coordination. Dahl and Lindblom (1953) have distinguished four principal forms of coordination: polyarchy, hierarchy, negotiation and market (pp. 21–4). Polyarchy refers to forms of democratic representation whereby the people check the behaviour of their political leaders. Hierarchy denotes central coordination which is found in, for example, bureaucratic organizations. In a market situation, it is the market mechanism that causes individuals to gear their behaviour to one another. However, behaviour may also be mutually adapted through interaction in the form of negotiation and consultation between actors.

Network management is aimed at stimulating this last category of coordination. As mentioned earlier, it should be distinguished from forms of central coordination which are associated with polyarchy and hierarchy. On the other hand, it also differs from mutual adjustment, in so far as that concerns adjustment without interaction (compare Lindblom, 1965). In a market situation, coordination between actors develops on the basis of individual choices which actors make independently of each other. In a network, such 'go alone strategies' on the part of individual actors are rendered problematic by the interdependencies between actors. There is too much uncertainty regarding the strategies which other actors will choose and which might have a serious impact on the options for achieving one's own objectives or even for being able to function adequately. Mutual coordination thus implies interaction: in interaction, actors adapt their individual strategies to those of other parties (Scharpf, 1978: 350–2).

Rogers and Whetten (1982) discuss three coordination strategies within networks: corporate strategies, alliances and mutual adjustment. In the corporate model, coordination is realized by formal rules, central authority and collective goals. In the alliance model, negotiation is central and mutual agreements apply. In mutual adjustment, autonomous goals prevail and mutual influence forms the central focus. In their book *Strategies for Managing Intergovernmental Policies and Networks*, Gage and Mandell (1990) develop another typology of coordination mechanisms. They make a distinction between unmediated and mediated coordination. Unmediated, voluntary coordination refers to coordination initiated by participating organizations. Mediated coordination is further divided into legally initiated vertical coordination and horizontal systems in which a third party takes up the role of mediator and initiates coordination. A common trait of both typologies is their threefold subdivision. A third intermediate category is placed between the two extremes of vertical, hierarchical, formal coordination on the one hand and horizontal, voluntary and informal on the other. Thompson et al. (1991), in a recent categorization, present networks as an alternative coordination instrument in addition to those of public sector and market.

The problem with these typologies is that they suggest three coordination mechanisms, two of which are all too familiar, and thus fail to add much to our understanding of network management (Kickert, 1991). We need to focus on the intermediate model in which coordination involves the furthering of joint problem solving through interaction.

Network Management: An Elaboration

Various authors have attempted to describe network management in more detail. As early as 1978, Hanf was talking of 'interorganizational coordination' which meant 'intervening in the existing structure of interrelationships in order to promote the interactions appropriate for mobilizing a concerted or coordinated effect consistent with the objective interdependencies of the problem situation' (1978: 12). In his study of intergovernmental management, Agranoff (1986) lists three characteristics of this type of management. In common with Hanf, he argues that the term 'management' implies that the existing organization structure is 'taken for granted' and the important thing is discovering how to deal with this system. Furthermore, he makes the issue of cooperation and coordination the central focus: 'joint efforts towards agreed upon issues'; in other words, problem solving through joint image building (pp. 5–8). Wright (1983) describes three comparable characteristics of intergovernmental management: strategic and 'coping behaviour', communication, and problem solving.

From these descriptions it can be deduced that network management comprises three elements: intervention in an existing pattern of relations, consensus building and problem solving. With regard to the first of these, however, opinions differ. Authors such as Scharpf (1978) and O'Toole (1988), in contrast to other writers, consider the restructuring of relations within a network as part of network management. As far as the two other characteristics, joint image building and problem solving, are concerned not everyone understands them to mean the same thing. O'Toole, on the subject of intergovernmental management, talks of 'mobilization for collective action' and 'multilateral coordination' (1988). Glasbergen (1995: vii) sees network management as 'a new approach . . . to deal effectively with environmental problems'. Furthermore, he makes a sharp distinction between consensus building and problem solving: 'It remains by no means clear that consensual politics inherently leads to better environmental policy' (ibid.: 14). In short, some authors refer to joint problem solving which must be reached through consensus building. In that case, consensus building and problem solving practically merge. Other authors, however, assume a fixed, objective problem situation, in which it is not certain whether consensus building will result in a solution to the problem. Table 3.2 summarizes the three main activities which make up network management.

Table 3.2   *Network management: three activities*

1	Intervening in existing patterns/restructuring of network relations
2	Furthering conditions for cooperation; consensus building
3	Joint problem solving

Network Management: A New Form of Steering?

To what extent, in a historical sense, is network management a new phenomenon? Some authors claim that network management is a new method of problem solving (Glasbergen, 1995). In some fields and in certain situations that may be true. Broadly speaking, however, this hypothesis is not tenable. Historically speaking, strategies and procedures may be encountered in numerous policy fields which might not be referred to as network management, but in retrospect may well be classified as such.

Richardson (1982), for example, pointed out the existence of policy styles. He contrasts a policy style aimed at imposing solutions on other actors with the policy style of accommodation, whereby social groupings, in exchange for contributing their know-how and information, are permitted to influence government policy. Richardson argues that this style underlay the development of neo-corporatist systems in Western democracies. This policy style led to the creation of consultation structures between social interest groups and the public sector which – as far as conscious attempts at institutionalization were concerned – could be considered as forms of network management.

As Chapter 2 discusses in depth, neo-corporatism does not constitute the only historical root of the network approach, either in terms of policy practice or theory formation. Consequently, in the policy practice of government steering over the last hundred years, numerous other forms of network management *avant la lettre* may be found.

3.5   Strategies for Network Management

In Chapter 2, it was stated that the policy network approach as an approach to governance underlines the highly interactive nature of policy processes, while at the same time highlighting the institutional contexts in which these processes take place. This statement has two major implications for network management. First, it means that in order to be successful, attempts to initiate and support the game or interaction process should take institutional factors into account, that is, the interdependencies between actors, their relationships, the rules that guide their interactions, etc. Second, it means that there are two points of intervention for network management strategies. In addition to strategies aimed at influencing the interaction processes directly, network management may be directed at the institutional context, the structure and culture of the network, in order to improve conditions for cooperation indirectly. Thus, two forms of network management may be identified: managing interactions within networks, or, as we have called it elsewhere, *game management*, and building or changing the institutional arrangements that make up the network: *network structuring* (Klijn et al., 1995). Views found in network theory and related literature regarding both these forms are discussed below.

Network Management as 'Game Management'

Network management conceived as the steering of interaction processes may involve activating networks to tackle particular problems or issues (network activation), establishing *ad hoc* organizational arrangements to support interaction (arranging), bringing together solutions, problems and parties (brokerage), promoting favourable conditions for joint action (facilitation) and conflict management (mediation and arbitration).

Network activation   Network activation involves initiating interaction processes or games in order to solve particular problems or to achieve goals. In this context, Scharpf (1978: 345–69) talks of 'selective activation'. An (empirical) network has many potential relations not all of which are constantly activated. Selective activation involves identifying and activating the parties necessary for tackling a particular problem or particular task. (Prescriptive) policy networks are thus mobilized. Friend et al. (1974) talk in this context of 'reticulist judgements'. These are decisions focused on:

1   the activation of links in a network (one or more people who occupy 'nodal positions') connected with the exploration of decision making issues; and
2   the nature and amount of information which needs to be sent through these links.

With regard to the activation of links in a network, an important issue is who should be involved and who not. The success of this activity depends among other things on the willingness of those who are invited to participate to invest their time and resources in the decision making issue concerned, and the willingness of those who are not invited to stand on the sidelines (Friend et al., 1974; Scharpf, 1978: 365–6).

With regard to the information which is provided, the important issue is which information should be given and how much. Scharpf (1978) talks of positive coordination if those involved are given the opportunity to hold an open discussion about alternatives. There is negative coordination if only one alternative is proposed.

Selective activation is seen by many authors as an important form of network management. O'Toole (1988) talks in this context of mobilizing the network for 'joint problem solving'. Mandell stresses the importance of establishing 'mobilization behaviour' in contrast to ex ante design: 'the managers do not necessarily achieve goals by formally setting them forth and then building strategies to achieve them. They may refine their ideas many times based on support for and against them before actually proceeding with them' (1990: 33). Glasbergen (1995) applies the ideas regarding selective activation to environmental problem solving. He sees network management among other things as the activation of the 'most relevant social interest groups'.

Arranging interaction   Joint problem solving assumes that actors will decide to participate in games. Such a decision is not taken without risk. Earlier, the dangers of opportunistic behaviour linked with cooperation, such as free-riders' behaviour and 'premature pulling out', were mentioned. Hence, actors will be more likely to choose cooperative strategies if they know that such dangers are minimized. To that end, they may proceed to arrange their inter-action, for example by entering into a gentlemen's agreement, a cooperative agreement, a contract, or a joint venture, or by setting up a new public-law or private-law body. These all formalize the agreements and rules which regulate their interaction. Thus they commit themselves explicitly once again to the agreed objectives, rules and procedures (Teisman, 1992).

An element of arranging is to provide conflict regulating mechanisms, which indicate how action should be taken in conflict situations and the way in which differences of opinion should be resolved (cf. Crozier and Friedberg, 1980). Game management may be directed towards bringing about *ad hoc* arrangements which facilitate the development and course of interaction processes.

These ad hoc arrangements are explicitly directed towards underpinning a particular game. Arranging should thus be differentiated from network struc-turing, which is aimed at influencing the culture and structure of a network. Permanent modifications are then introduced which will affect to a greater or lesser extent most of the games within the network.

Brokerage: matching problems, solutions and actors   Network management as guided mediation may mean (the responsibility of) taking on the role of 'broker' or furthering the performance of this role by others. A broker is an 'intermediary, a go-between' (Mandell, 1990: 47; compare also O'Toole, 1988).

Kingdon (1984) argues that as a result of the fragmentation of policy processes into 'loosely coupled structures', problems, solutions and partici-pation develop relatively independently of each other, and that for agenda building and decision making it is necessary for them to be brought together. This role is taken on by entrepreneurs, 'people willing to invest their resources in return for future policies in their favour' (Kingdon, 1984: 214). Entrepreneurs not only raise problems and suggest solutions, but also act as brokers. They deal in ideas and solutions and link up actors who would not have found each other by themselves. Entrepreneurs' motives may range from pursuing self-interest or promoting certain proposals to genuine concern about certain developments or simply enjoying participating in interaction processes.

Mandell (1990: 47) identifies three kinds of 'broker':

1   the orchestra leader who can envisage exactly how the product of the 'concerted action' should look;

2   the *laissez-faire* leader who is solely focused on bringing parties together and who has no interest in the content of the outcome of the interaction;
3   the 'film producer' who is highly involved, but due to his dependencies on others is intent upon keeping them involved in the process.

The importance of the role of broker lies in the fact that their activities contribute to tapping and utilizing the diversity of ideas, insights and solutions which are present within a network, but which without their efforts would not be mobilized for tackling a problem. By creating such a diversity it becomes easier to find solutions which are acceptable to those involved. At the same time, this means that brokerage activities may make a significant contribution to the creation of conflict because of the fact that, partly owing to the broker, 'advocacy coalitions' form around certain problem definitions or proposals which then conflict with one another (cf. Sabatier, 1988).

Facilitating interaction   Game management may also be aimed at creating conditions for the favourable development of strategic consensus building in interaction processes. In such a case, the network manager acts as 'facilitator', as process manager (O'Toole, 1988). Facilitating covers a large number of activities, all of which are of a procedural nature. As Susskind and Cruikshank (1987: 152) put it: 'the facilitator focuses almost entirely on process, makes sure meeting places and times are agreed upon, sees that meeting space is arranged appropriately, and ensures that notes and minutes of the meetings are kept . . . facilitators monitor the quality of the dialogue, and intervene with questions designed to enhance understanding'. In order to foster conditions for consensus building, the facilitator may employ a number of 'techniques', such as organizing workshops, conducting surveys, organizing brainstorming sessions, initiating role play and promoting collective image building (p.154). These activities contribute towards increasing an understanding of the issues at stake, the diversity of ideas, the ability to appreciate each other's viewpoint and the dedication to joint problem solving.

The strategies listed by Agranoff (1986) under the heading of intergovernmental management could easily be seen as facilitating. He argues that this type of management should contribute to an open exchange of ideas and opinions; exploring creative and mutually beneficial solutions; confronting opinions and entering into commitments (1986: 180–2). He, too, emphasizes the importance of promoting collective image building: intergovernmental management is directed towards realizing a 'joint task orientation'.

Glasbergen (1995) points out the importance of structuring the interaction process in a number of steps. Facilitating in that case may involve getting participants to agree upon which subproducts will be delivered when. An ideal phased development for an interaction process does not exist, but the steps which are taken should constantly be adapted to circumstances. Agranoff (1986: 177), on the basis of empirical research into intergovernmental management in six metropolitan areas, argues that interaction processes are characterized by many 'loops' and steps backwards and forwards. There is reflection and communication about how the process is developing: watches are synchronized continually.

In Forester's view (1989: 90), facilitating may be defined as 'premediation': 'articulating others' concerns well before they erupt into conflicts'. Facilitating is therefore not only directed towards the reduction of conflict and consensus building, but its objective may on the contrary be to provoke conflict and organize confrontations between participants. The underlying rationale is to prevent interests, views and ideas from remaining unarticulated or being suppressed. In later stages, this can lead to blockades and deadlocks, but it also compromises the quality of the interaction and the joint solution (Brown, 1983).

Mediation and arbitration   Mediation and arbitration may be distinguished from facilitation on account of the fact that they are implemented at a time when conflict exists and the interaction process finds itself in an impasse. A distinctive feature of mediation is that the responsibility for reaching a particular outcome rests with the participating parties (Susskind and Cruikshank, 1987: 162). Mediation is implemented by a party which is not involved in the conflict, and which maintains no direct ties with either of the disputing parties concerned. During the process, this independent position must be preserved (Glasbergen, 1995: 168). Mediation can occur spontaneously, but alternatively, an actor might be invited by the parties to act as mediator.

Activities which the mediator may undertake are:

1   ensuring that relations are maintained; opening up channels or keeping them open. This also includes calling on parties to recognize and respect the interests of other parties (Moore, 1986; Forester, 1989: 93–5);
2   keeping an eye on procedures and making procedural and, on occasion, substantive proposals (Susskind and Cruikshank, 1987: 162–5);
3   signalling which resources are necessary to resolve the conflict and making suggestions as regards making use of them. These might include such things as carrying out research, involving legal or technical exports and so forth (Moore, 1986);
4   exploring standpoints; exploring possible solutions, through, for example 'shuttle diplomacy' and putting out feelers (Susskind and Cruikshank, 1987; Forester, 1989: 92–3);
5   confronting the parties with the perceptions and interests of the 'outside world'. This might include calling into question unrealistic claims, or taking into account unrepresented or underrepresented interests (Moore, 1986; Susskind and Cruikshank, 1987);
6   endeavouring to make parties enthusiastic about and getting them committed to the proposed solutions (Susskind and Cruikshank, 1987).

Apart from (promoting) mediation, network management may also involve seeking arbitration for the solution to conflicts. Arbitration means that parties ask a third party to intervene and impose a solution on them. This might happen, for example, when parties sue: a practice which occurs far more frequently in the USA than in Europe, but which is also becoming increasingly common there. The disadvantages for the parties concerned are that the conflict is no longer in their hands, that procedures are prolonged and costly, and that judges do not command the knowledge and expertise to devise an effective solution. Furthermore, constitutionally speaking it is not always possible for public-law parties to go to court, and is often unorthodox.

As an alternative, therefore, forms of non-binding arbitration are also implemented. The conflict is then presented to a person or committee which suggests a solution but does not impose it. It is possible, however, that parties undertake in advance to accept the proposed solution as binding, but to what extent this can be enforced is debatable (Susskind and Cruikshank, 1987: 176). Appointing a committee of 'wise men' who come up with solutions for getting out of the impasse is a tried and tested method.

Network Structuring: Tinkering with the Network

If it proves impossible to solve problems within the existing network, one might consider modifying the network. Scharpf refers in this context to a misfit between the empirical structure of the interorganizational network and the prescriptive task structure of required policy interactions (1978: 363). He sees this misfit as a strong predictor of policy failure. At the same time, he cautions against reorganizations in connection with the 'multi purpose structure' of networks and organizations. An organization structure rarely corresponds to the ideal scale of one particular task. For this reason, it should not be expected that an ideal organization form will be found for the interactions concerning specific tasks. A second argument is that reorganizations are expensive and time-consuming.

Ostrom (1990), too, cautions against radical reorganizations or organizational innovations. Her argument is that within existing networks there are forms of self-regulation which are based, among other things, on knowledge of local circumstances and shared rules and perceptions. Attempts to alter arrangements or to introduce new ones may result in the destruction of this 'social capital'. Ostrom refers to the introduction of state management in connection with the threatened destruction of the tropical rainforest in Brazil, which led to existing forms of self-regulation based on local rights of ownership being destroyed without the state being able to replace them with any new, effective protection for the forest (Ostrom, 1990: 18). At most, she envisages opportunities for an incremental restructuring, whereby new arrangements and 'sets of rules' do not replace existing ones, but are built onto existing ones (Ostrom, 1990: 189).

These warnings do not dissuade other authors nor Scharpf and Ostrom themselves from seeing tinkering with the network as an option. O'Toole (1988) points out the options for promoting cooperation via a number of 'strategic variables'. Two of these relate to the network. According to O'Toole it is possible, by means of influencing the 'formal policy', to influence the division of resources within the network and thus alter the actors' positions.

In this way, possible 'veto points' might be either established or removed.

In the formal policy, an actor may be designated as 'lead organization', that is, network manager. Not only relations but also rules may be influenced via the formal policy: the guidelines which regulate, among other things, interaction and participation. Although O'Toole indicates that the influence of the formal policy is limited by, among other things, informal power relations, in his recommendations he nevertheless acknowledges its importance. This may be explained in part by the fact that he is talking about implementation issues. It should be borne in mind, however, that in many processes in networks a 'formal policy' as such does not exist other than various actors each pursuing their own policy or strategy.

O'Toole's second strategic variable is formed by the structure of mutual dependence and the decisions which are taken in this regard within the network. Involved here are the number of units within a network and their interrelationships. O'Toole points out the problem of the optimal size of networks. The literature is peppered with warnings against too many actors in connection with high coordinating costs. This is not to say that the smallest network must necessarily be the best. Owing to the uncertainty about future developments, maintaining redundant relations is essential (Landau, 1969).

O'Toole sees a relation between network features on the one hand and process development and network management on the other. Restructuring policy fares better in professional networks; development programmes require politicized networks. In an 'assembly line' there is a need for a network manager to act as 'fixer' (Bardach, 1977); whereas a complex network is more likely to need a mediator.

In addition to changing relations, resources and rules, network management can also imply changing the existing values, norms and perceptions of actors within the network. By directing 'internalization processes' the manager can attempt to steer the value and interest definitions of a target group in a desired direction (In 't Veld, et al., 1991). This strategy is quite popular in the field of environmental policies. It is carried out by means of intensive and expensive mass information campaigns, but also through information strategies directed at specified target groups (Neumann, 1995).

A more drastic method is that of 'reframing', an intervention which challenges actors' frames of reference (Rein and Schön, 1986, 1992). The objective is to effect an illogical, irrational leap which can be compared to a 'paradigmatic shift' (compare Kuhn, 1962). 'The approach results in changing perceptions, behaviour and relations,' according to Levy and Merry (1986: 96). Striking, shocking events often serve as a trigger for reframing, whether consciously directed or not. Reframing can be organized by confronting representatives of different coalitions or organizations. Techniques used include gaming and simulations.

Opinions are divided regarding the options for influencing networks in a specific way. Earlier, the reservations of Scharpf and Ostrom were presented. March and Olsen (1989) caution that given the complexity of reorganization processes, these sometimes degenerate into garbage-can processes with entirely unexpected outcomes. There is a consensus that network structuring is not simple. Nevertheless, some authors have greater expectations than others of the opportunities for social engineering. Others see network structuring less as a possibility for influencing networks in a certain direction. Instead, network management is associated with mobilization and conflict, and with 'management by chaos'. Richardson, for example, points out that existing networks may be broken into by new coalitions or, alternatively, issue networks (Heclo, 1978; Richardson, 1982). By provoking such a mobilization, it is possible to put pressure on existing 'closed circuits' and, if enough pressure can be applied, to break them open.

Kickert (1993b) states that ideas about the self-referentiality of systems, networks and organizations do not imply that it would not be possible to disturb the internal balance. By drastically disrupting the environment of the system, it may be brought out of balance to such an extent that a leap to a new internal balance becomes possible. In this way undesirable forms of 'dynamic conservatism' may be dealt with. Note that the new balance is not imposed, but must come about through the self-regulating capacity of the system. Table 3.3 sums up the strategies for network management which we have discussed above.

Table 3.3   *Strategies for network management*

Game management	Network activation
	Arranging
	Brokerage
	Facilitating
	Mediation
	Arbitration
Network structuring	Influencing formal policy
	Influencing interrelationships
	Influencing values, norms, perceptions
	Mobilization of new coalitions
	Management by chaos

3.6   Conditions for Network Management

Empirical studies of network management and its effects are scarce. Systematic research into its effects and effectiveness are almost wholly lacking (exceptions: Ostrom, 1990; Agranoff, 1986). Yet various authors have mentioned preconditions for the method and potential success factors. There now follows – with no claims to exhaustiveness – an overview of these frequently mentioned factors.

The Number of Actors

Many authors assume that the more actors are involved in interaction processes, the more difficult it becomes to reach agreement. Perceptions from game theory, however, show that the number of actors is not the crucial factor which promotes or impedes cooperation within game situations. After all, a prisoner's dilemma occurs between two actors. On the basis of empirical study, Ostrom (1990) concludes that even in situations involving many actors, they are nevertheless able to achieve cooperation. Owing to the need for keeping or making situations of collective action manageable, endeavouring to reduce the number of players is understandable. This is expected to enhance control of the situation. The concept of selective activation also appears to fit in with this line of argument: in a process or game, involve only those who are indispensable.

In reality, however, it will not always be possible to exclude actors, simply because of the existing relationships of dependency. A considerable risk is that actors might misjudge their external dependencies and exclude actors without whom they are unable to achieve their objectives in the short or in the longer term. Furthermore, given the uncertainties surrounding strategic interaction processes, dependencies are very difficult to assess. Instead of aiming at reducing uncertainty, making use of uncertainty is often a more prudent strategy. It should be borne in mind that an increase in the number of actors causes not only increased complexity, but also an increase in the number of permutations for achieving an adequate approach to problems. Moreover, attention should be drawn to the importance of maintaining redundant relations in connection with uncertain future developments. Of course, network management is not a case of 'the more the merrier', but rather of finding an adequate level of participation.

Diversity within Networks

The complexity of policy networks finds expression in, among other things, the multiformity of the actors who are part of them. Whereas central governance implies a generic approach to target groups, network management signifies a more differentiated approach to actors within networks. Attempts to influence the behaviour of actors are tailored to the specific features of actors (fine tuning). Fine tuning makes heavy demands on the network manager, as regards not only their knowledge about specific actors and the strategic skills of the steering organization but also their capacity to simultaneously manage different strategies and instruments (De Bruijn and Ten Heuvelhof, 1991). Multiformity sets limits to traditional management methods.

Consequently, an alternative to fine tuning is formed by management at a distance, whereby an organization endeavours to steer without getting bogged down in the details of the internal processes of the organizations or networks concerned, and without the risk of becoming involved in internal processes (Kettl, 1988). Furthermore, agreements may be made regarding the preconditions which will apply to collective efforts at problem solving. Network management then takes the form of 'management at a distance'.

In other words, the success of network management will depend on the degree to which efforts to influence games and networks take account of the multiformity of the network and the actors who operate within it.

Closed Nature of Networks

In addition to multiformity, closedness also represents an important problem area as regards the options for steering. The concept of closedness originates in systems theory. The closedness of systems does not mean that they do not receive any inputs from the environment, but that they process these inputs in their own way. Complex social systems are highly self-regulating. Within the system there are divergent, conflicting forces which balance each other out. If this equilibrium is disturbed by external influences, these forces then seek a new point of balance (Kickert, 1993b). This idea from cybernetic systems theory has been developed by Luhmann (1990) among others in a theory on self-referential social systems. While coping with disturbances from outside, self-referential systems refer only to themselves. They are self-referentially closed. Self-referential systems have recently acquired the name of autopoietic systems, based on a model of living systems called autopoieses (Varela et al., 1974). This biological model envisages a living system which is able not only to produce or reproduce its elements, but in particular to generate and reproduce its organization, the interactions between elements that compose the system. These ideas have more recently been applied to organizations (Morgan, 1986), legal systems (Teubner, 1982) and governmental steering (In 't Veld et al., 1991).

If networks are conceived as systems which are to a large extent closed off, then the opportunities for network management will be limited. Thus, Scharpf (1978) states that selective activation assumes loosely coupled structures instead of rigid, traditional hierarchies of tightly knit networks. Two implications may be linked with closedness. The first has negative implications. Closedness implies that steering signals do not penetrate into the system. In so far as that does happen, there is uncertainty as to how the system will react to it.

The second implication has a more positive aspect. The underlying idea is that this self-referential nature forms the pivotal factor for exerting influence. Dunsire introduces the concept of 'collibration' to describe this: 'under certain conditions, although you may not know what the point of balance between rival forces is likely to be or should be, you may be able to bias that location to suit yourself, within limits, by intervening in the equilibration process' (1993: 26). 'Collibration' does not by definition serve to promote joint action. It can evidently also be used for less high-minded motives, namely 'to suit yourself' (ibid.). Ostrom (1990) argues that efforts to prompt actors into collective action should take advantage of the 'social capital' available, that is, existing forms of self-regulation, based among other things on prevailing 'sets of rules'.

From this perspective, network management involves taking advantage of the capacity of a system for self-management, thus causing it to be 'adjusted' using minimal coercion and resources. Network management then entails 'balancing social forces and interests and enabling social actors and systems to organize themselves' (Kooiman, 1993: 256).

Conflict of Interests

The absence of too sharp a conflict of interest is also considered by most authors to be a precondition (Agranoff, 1986; Ostrom, 1990; Kooiman, 1993). Attention is often drawn to the fact that joint action assumes a convergence of interests. In situations in which interests are divergent or even clash, reaching consensus is rendered impossible by lack of alternatives and by conflict. Such a statement, however, is based on a structuralist orientation. It assumes that interests are fixed and embedded in the objective division of resources within the network.

At first sight it resembles the position which Scharpf et al. (1978) take up where they argue that the conflicts of interest between actors and their veto power limit the margins within which solutions may be sought. However, they also argue that efforts to exert influence may be directed towards influencing actors' definitions of interest. In other words: interests are not fixed, but are social constructs which might be modified through interaction. Although Scharpf in his concluding chapter (1978) remarks that as long as game theory is still in its infancy a structuralist approach is preferable, this nevertheless places him much nearer to the social constructivist game theory of for example Crozier and Friedberg (1980) than he admits.

The ideas of March and Olsen (1976a) are also consistent with a game approach. They have pointed out the ambiguous nature of many interaction situations. Actors initially have no idea where exactly their interests lie. They only develop this idea when they start to gain information on the subject during the course of the process and through the contributions of other actors. In short, the scope for finding a joint solution is far greater than may be inferred from the reference to conflicts of interest, because interests are not an objective fact but are defined by actors in the course of interaction processes.

If, based on Scharpf, we assume that interests are defined by actors themselves, this means that network management should then be directed towards influencing interest definitions. We would not go so far as to say that overcoming alleged conflicts of interest is always possible, but this precondition is certainly less 'rigid' than is often intimated.

Costs of Network Management

There are costs involved in network management. The higher these costs, the less actors, including public organizations, will be inclined to take this role upon themselves. The success of network management, in terms of the costs entailed in it, depends partly on the way in which it is implemented. De Soet (1990) finds a connection between the seriousness of a conflict and the comprehensiveness of the mediation. Minor forms of conflict require facilitating, more serious forms need mediation and major situations require arbitration.

Ostrom (1990) draws attention to the need to reduce the enforcement costs of agreed solutions. An essential element of successful joint action is that agreed solutions should also be enforced. Enforcement implies monitoring, an activity which requires the intensive gathering of information, possibly followed up by the imposing of sanctions. This gathering of information may be extremely expensive, as might the imposing of sanctions which, as experience with the enforcing of fishing quotas in Europe has shown, are not always workable and occasionally even dangerous.

By recognizing and making use of the know-how which the parties concerned possess and their problem perceptions and interactions, in short by the self-regulating capacity of networks, it is possible to minimize the costs of network management. Thus, Dunsire – inspired by the cybernetic systems approach – argues that 'Government could never govern if the people were not self-governing' (1993: p. 26). Management of networks should be harmonized as far as possible with the self-governing capacity of networks.

Political and Social Context

A number of authors have stressed the importance of the role of the political and social environment. In this connection, Glasbergen (1995) talks of the macro context, the environment in which networks find themselves and which can influence the functioning of networks and even threaten their existence. Political and social involvement may underpin the course of interaction processes within networks, but may also disturb it.

Agranoff (1986) argues that intergovernmental management must take account of political developments. In Kingdon's conceptual model, the stream of political developments forms the central focus (Kingdon, 1984). In their efforts to establish support for proposals, the entrepreneur should take full advantage of these developments. Lynn (1981) argues that public managers need to participate simultaneously in games at both the meso and the macro level. In short: processes which take place within a network may be strongly influenced by developments in the network environment.

These may lead to networks being broken open, game rules and perceptions being changed and the conditions in which interaction occurs being altered drastically. As a result of this, interaction processes may take an unexpected turn or become blocked. It is also feasible that solutions which were accomplished through exemplary processes of joint decision making will be superseded or will not be accepted by the broader social or political environment. An example of this can be found in the recent developments regarding the establishing of a regional government in the Rotterdam region. After the local, provincial and national authorities had reached agreement on the forming of a new province in the Rotterdam region, as a result of which the major city of Rotterdam (pop. approx. 600,000) would be divided into smaller units, opposition to these proposals arose. In a Rotterdam referendum, a significant majority of the voters expressed dissatisfaction with the plans and, as a result, the agreed solution was dropped. It is essential that network management should also reflect developments of this kind in the network environment and endeavour to anticipate them, for example by confronting the actors within policy networks with the possible effects of developments outside the network and with 'perceptions from the outside world'.

Leadership and Commitment Power

The results of network management are determined by the capacity of actors to demonstrate leadership in interactions by devising new options, speaking out for them to their organization and in addition by succeeding in getting their organization to keep to the agreed procedures. Network management, however, rarely directs itself to organizations as a whole. Interactions take place between representatives of 'corporate organizations', whose representativeness and commitment power is not always guaranteed. In network management it is important not only to create consensus between the representatives of organizations regarding a joint course of action, but also to establish support for these ideas within the organization. This calls for leadership qualities. Representatives in organizations must be willing to take risks during negotiations by accepting new ideas and being prepared to speak out for them to their organization. In other words, the success of network management largely depends on the quality of the leadership and the commitment power possessed by the representatives of the organizations involved.

Skills

Finally, attention should be drawn to the quality of network management as a precondition. Friend et al. (1974) emphasized the importance of reticulist skills: the ability to correctly assess who should be involved in interaction processes and which information should be given to them. The 'mediation literature' mentions skills such as being able to negotiate and mediate (Susskind and Cruikshank, 1987). A network manager must be able to operate in a complex domain and needs to be able to distinguish between diverse target groups and to make use of various methods of approach at the same time. Others point out the importance of the availability of information and know-how.

Although it would hardly be possible for a network manager to be an expert in every issue that happens to require their attention, a certain amount of expertise is nevertheless indispensable (Ostrom, 1990). In addition, they will need to possess the necessary 'tactical and strategic' know-how: knowledge about the actors involved and their idiosyncrasies, and the shared perceptions and game rules which affect the behaviour of actors within the network. The degree to which the network manager is able to retain their independent position is also mentioned in this context, although authors have indicated that a network manager need not by definition adopt an impartial stance towards the outcome of the interaction (Friend et al., 1974; Kingdon, 1984; Mandell, 1990). Of particular importance also is the extent to which other actors consider the network manager legitimate. In short: the qualities and skills of the network manager constitute a crucial precondition for success. Thus not every (public) organization will be capable of adequately fulfilling this role.

3.7   Governmental Organizations and Network Management

Governmental organizations operating in networks frequently come up against deep-rooted opinions about what government is or should be. This is linked with the fact that the phenomenon of 'policy networks' has been subjected to considerable criticism. They are considered to be non-transparent, impenetrable structures of interest representation which block essential, broad-based policy innovations and constitute a threat to the effectiveness, efficiency and democratic legitimacy of government performance (Marsh and Rhodes, 1992: 249–68). Although this criticism is primarily aimed at the functioning of policy networks in practice, it also implies a rejection of policy networks as a steering model. Government should try not to manage networks but to combat them.

This position does not detract from the fact that governmental organizations often find themselves in complex arenas which do not always allow them to ignore networks. Whether they want to or not, in order to be able to function they will have to enter into relations with organizations in their environment. Often, however, there are more positive reasons for joining a network or adopting network management strategies. Networks frequently offer the prospect of results which could not be attained by government's go alone strategies. Negotiating government and network management are forms of steering in which the public sector is highly dependent on other actors and where the alternatives, market and hierarchy, encounter normative or practical difficulties.

Theoretically, governmental organizations may respond to the existence of policy networks in a number of ways. They may refrain from engaging in network processes, they may join networks as a 'party among other parties', they may attempt to impose solutions on other actors within a network by means of hierarchic interventions, and they may take on the role of network manager (see Table 3.4).

Table 3.4   *Attitudes of governmental organizations towards networks*

1	Refraining from engaging in network processes
2	Participating as party among other parties
3	Participating as 'special party'; imposing solutions on parties in networks
4	Taking up the role of network manager

The first alternative implies abstaining from policy and this choice might not even be open to public organizations, for example because political superiors demand results. Neither is joining networks as 'a party among other parties' always permitted. An example of this might be the restrictions which are imposed on public organizations in combating organized crime. In other situations, however, this option is undisputed, but the question remains of to what extent government is capable of fulfilling its task in negotiating processes. Third, a public actor may attempt to impose solutions on other participants in the policy network. This may lead to high enforcement costs.

This avenue is sometimes feasible or necessary, but is not an option which could simultaneously be implemented in a large number of cases. There are also restrictions associated with the last alternative: choosing to take on the role of network manager. If serving a clearly defined interest is demanded of a public actor, the more process-oriented role of network manager may then conflict with this.

One argument for government taking on the role of network manager is that to do so might mitigate objections linked to networks. Public organizations are in an obvious position to ensure that the interests of unrepresented or underrepresented groups are safeguarded. As far as that is concerned, government might be a far more suitable candidate for playing the role of network manager than other parties.

3.8   Conclusion

In the literature, theories regarding the consequences of policy networks for governance and public management have not been elaborated in detail. There are few publications on this subject. There is literature available, however, such as the so-called 'mediation literature', which does not deal explicitly with this theme, but offers relevant insights into our subject. In the network literature, moreover, a considerable conceptual multiformity can be found which is evident, for example, from the abundance and diversity of concepts and strategies. On some points the conceptual distinctions are inadequate. Thus, authors scarcely distinguish between government operating as 'an actor among many' and government playing the role of network manager. Similarly, authors stress different theoretical and normative features. Some authors emphasize the importance of a process approach and consensus building, while others attach more importance to 'good policy' and effective problem solving.

Nevertheless, a certain convergence of ideas is apparent, which could form the primary focus for the further development of perspectives on network management. Most authors agree that network management is directed towards promoting cooperation between actors within a set framework of interorganizational relations. Some authors restrict network management to the influencing of interactions within fixed relationships; others also include the modifying of those relationships. In spite of these differences, it may be argued that there is conceptual agreement regarding making a distinction between a game level and a network level. Management strategies can be directed towards both levels. Thus, a distinction may be made between what we have termed game management and network structuring. The diversity of the network management strategies which are discussed in the literature are dealt with in the light of this dichotomy.

This chapter has examined the conditions for successful network management and the role of public organizations as network manager. It has been established that this role is not always open to public organizations, that they are not always equal to it, but that generally speaking it is vital that public organizations play this role because they are eminently suited to reducing or removing a number of disadvantages connected with the functioning of policy networks.

This chapter has provided an overview of the state of affairs with regard to the perspectives on steering and public management in policy networks. This state of the art is intended to provide a point of departure for the chapters that follow, in which a number of theoretical, conceptual and empirical themes are discussed and elaborated in order to gain a more thorough and systematic understanding of what network management involves or could involve.

PART II
NETWORK DYNAMICS AND MANAGEMENT

4

The Dynamics of Closedness in Networks

L. Schaap and M.J.W. van Twist

4.1 Introduction

Most network theorists agree that policy networks are not easily managed. There is also agreement up to a point about why the options for steering in policy networks are limited. Many authors have tried to find the key for this in the (relatively) closed nature of (the actors within) the network, although a systematic theoretical underpinning of this interpretation is sadly lacking. In order to explain the (relatively) closed nature of policy networks, most authors draw attention to the balance of power and resources in the network (Hanf and Scharpf, 1978) or to actors' self-interest (Sabatier, 1986; Rhodes and Marsh, 1992). In our view, such explanations are inadequate because they fail to focus on the question of where interests arise, whether a difference in perception with regard to the balance of power and resources is possible, what the consequences of this then are and whether the (relative) closedness can be surmounted by management interventions. Similarly, the question of the relationship between the closedness of the separate actors and the closedness of the network as such has hardly been dealt with. Yet such questions are relevant to an analysis of the options for steering networks and also to any recommendations which might then ensue. The literature on the closed nature of policy networks is characterized by such a wide variety of interpretations of the concept of 'closedness' (linked to a lack of systematicity) that a number of questions are left unanswered (see In 't Veld et al., 1991).

In this chapter our aim is to develop a public administration model of closedness which can provide an instrument for analysing network management in policy networks and any subsequent problems that arise. We have chosen the following approach. First, we examine the various forms of closedness. On the basis of this, we then develop an analysis model. Based on this analysis model we try to find clarifications for the various forms of closedness. We discuss three of these: veto power, frames of reference and network culture. We attempt to prove that there is interference between these three clarifications. Subsequently, we make a detailed examination of network culture as the cause of closedness, part of our intention being to illustrate how the culture of the network relates to the individual frames of reference of the actors in the network. Finally, the dynamics of the relationship between steering and networks will emerge as a central focus.

4.2 Some Forms of Closedness from the Literature on Networks

In the literature on networks, we can find various insights into closedness and policy networks (e.g. Rhodes, 1980; Jordan, 1990a; De Bruijn and Ten Heuvelhof, 1991). On the whole, insufficient attention is paid to whether it is the closedness of separate actors or the closedness of networks which is at issue, in other words, the closedness *within* networks or *of* networks. In the following sections, we shall present an analysis model in which we explicitly introduce that distinction. First, we describe a number of forms of closedness, based on a distinction between the social and the cognitive dimension of the interaction within networks. We have not attempted to provide a full description.

Closedness in the Social Dimension: Inclusion and Exclusion

Closedness in the social dimension occurs when certain actors are excluded from the interaction, for example because other actors fail to appreciate their contribution or do not consider it relevant. In that case, the range of possible links between actors in the network is consciously restricted. Elsewhere, this has been called social fixation (Van Twist and Termeer, 1991). Social fixation can be of a formal or informal, conscious or unconscious nature.

The entry of actors into the network (and the concomitant relative closure in the social dimension) can be made formally verifiable by, for example, introducing institutionalized membership as a condition of participation in interaction (Jordan, 1990a: 327). There are numerous examples of networks which clearly display closedness in the social dimension, for example religious communities or associations of professionals. Illustrative of the closed nature of professional associations is the strong aversion traditionally shown by the Dutch medical profession to admitting 'alternative healers' to their ranks. The closedness of networks in the social dimension does not always have to be formally confirmed, however. Frequently, informal rules of behaviour are developed within a network which in fact regulate the inclusion of actors in and their exclusion from the interaction within the network, without this being explicitly indicated in formal rules.

The exclusion of actors may be formally or informally arranged, but it can also be the result of a conscious strategy (such as that of the traditional medical fraternity) or of unconsciously applied rules. In the academic world, for example, there would appear to be only minimal closedness: the quality of academic debate and fraternal equality are keynotes in the scientific community, which is devoted to the search for truth. In science, truth is often linked with intersubjectivity, with harmonization in the academic forum. However, a necessary precondition for this intersubjectivity is to form a part of that academic forum, and it is not always simple to gain access to it. Various rules apply, some of which can unconsciously lead to social exclusion: knowing the jargon, being highly respected within the field of study concerned (for example having published widely or having obtained one's doctorate), having a position at a reputable university or department (Kuhn, 1962). However marginal they may seem, all of these are rules which are important if one is trying to become established in the academic world. The academic forum appears to be very open, but here, too, self-selection (often unconscious) and thus closedness in the social dimension are found.

Closedness in the Cognitive Dimension: Inability or Unwillingness to Perceive

In addition to closedness in the social dimension, closedness in the cognitive dimension can also occur. Two forms of cognitive closedness (also called cognitive fixation) can be identified: closedness in the sense of *an inability* to perceive and closedness in the sense of *an unwillingness* to perceive. The latter is a conscious strategy, whereas the former is not.

   In the former case, none of the actors in a network have direct access to the reality 'outside'. They first have to perceive that reality and ascribe meaning to it before it can play a role in their decisions. For this purpose, actors have their own frame of reference (Rein and Schön, 1986); a frame of reference which organizes their perceptions and thus enables the interpretation of a complex reality. Frames of reference have a selective and regulatory effect which facilitates the ascription of meaning, and this effect is a requirement for interpretation since it is impossible to fathom reality the way it 'really is' for actors in all its complexity. The fact that actors by definition ascribe selective meaning (supported by their own frame of reference) to reality, results in a certain degree of cognitive closedness. Actors are then cognitively closed to those aspects of reality to which they do not ascribe any meaning or to which they ascribe a different meaning.

   In addition to closedness in a cognitive sense, resulting from an inability to perceive due to the selective interpretation based on the frame of reference, cognitive closedness stemming from an unwillingness to perceive can also occur. The latter is the case when actors declare a particular line of approach to be out of order. Phrases such as: 'we're not discussing that now', or: 'you can't consider every angle' are symptomatic of this. In contrast to the first type of cognitive closure, this constitutes a (goal) conscious strategy to reduce complexity.

Interference between Forms of Closedness

Social and cognitive closedness can be analysed not only as separate elements, but also as relative to each other: the latter method illustrating that the two forms of closedness interfere with each other. By excluding certain actors (social closedness) it becomes possible to promote the exclusion of particular points of view (cognitive closedness). Conversely, downplaying (consciously or unconsciously) certain aspects of reality as they are perceived (cognitive closedness) can result in certain actors not being involved in the interaction (cognitive closedness). Thus, the two types of closedness are able to reinforce each other.

A Model for Determining (Types of) Closedness

This overview offers us two distinctions: between the social and cognitive dimension of closedness and between conscious and unconscious exclusion. One distinction which has only been implicit up to this point is that between actor and network. In the introduction we stated that in the network literature, arguments about closedness often fail to make clear whether it is the closedness of actors or the closedness of networks which is at issue. In our view, the various types of closedness are as likely to occur at the network level as a whole as at the level of the actors within it. We are defining actors here as the individuals, groups or organizations which are active in a network. The distinction between them is of an analytical nature and can be defined empirically in a number of ways. What we consider an organization can also be defined as a network and, conversely, what is defined here as a network may be regarded as an organization. The distinction, then, is only intended as an aid to analysing (steering problems resulting from) conscious or unconscious, social or cognitive closedness. When we use the term 'actors', here, it is understood that any further interaction on their part is not the subject of our research. The term 'network' indicates the opposite: here, it is precisely the interaction between actors and the impact which this interaction has on the policy making process and the culture of the network which we wish to highlight.

We can now represent schematically the forms of closedness we wish to identify using the three distinctions we have introduced for this purpose. Table 4.1 can serve as a basis for diagnosing the problems that occur in the management of and within policy networks.

Table 4.1   *Forms of closedness*

Social closedness		Cognitive closedness	
Unconscious exclusion by actors	Conscious exclusion by actors	Actors' inability to perceive	Actors' unwillingness to perceive
Unconscious exclusion by networks	Conscious exclusion by networks	Networks' inability to perceive	Networks' unwillingness to perceive

The table shows that we are dealing with eight forms of closedness: two types of closedness (conscious and unconscious) in two dimensions (social and cognitive) and at two levels (actor and network). In the following sections we examine the causes of these forms of closedness. We identify three:

- the veto power of actors (4.3);
- frames of reference (4.4);
- the culture of a network (4.7).

The last of these is dealt with in depth. We shall indicate the forms of closedness resulting from each of the three causes.

4.3 First Clarification for Closedness: Individual Veto Power

The clarification for closedness which usually receives most consideration in the literature is the veto power which actors in the network command: the veto power by means of which 'obstructive' management interventions, that is, management interventions which are not acceptable to the actors, can be averted. This clarification for closedness will be dealt with first.

The term 'interdependence' is an important concept in analyses of policy networks. This term implies that the actors in the network are dependent on each other for obtaining the resources which they (think they) need in order to realize their objectives (Aldrich, 1979; Benson, 1982). The actor who needs resources from another actor in order to achieve their objectives is dependent on that other actor (or on others who may take their place). Interdependence with regard to resources compels actors to interact in order to achieve their own objectives.

The central theme of the steering issue of policy networks thus also concerns the structure of the interdependence, as has been argued in earlier chapters. Steering in a network cannot be achieved by setting an empowered hierarchy at the top of the network. This type of hierarchic approach to steering fails to take into account mutual dependencies. In network management, it is not coordination and integration which are the key terms but mutual dependence and balance of power. Steering a network means influencing the balance of power (Kickert et al., 1985: 132–5). Actors who are dependent on each other to achieve their objectives will be prepared to surrender only precisely the amount of autonomy necessary to achieve those objectives (Wassenberg, 1984: 200). Thus, managing means operating constantly in a field of tension between dependence and autonomy. The actors in the network will not automatically accommodate the objectives of one actor, even when that one actor is 'government-related' (Kiser and Ostrom, 1982). In this field of tension, steering will take place through negotiation and exchange, persuasion, the forming of coalitions and strategic cooperation.

For our argument about closedness it is necessary to establish that actors in the network are always relatively autonomous and thus to some extent are able to cut themselves off from the steering interventions of other actors. The mutual dependence implies that each of the actors possesses veto power. Our hypothesis[1] is that this veto power can result in a number of forms of closedness:

1 *Conscious social exclusion at actor level.* Actors can deploy their veto power to exclude certain actors: 'In principle, we are quite happy to cooperate, as long as they keep out of it.' Actors are not in agreement, are

not prepared to provide another actor with resources and therefore refuse to interact.

2   *Actors' conscious cognitive closedness.* Actors can also deploy their veto power to ban certain points of view: 'In principle we are quite willing to participate in the brainstorming as long as that point is not raised.' This type of problem is often what is being referred to when the network literature talks of closedness as a barrier to steering. Actors close themselves off in this way to other points of view, to certain problem definitions and to problem-solving processes.

3   *Conscious social exclusion at network level.* Finally, a network as a whole can also be closed by veto power to actors outside the network, either through the veto power of a number of actors, or through the veto power of the network. To illustrate this we remind the reader of the example of the professional associations discussed earlier.

4.4   Second Clarification for Closedness: Actors' Frames of Reference

A second clarification which we come across in the literature is the existence of actors' 'frames of reference' (Rein and Schön, 1986). An actor's frame of reference functions as a filter. The world an actor perceives is a reality which is filtered through their frame of reference. Actors only perceive 'the' facts if, and in so far as, their frame allows. This offers an explanation for the relative closedness which occurs when there is a confrontation between different points of view and actors try to reach a consensus by means of a 'closing' argument based on 'the' facts. The filtering effect of the frames determines the receptivity to new developments, as well as the actor's explanation for them. Information from other actors is not perceived in the way it is intended but in the way that this, modified by the filtering effect of the frame, is interpreted by an actor. Sometimes, actors can only ascribe meaning to totally new developments and facts by having a different frame. To achieve such a 'reframing', however, the actor needs at the very least to clearly understand why their present frame of reference is inadequate for perception. This is not as easy as it seems, because in order to understand this the actor needs to see what they have been unable to perceive, and in order to be able to see that, they first need to undergo 'reframing'.

The conclusion is: actors' frame-bound perception is self-referential (it refers to the actor's frame of reference) but not self-interpretive, that is, it does not call the frame itself into question. In order to assess one's own frame it is first necessary to get a new frame – a different frame of reference with which to assimilate and interpret the available facts. However, even after the frame has been changed, the perceptions still remain self-referential and not self-interpretive; the actor still does not see what they are unable to see (at most they can suspect its existence) (In 't Veld et al., 1991). Actors tend to become fixated on the frame of reference which they have at a particular point in time and with which they ascribe meaning to reality in public administration. This is another reason why it is not always easy to arrange for actors to exchange one frame for another. Incidentally, this does not imply that the existence of frames should be seen in a negative light: actors need a frame in order to be able to gather information at all.

Our provisional hypothesis (which needs to be further assessed by means of empirical research) is that the actors' frames of reference cause the following forms of closedness:

1   *Actors' unconscious cognitive closedness*, previously referred to as 'inability to perceive'. This is not, as we mentioned, a conscious strategy but a result of the differing frames of reference which actors have. Actors in the network are not always able to question the frame of reference with which they ascribe meaning.

2   *Actors' conscious cognitive closedness*, 'unwillingness to perceive'. There are times when (for strategic reasons) it just does not suit actors to look at policy from another perspective. However, it is important to realize that this is by no means always a conscious choice. Sometimes it is simply that actors are unable to see it.

3   *Unconscious social closedness*. It can also occur that actors are prepared to interact but fail to see that, owing to their frame, they have excluded some actors from the interaction, for example, because they have simply overlooked them.

4.5   Interference between the First and Second Clarification for Closedness

Actors' veto power and their frames of reference can be analysed in two ways: separately, or in relation to each other. If we choose the latter, it becomes clear that the two clarifications for closedness interfere with each other. The position of power which actors hold in a network influences the way in which they perceive: 'where you stand depends on where you sit'.[2] Conversely, the frame of reference with which actors perceive the network determines their perception of the power, the objectives, the resources and the interests of the other actors.

In that sense, the two clarifications for closedness referred to above can be considered as two equal, alternative, even competing clarifications each of which influences the other. However, we prefer the second clarification, and consider it to be better founded and more comprehensive. If the emphasis is placed on the possession of veto power and on actors' own goals and interests, then underlying this is the assumption that power, goals and interests are objective, that is, independent of perception. We do not believe in this type of objectivist model. Earlier, we argued that each actor ascribes (selective) meaning through their own frame of reference and bases their actions on this interpretation and perception. Thus it is clear that all actors' opinions about their own negotiating options or those of someone else, of their own position of power or that of someone else, every idea about their own interests or the interests and motives of the other actors in the network, are inevitably the result of a process of ascribing meaning; a process that cannot be isolated from this actor's frame of reference.

This would appear to conclude our argument. The message might now be: analyse the frames of reference of the actors in a network and the meanings which they ascribe to management attempts based on these and, armed with this knowledge, you might find ways to intervene successfully. This is unsatisfactory for two reasons, the most important being that it offers a rather too static view of the world. Frames do not appear out of the blue, nor are they immutable. Communication between actors is possible, and that interaction can lead to changes in thinking. The second reason is that we do not want to reduce the closedness of networks to an analysis of closedness at the level of the individual actors. Perceiving the closedness of individual actors is certainly of considerable importance, but that does not mean that it is sufficient for comprehending the steerability of networks. Because in the interaction between actors, too, in the 'network in action', closedness can and will occur, even closedness which goes beyond the (intentions of) individual actors. In the following section, therefore, we examine communication and interaction in networks focusing on the particular significance of discourse as a component of the network culture.[3]

4.6 Communication between Frames: The Formation of a Social Reality

Actors communicate with each other. A communication process is usually described in terms of an 'information transfer' metaphor: one actor broadcasts a message, the other receives it, preferably unaltered. This metaphor needs to be adjusted in at least one area: i.e. the receiving (cf. Luhmann, 1984: 193; 1990: 32). In the previous section we showed that actors have their own frame of reference which filters their image of reality and on the basis of which they interpret reality. This then also applies to the messages which other actors broadcast. In other words: the message undergoes translation and the odds are that it will become distorted and take on a different meaning.

Language (together with other socio-symbolic, non-verbal cultural elements) is of great importance in communication. A major part of 'the' reality reaches us (indirectly) via language in texts. Linguistic forms and the symbolic actions associated with them provide us with a substantial proportion of our convictions and assumptions. This is not only the case when we are learning to talk, a lengthy game of learning words that apply to objects which we see and in which we are corrected by our parents. It also applies to communication in later life, for example about what social problems are, what they are caused by, the reasons why a particular solution is or is not successful, which aspects can be influenced or, conversely, are an invariable part of policy making, what impact the problems have on people, which are the appropriate authorities to tackle the problems, which advantages and level of competence the actors involved have, the criteria for evaluating policy, and even who are friends and who are foes. Symbolic and linguistic signals might not be all-determining, but their importance to the defining of each person's political world should not be underestimated (Edelman, 1971, 1977). Describing in language evokes a reality which is perceived and experienced by actors.

In administration in practice, too (and in the science of public administration), actors constantly present their own (not 'the') reality, by very patiently but very firmly 'explaining' that the subject under discussion needs to be named (and thus needs to be defined): these people are unable to work, those are not; this is an unemployed person, that one is not; this is poverty, that is not; loosening the ties with the public sector is a form of privatization (or vice versa). In this way, the 'babbling' which people hear in others is corrected and at the same time, during the process of communication, the target group, the legitimacy and the key factor for policy are determined. The following example illustrates this:

The Netherlands, in common with many other countries, has a refugee problem. Countless public bodies tackle the issues concerning the admittance of newcomers and their circumstances. The policy on this issue has been and is being talked about at great length, and even the name of the policy concerned is not a constant. It is variously called the aliens policy, the minority or foreigners policy, or the asylum seekers or newcomers policy. This debate about the naming of the policy is not just casual word-play but a battle about interests and outcomes. The term 'foreigners', for example, does not include people from the remaining Dutch colony (the Netherlands Antilles) nor some emigrants from the former colony of Surinam. The term 'aliens' needs to include immigrant Americans, Germans and Belgians. The term 'immigrants' does not include their descendants. And the term 'ethnic groups' in fact also includes the autochthonous Dutch. So it is not surprising that creative minds finally come up with a euphemism like 'fellow inhabitants'.

The people concerned who are being described in this way, though, generally do not think of themselves in these terms: people see themselves as Antillean or American and not as an ethnic minority; people consider themselves Turkish, rather than 'foreign'. However, the (provisional) outcome of the discussion on naming policy has an impact on them, too, because that outcome affects the division of responsibilities between the politicians, the balance of power between the departments concerned, the policy direction, the division of resources, the impact of social discrepancies and thus, indirectly, has an impact on these people's sense of identity. As far as policy is concerned, some things are (can and may be) said at a particular time and others definitely not. This determines both what actors see and what they fail to see, for example as far as the composition of the network is concerned. At the same time, this establishes which actors have veto power and which do not, which actors are friends and which are foes, and for example what the game rules are or the division of powers in the network.

4.7   Third Clarification for Closedness: Network Culture

The fact that actors are part of a network places specific restrictions on an actor. These restrictions take the form of values and norms, customs and rules which together form the culture of the network.[4] In our view, there is both a social and a symbolic side to network culture. The symbolic side of the network culture concerns all those external phenomena which generally receive a lot of attention when we talk about culture: the traditions, the ceremonies, the rites, the myths, the hero figures and so on and so forth. Then there is the social side, the (underlying) rules of interaction, which determine what is and is not correct in interaction between actors, what is good and what is not, what is appropriate and what is not. This includes aspects such as: with whom you should speak, who needs to be involved in a particular issue; are personal attacks or polemic debate allowed; are discussions mainly concentrated on negotiation and/or conferences; is publicity permissible? One essential component of the social side of the network culture is discourse. What is understood in a network by 'comprehensible' and 'intelligible' usage is determined in the discourse. In the remainder of this chapter we shall restrict ourselves to this aspect of network culture, since the other aspects are dealt with elsewhere in this book.

The condition of intelligible and comprehensible linguistic usage might at first sight seem to be an innocent one, but it most certainly is not (Stuurman, 1985). More is involved than simply the requirement of speaking Dutch or English. The condition of intelligibility and comprehensibility may (but does not necessarily) relate to the terms which are used. Certain words can be labelled as being carelessly chosen, incorrect, not specific enough or incomprehensible jargon. By consistently imposing this type of qualification on the use of words in a network, specific language forms can arise: network dialects, which facilitate the expression of some things while making it impossible (by means of exclusion) to say others. The condition of intelligibility, however, can also relate to other aspects of linguistic usage (Stuurman, 1985). The sentence structure, for example; this can be criticized as too contrived or too complicated. Then again, it is sometimes the style or the tone of the piece which is implied in the requirement of 'comprehensible' and 'intelligible'. Sometimes the structure of a text is involved and might be criticized as illogical or inconsistent. We use the term 'discourse' for all the language rules which are specific to a network.

Actors who wish to continue to participate in the discussion must obey the rules of the discourse in order to be heard, irrespective of whether they wish to express approval or criticism. If they fail to do this, their contribution will be incongruous and there is even a chance that it will be ignored as irrelevant, because it is 'unintelligible' and 'incomprehensible'. We indicated earlier how such rules affect the apparent openness of the academic forum, but the same applies to policy in practice. For example, regarding the proposed construction of large-scale infrastructural projects, the authorities arrange public meetings with the intention of giving local people a say in their implementation. Anyone who has attended such a meeting will have been struck by the communication problems which arise when pragmatic civil servants who are used to talking in terms of noise standards and risk contours are faced with emotional members of the public voicing their fears of noise and danger. There is a very real chance of these sentiments being ignored as incomprehensible or unintelligible.

The network culture, of which in our opinion discourse is an essential component, offers the third clarification for closedness, this time of networks as a whole. As a touchstone for further empirical research, we will (provisionally) assume that the network culture causes a number of forms of closedness:

1 *Unconscious cognitive network closedness.* Network culture causes this form of closedness due to the fact that each discourse has its own symbols, its own rules for correct use of language. Communication with and in the network is only possible if one speaks the network language.
2 *Conscious cognitive network closedness.* Conscious closedness also occurs. In the network, reflection on one's own discourse is possible; if this does not dispel the closedness, which it usually does (even if the language is changed), then there is conscious cognitive closedness in the network.
3 *Unconscious social network closedness.* The network culture can also lead to social closedness in the network. Procedures, practices and so forth can, unconsciously, be so deeply embedded in the network that certain actors are effectively excluded from communication.
4 *Conscious social network closedness.* Finally, the network culture can also lead to conscious social isolation, that is, if it becomes clear during the communication that certain actors are unable to participate, and the network culture is consciously not modified so that the excluded actors remain outside the interaction.

4.8   Network and Actors

Initially, the conclusion of our argument about network culture would seem to be that actors simply have to put up with it. If they fail to comply with the rules of intelligible and comprehensible usage, and if they do not conduct themselves appropriately, the network closes itself off from them: they cannot communicate with it and they no longer form a part of it. Such a conclusion, however, would be rather too simple. Actors in a network are not weak-willed creatures who automatically go along with the rules of the game, if only because they have their own interpretive framework, their own frame of reference. They are able to react in different ways to the network culture, whether it involves the codes of conduct required of them, or the condition that they speak comprehensibly and intelligibly. We will discuss a number of concepts here which shed light on the relationship between the network and the actors.

In order to describe the attitude of actors, we identify, following Pêcheux

(1982), three types of behavioural reaction: identification, contra-identification and dis-identification.[5]

Identification occurs when actors conform without protest to the rules which the network lays down for 'correct' communication. Actors who react in this way we shall term the 'conformists'. Then there is contra-identification. This concerns the behavioural reaction of actors who oppose the rules, images and meanings which are held up to them (under the guise of intelligible and comprehensible usage): 'what *you* call a problem', '*your* solution', '*your* social sciences', '*your* way of behaving'. Actors who remonstrate in this way we could term the 'revolutionaries'. Identification and contra-identification are diametrically opposed. In addition to these two types of behaviour, there is also behaviour 'based both *on* and *against*'. This involves simultaneously both building on and opposing dominant practices. We term actors who behave in this way 'evolutionaries'. An example of this can be seen in members of the public who make a determined attempt to voice their fears and emotions concerning the construction of a railway or the building of an airport in such professional jargon that it also becomes intelligible and comprehensible to civil servants.

We have now described three attitudes which actors can take up *vis-à-vis* the network, but this does not yet fully describe the relationship between the actors and the network, since for that interrelationship it does not in fact make any substantial difference whether they tacitly submit to the culture (as the conformists do) or whether they make some protest against it, either evolutionary or revolutionary. As long as actors communicate with each other, they form part of the network. It should be emphasized once again: actors are not weak-willed creatures. They are empowered to use their own discretion and to react in very different ways to the rules which the game imposes on them. But that does not mean that they can shirk the disciplining effect of these rules. Irrespective of how they react, they are participating in the communication simply by reacting at all, and thus become the subject of communication.

By continuing to participate in the communication, actors create the possibility of becoming the subject of the communication, that they themselves acquire meaning in the communication and that expectations are created with regard to them (Luhmann, 1984, 1990). Actors thus become accessible to others: 'so my problem isn't yours, then' or: 'so you don't think this is poverty?' However an actor talks, they remain a player in the game and as such is accessible. Foucault (1971) talks in this context of subjectification. In the language of the network, the subjectification of actors enables exclusion and oppression, manipulation and censoring, masking and revealing: in short, it offers the opportunity for the exercise of power.[6] Foucault's concept of 'subjectification' concerns the relationship between humans and society (the individual and the discourse). We use it here to indicate the relationship between actors and network culture: the subjectification of actors by the culture of the network. We develop in detail the concept of 'subjectification'.

Foucault (1971) describes the subjectification in the discourse as a process that falls into three modes: 'sharing practices', 'classification' and 'subjectifying'. The gist of it is that first of all distinctions, categories, types, groups and classes are introduced into the discourse (as a network-bound language game). Actors are subsequently divided by a process of classification: you are this (good-looking, rich, clever) and you are that (ugly, poor, stupid). Finally, these labels can, in the long term, become internalized by the subject and may start to determine their self-image.[7] Training and courses can illustrate this point. Training separates, analyses, differentiates and implements procedures from decomposition up to the level of 'single units'. Training disciplines and also individualizes by making it possible to measure anomalies, to differentiate between levels, to fix specialities and to retain differences. What training and courses do for actors is: separate and divide in order to unify, disperse in order to break down into parts, segment in order to totalize and individualize in order to expel differences (Poulantzas, 1978). Actors are described in all their individuality, evaluated, measured and compared; in this way they are trained, corrected, classified, normalized and either included or excluded.

What Foucault is describing here is applicable to many aspects of human existence; making distinctions is a very human trait (De Beus and Van Doorn, 1986). In our personal lives we divide people into friends, acquaintances and colleagues, into wise guys and idiots, into the powerful and the weak. Many classifications lie ready-made in the language we have learned to speak. They order our world and we gratefully make use of them: we differentiate between town and country dwellers, single and married people, the employed and the unemployed; and the actors in a network are no different. However, the differences can be found in what is involved in that differentiating and its consequences. In a policy network we cannot arbitrarily divide people into old and young, adults and children. For in a policy network, making such divisions simultaneously involves the concomitant interpretation of, for example, compliance with compulsory education, awarding study grants or allocating pensions, or placement in a juvenile detention centre. Dividing here thus also means: differentiating, sorting, classifying, individualizing, discriminating, labelling, stigmatizing.

4.9 Interference between Network Culture and Frames of Reference

Thus we can ascertain that an interaction exists between actors and networks. The behaviour of actors gives structure to networks. Through their communication in the network, actors become subjects, so can never entirely control the meaning ascribed to their own actions. At the same time, actors can, through their behaviour, stimulate the communication in the network. By adopting a critical stance *vis-à-vis* the network culture, they force reflection on that level.

Once again interference is found; the culture of the network (more especially the discourse) and the actors' frames of reference influence each other. Rein and Schön (1986) talk in this context of a complementary process of 'naming' and 'framing'. They describe 'framing' as the process of selecting, organizing and interpreting and subsequently giving meaning to a complex reality, in order thus to define the limits of knowing, analysing, reasoning and acting. A second process occurs to facilitate 'framing', that is, that of giving a name to a situation which is experienced as problematic. This process, described as 'naming', is a contributory factor in the direction and intensity of the attention paid by actors; by giving it a name, a label, certain aspects of the situation are highlighted while others are glossed over and fall outside the field of vision.

We can extend this distinction between naming and framing to the relationship between network culture and individual frames. Actors interpret the world, including a network, via their frame. On the basis of this they adopt attitudes and attempt to communicate them. They will then reach the conclusion that, at least in a network, there are some things they may say and do, while there are others which they absolutely cannot. They get to know the network culture and learn to fit into that culture by, for example following the 'correct' language rules. Their frame of reference might change as a result. In this sense, culture changes the frames. At the same time, actors themselves become the subject of the communication, and the discourse and the entire network culture can undergo a change through their behaviour and their input. There are thus two complementary processes here which interfere with each other.

4.10 Explanatory Model for Determining Clarifications for Closedness

Let us now return to our argument about the relationship between the three clarifications for closedness. Earlier, we argued that the possession of veto power is not an objective fact which is independent of actors' perception, but on the contrary only attains meaning for actors through the frames of reference via which they identify that veto power, in order subsequently to be able to attach consequences to them. Actors' positions of power and the way in which these actors 'frame' reality influence each other, but the frame level is the most fundamental of all.

Extending this argument, we can now state that actors' frames of reference develop in communication processes, processes which are embedded in the culture of a network. Obviously, the frames and the network culture influence each other, but once again we ultimately consider only one of them to be the most comprehensive, i.e. network culture. We are not falling into a sort of collectivism or structuralism but are simply making the choice consistent with the object of our study. If we describe the object of study as the management of (actors in) networks, the frames of reference of the individual actors are hardly relevant, *if and in so far as they are given meaning in the network culture*. Actors' interpretations can, in any case, only become socially relevant at the moment when communication about that perception becomes possible, thus at the moment when the interpretation between actors becomes nameable. In this sense the network culture, and in particular the discourse, forms a condition for framing in networks. Furthermore, the discourse not only describes what actors perceive but also has a structuring effect: it also evokes a reality. By 'articulating' reality, certain aspects of reality are highlighted, while other aspects are glossed over and thus fall outside the (intellectual) field of vision.

The cohesiveness between the three (interfering) clarifications for closedness is represented schematically in Figure 4.1.

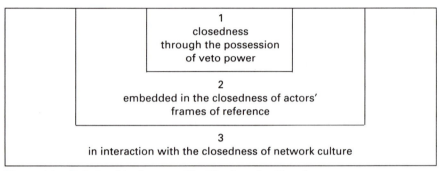

Figure 4.1   *Relationships between Clarifications for Closedness*

4.11 On Fashionable Interventions and Problems of Network Management

So far, our discussion on closedness has been of a descriptive and interpretive nature. In the preceding sections, we have attempted to disentangle its various forms. To that end, three distinctions were introduced: between the social and cognitive dimension of closedness, between actors and networks and between conscious and unconscious closedness. The combination of these distinctions yielded eight different forms of closedness. Subsequently, we looked for clarifications and found that there were three: actors' veto power, their frame of reference and network culture.

The cohesiveness which exists between the steering problems of the public sector and (the forms and causes of) closedness compel us to go further, however, and to explore the possibility of making some relevant prescriptive comments. We consider that our explanatory model can make a useful contribution to a consideration of this subject.

Earlier, we defined the veto power of actors as the cause of conscious forms of social closedness in actors and networks and of actors' cognitive closedness. An attempt to break through these forms of closedness, in our view, can only be successful if this consciously used veto power is accounted for. If this is not done (or is incompletely done) then the attempt to force openness will prove to be no more than a superficial, effect-related treatment. For example, a network management strategy which might be proposed for breaking through the form of social closedness in question is that of selective activation (see Friend et al., 1974; Scharpf, 1978). Introducing new actors and blocking entry to the network for other actors can, however, only be successful when it is carried out in conjunction with breaking through the actor-linked veto power; this veto power has, after all, brought about the closedness *vis-à-vis* certain actors and allowed its continued existence.

The same is true of actors' conscious cognitive closedness. A network management strategy which is sometimes suggested in this context is that of 'reframing': here the intention is that actors reflect on their own frame of reference by being made conscious of the existence of alternative frames of reference and other possibilities for giving meaning to reality (Levy and Merry, 1986: 99). There is little point in such an intervention if actors consciously declare those alternative frames of reference to be out of order, and *refuse* to recognize that other situation definitions are possible. Superficial, effect-related treatment can be prevented here by looking for the point of intervention where its cause is located: in actors' veto power. (Fashionable) network management strategies are formulated far too easily and fail to combat the cause of closedness but address instead its manifestations. This ensures that they are rarely effective. Calling in an external adviser, recruiting new personnel, appointing a committee, introducing new ideas, stimulating reflection or arranging reframing in order to break through *consciously desired* forms of closedness can only be successful if at the same time the veto power of actors in the network is also broken through.

Incidentally, the situation is very different if actors' closedness is not consciously desired. With unconscious cognitive closedness (which can be accounted for by the frame-based perception of actors) the network management strategies mentioned above can certainly offer a solution. In that situation, openness can be achieved in two ways: via the social dimension (the introduction of a third party actor) and via the cognitive dimension (the introduction of a third perception). For a discussion of this, we refer the reader to Termeer and Koppenjan (Chapter 5 of this book).

Finally, we come to the closedness of networks, in all four of the forms which we have identified. We have tried to find the clarification for this in the role and the interests of the network culture. We have understood this to mean the game rules which are laid down by the network regarding the 'correct' behaviour and 'correct' way of speaking for actors. We will now briefly summarize our reasoning. The culture of a network contributes to the inclusion and exclusion of actors and views in the network. Actors can distance themselves from the dominant network culture, which may lead to reflection at that level, but that distancing does have its limits. For if the actors totally fail to comply with the game rules of the network, they are literally sidelined. In this sense, culture functions in a structuring way: through the network culture, actors become subjects, they are given a meaning in the communication which they are not entirely able to determine or to control.

As a remedy for this form of closedness, language interventions are sometimes recommended. However, our discussion exposes how badly such a fashionable remedy fits the fundamental steering problem which is at issue here. It is characteristic of (the cause of) this form of closedness, in any case, that it goes beyond the level of the individual actors. The idea that an actor – here, the network manager – can control and manage the rules of intelligible and comprehensible usage, for example, discounts the central focus of our analysis. The search for solutions to the steering problems with which our modern society is faced has certainly not yet reached an end.

Notes

1 We must emphasize that we are talking of a 'hypothesis' here, because the exact connection between the forms of closedness identified by us and the clarifications for these needs to be further assessed in empirical research.

2 Cf. Allison's Model II (Allison, 1971).

3 We shall base our case on the French post-modern philosophy which examines in particular the reality-forming nature of language (Foucault, Pêcheux, De Saussure), and on the new (autopoiesis) system theory which provides us with insights into the relationship between people and social systems, here: actors and networks.

4 We use the term 'culture' here and not 'belief system', because the culture concept is more expressive of the fact that the practice of communication, the actual ascription of meaning, is important for an analysis of the (closedness of) networks; cf. Erickson, 1982: 163.

5 Pêcheux sees these behavioural reactions as mechanisms which regulate the subjectification of people in the discourse.

6 If we follow Foucault (1984), then we would even have to go so far as to deprive the actor (or the actor's substitute) of the role of originator or creator of the discourse. In Foucault's view, the actor is not the author (producer) of the discourse. For him it is the other way around: the discourse produces actors as a semantic artefact, as a result of the discourse. The actor is conceived of as a function of the discourse (Foucault, 1971). Through this reformulation of the relationship between subject and discourse, questions such as: 'how do actors steer the communication process?', 'how does an actor generate meaning?' and 'how can the actor activate the rules to this end?' are no longer key issues to him. Instead, entirely different questions suddenly intrude, such as: 'how, and under what conditions, can such a thing as "the actor" appear in the process of the discourse?' or 'what is the position and what are the functions that the actor can achieve through communication?'

7 Foucault here is more deterministic than we dare to be.

5

Managing Perceptions in Networks

C.J.A.M.Termeer and J.F.M. Koppenjan

5.1   Introduction

It is often stated that conflicts of interests between interdependent actors are
the main reason why policy processes give rise to chaotic and lengthy debates
and stalemates, with the result that urgent societal problems remain unsolved.
For instance, the manure which is produced by extensive livestock breeding in
the Netherlands was already being viewed as an ecological problem in the
early 1970s. Up till the present day, the policy debate has not yet produced an
adequate policy to tackle the problem. In this chapter we argue that blockages
in policy processes are not only caused by conflicts of interest and power relations, but equally by the *perceptions of the situation* of the actors involved.
Actors have their own definition of the world that surrounds them, which
consists of their definition of the problem, their image of other actors in the
policy network, the nature of their dependency upon others and vice versa,
and the advantages or disadvantages of working together. People seek to give
expression to these perceptions in policy programmes (Sabatier, 1988: 142).
These perceptions are stable and difficult to change. However, in order to
accomplish joint decision making about solutions to social problems – a prerequisite for problem solving in policy networks – a mutual adjustment of
perceptions is essential. In this chapter the question is raised of how actors in
networks can be encouraged to adapt their perceptions in such a way that collective action with regard to policy problems becomes possible.

First, in section 5.2 we show that the inability or unwillingness of actors to
reflect on their perceptions may lead to fixations in interaction processes.
Blockages in policy processes are one result of these fixations. In section 5.3,
we explore the nature of perceptions and explain why perceptions are so persistent. Their persistent nature, however, does not imply that they do not
change or that it is impossible to influence them. Efforts to influence perceptions need to be adapted to the specific dynamics of perceptions. In section
5.4, these dynamics will be described. Perceptions are constructed and reconstructed in interactions. A condition for the adapting of perception is the
existence of variation. Management efforts to modify perceptions should
take these insights into account. Sections 5.5 and 5.6 deal with possible ways
to manage perceptions. Perceptions can be influenced indirectly, by strategies
aimed at the social dimension of interaction. These indirect strategies are

discussed in section 5.5. Strategies aimed directly at perceptions are dealt with in section 5.6. In section 5.7, the normative implications and the risks of managing perceptions are discussed. The chapter concludes with a summary of our findings.

5.2   The Role of Perceptions in Interaction Processes: Joint Action and Fixations

In order to solve social problems in policy networks, joint action is needed. These processes of problem solving are often frustrated by the existence of divergent or conflicting perceptions concerning the problem involved, the best solution and the actors who should participate. Sometimes the actors disagree with one another not only about goals or means, but also about the nature of their disagreements (Rein and Schön, 1986: 4). To resolve these blockages in interaction, actors need to adapt at least some aspects of their perceptions or try to recognize and accept the existence of different perceptions. However, actors are not always capable of or willing to adapt their perceptions. In that situation 'fixations' occur. Policy processes can become 'dialogues of the deaf'. Actors talk at cross-purposes, arguments are constantly repeated in a ritual way and none of the participants is willing to

---

Fixations in the Dutch Manure Policy

The case of the Dutch manure issue provides a good illustration of the way in which cognitive and social fixations can block policy processes. In the early 1970s, the environmentalists warned us that manure would develop into a severe environmental problem. At that time agricultural actors saw manure as a very useful product. They could not believe that manure caused damage to the environment. A social fixation by both parties complicated the process of communication. The agriculturalists saw the environmentalists as their enemy and were unwilling to talk with them. The environmentalists saw no use in communication because they did not trust agriculturalists. When after 15 years the blockages were broken through and the existence of a manure problem was recognized, a cooperative approach was still very difficult because both parties used different problem definitions. Although the social fixation was resolved, problem solving remained blocked by a cognitive fixation. Environmentalists saw the manure issue as a problem of too many chicken and pigs. Policy had to be focused on reducing livestock. Farmers, on the other hand, saw the manure problem as one of transport: the problem could be tackled by developing a sophisticated transporting system. (Termeer, 1993)

reflect on their own arguments. A well-known example is the energy debate in the United States during the 1970s. The debate between opponents of 'soft' versus 'hard' energy resulted in an enduring blockage of the policy process (Wildavsky and Tenenbaum, 1981; Sabatier, 1988: 155).

Fixations arise when the actors involved take their own perceptions so much for granted that they no longer reflect on them. Voogt (1991) distinguishes between cognitive and social fixations. In a situation of *cognitive fixation* actors included in the interaction have already dealt with the same problem definition for a long time and none of them wants to change it. *Social fixation* means that mutual relations and interaction rules are no longer subjects of reflection. Introducing new actors or new ways of handling problems is no longer considered.

Conflicting perceptions and, what is more, the reluctance of contestants to adapt their interpretations of the problem situation, can be seen as the main causes of blockages in the policy processes (Van Twist and Termeer, 1991). The question is: why are perceptions so persistent and how can they be influenced? To answer these questions we first have to examine the nature of perceptions.

5.3 Perceptions, Policy Networks and Configurations

Perceptions play an important role in interaction processes within policy networks. Perceptions are often persistent and may result in fixations which block joint problem solving processes. But perceptions can change. In this section we will examine the concept of perceptions more thoroughly, and will demonstrate that perceptions are produced and reproduced in interaction processes and are embedded in social configurations. Both features make up the dynamics of perceptions. In order to influence perceptions, their dynamics must first be understood.

Perceptions

The concept of perceptions can be approached in different ways. One approach is based on the assumption of a reality which exists outside a social context and which is independent of the subject as observer. Perceptions are seen as one of the variables in the process of policy making together with such factors as resources, problems and solutions. In addition to cognitive processes there is a real world which changes (Sabatier, 1988: 134). According to this approach there are perceptions which are right, because they reflect reality, and perceptions which are wrong.

This view can be criticized. Smith (1992), for example, argues that when actors in a network construct their own world, 'impersonal' or 'objective' forces, such as socio-demographic or economic change, also have to be interpreted (compare Rhodes and Marsh, 1992: 195). Facts do not exist outside a social context: 'Organizations have a major hand in creating the realities which they then view as facts to which they must accommodate' (Weick,

1979: 13). In the controversy between those who are looking for a 'best perception' and those taking a 'relativistic' point of view we subscribe to the latter (compare Rein and Schön, 1986: 6).

A perception is an image through which the complex, ambiguous world which surrounds actors can be made sense of and be acted upon. It guides the process of the perception of stimuli and the shaping of responses. In the literature, several concepts are used which, although they do not have exactly the same meaning, all more or less refer to this phenomenon: frames (Rein and Schön, 1986), belief systems (March and Olsen, 1976b; Sabatier, 1988; Smith, 1992), theories in action (Argyris and Schön, 1978); causal maps (Weick, 1979), paradigms (Hall, 1993).

Perceptions can be applied to the way actors define problems. Rein and Schön talk of the 'framing' of a problem. The hotel anecdote is a well-known illustration of this insight. The manager of a hotel received complaints from his guests about the long waits for elevators. The engineer he consulted provided him with two expensive alternatives: speeding up the elevators or installing new ones. The manager also asked a psychologist for advice. He suggested placing mirrors or interesting or informative items in the hallway alongside each elevator. According to him, guests experienced the waiting as boring. Thus, the same problem can be defined in different ways. Or rather: if we deal with problems as social constructs, we are no longer able to say we are referring to the same problem, because each perception selects different, at best overlapping phenomena, for its attention (Dery, 1984: 16; Rein and Schön, 1986: 8). Problem definitions can be described as interpretations of the gap between the present or expected situations and a desired situation, and the instrumental relations between both (Dunn, 1981). The way the problem is perceived determines what the interaction is about, which solutions are appropriate and which actors should be involved (compare Schattschneider, 1960; Cobb and Elder, 1983). Crozier and Friedberg argue that the definition of the problem forms the 'bounded rationality' which actors use to select their strategies (Crozier and Friedberg, 1980: 201).

Perceptions are not restricted to the definition of problems, though. According to Sabatier (1988: 139), a belief system includes problem definitions, causal assumptions and basic values. Basic values are part of the 'deep core' of the belief system which defines the person's, organization's or coalition's underlying identity and which is much more resistant to change than both the 'outer' policy core (which consists of basic strategies and policy positions) and the secondary aspects (a multitude of instrumental decisions). This distinction between more or less changeable aspects of perceptions is found in the work of many others. In learning theories this distinction corresponds with two forms of learning. Single loop learning is about correcting mistakes with regard to instrumental aspects of theories in action. Double loop learning refers to learning about goals, values and assumptions, and is far more difficult, because 'prohibiting learning mechanisms' protect the theory in action by suppressing or transforming deviating or threatening information (Argyris and Schön, 1978).

The Social Embeddedness of Perceptions: Configurations

How do perceptions come about? Perceptions are constructed and reconstructed in interactions with others (March, 1978). People prefer to talk to people with whom they share perceptions. Actors engage in interactions depending on the perceptions that they possess. Those interactions subsequently influence the perceptions of reality that are being constructed. In interaction processes, actors develop common perceptions which form the starting point for further action. Since people interact chiefly with people who share their perceptions and since their perceptions will be reaffirmed in these interactions, there is little opportunity for achieving a fundamental change in those perceptions.

As a result of these interactions *social configurations* develop: groups of actors who can be characterized by their matching, relatively stable interaction patterns and shared perceptions (Weick, 1979: 35). A configuration is an empirically derived record of a particular moment in a process of change. Sabatier refers to 'policy advocacy coalitions' composed of people from various organizations who share a set of normative and causal beliefs and who often act in concert (Sabatier, 1988: 133). As a result of this social embeddedness of perceptions, it is clear that the perceptions of individuals are not easily changed in specific interaction processes with regard to a certain problem. They cannot simply be influenced in the way the traditional stimulus–response model suggests (Stones, 1992). According to this model, it is assumed that by using a strategy of persuasion people can be induced to change their perceptions and behaviour in a desired way. However, this idea fails to take into account the social embeddedness of perceptions. When a new perception is introduced it becomes part of the interaction within the configuration in which it will be reconstructed. It is not possible to predict the outcome of this process.

Configurations within the Agricultural Policy Network

For many years, the agricultural policy network in the Netherlands could be seen as one configuration. The close interaction patterns were combined with a shared ideology. More recently, however, this old ideology is no longer shared by all the actors in the network. Due to new issues such as environmental problems and changes in the policy regarding quality and agricultural prices, perceptions have become increasingly diverse. Within the agricultural network several configurations have developed, which renders the interaction between actors within the network increasingly complex. (Termeer, 1993)

Social configurations may coincide with formal institutional arrangements and policy networks, but in most cases more than one configuration can be distinguished within any one organization or network. This means that the

problem solving process within the policy network may involve the cooperation of actors belonging to different configurations and who hold different
and perhaps conflicting views. Owing to the existence of 'multiple social realities' and the lack of what Rein and Schön (1992) might call 'meta frames',
interactions will not take the form of policy disagreements, which arise within
a common frame and can be settled by appealing to established rules, but of
policy controversies, which derive from conflicting perceptions. Joint problem
solving requires a minimum of consensus and therefore a mutual adjustment
of the perceptions of representatives from different configurations. Thus,
resolving persistent policy controversies involves learning across social configurations or policy coalitions (compare Sabatier, 1988).

Perceptions therefore play a crucial role in interactions within policy networks, especially when problem solving involves representatives from more
than one configuration. Owing to the absence of shared perceptions, enduring policy controversies may evolve. Resolving these controversies requires the
mutual adjustment of at least a part of the perceptions of the actors involved.
This may prove to be very difficult, because perceptions are related to the
basic beliefs of the actors involved, which define their identity and guide the
processes by which they select information. Furthermore, perceptions are
socially embedded in interactions that take place within social configurations. Perceptions do change, but have their own dynamics, which makes it
very hard, if not impossible, to consciously influence them.

5.4 Variation and Confrontation as Conditions for Change

The development of perceptions has its own dynamics. The managing of
policy processes is only possible if good use is made of these dynamics.
Perceptions are constructed, reaffirmed and changed in processes of social
interaction within configurations. When actors communicate only with actors
who have the same perceptions there is no reason for change. In such interactions perceptions can only be reaffirmed. Only a *confrontation with other
perceptions* can create the opportunity for change. Confrontation can be seen
as the driving force for change.

However, not all confrontations automatically imply change. Theoretically,
three steps along the path of change can be identified: actors must recognize
the differences between their own perceptions and those of others; they must
experience the differences as problematic; and they must be willing to reflect
on their own perceptions. Only when these steps are taken may a confrontation with other perceptions or other actors result in change (Termeer, 1993).

A prerequisite for confrontation is the existence of cognitive or social variation. A policy process is characterized by *cognitive variation* when a variety
of perceptions about the policy content, that is to say problems, solutions and
underlying values, are put forward. *Social variation* refers to the presence of
representatives from different configurations, which results in a variety of
ways to act.

Cognitive Variation

The presence of a variety of perceptions about problems and their solutions in policy debates creates a condition of cognitive variation which is favourable for confrontation and the mutual adjustment of perceptions. However, the susceptibility to new ideas by the parties concerned will depend on the extent of the correlation between these ideas and the other perceptions. If actors perceive new ideas as a threat to what they see as their vital interests and values, they will not be anxious to take these ideas into consideration. An important explanation for the reluctance of actors to find out about new ideas and solutions is a lack of trust.

Cognitive variation may arise from developments in the environment of the policy process as a result of technological, economic, ideological or institutional developments (Rhodes and Marsh, 1992: 193; Hall, 1993; Sabatier and Jenkins-Smith, 1993). These developments may lead to reflection on positions and ideas by the participants within a configuration. Developments in the environment do not directly influence cognition. Such 'impersonal' or 'objective' forces as, for example, socio-demographic change have to be experienced and interpreted (Weick, 1979: 130; Smith, 1992: 195). The chance of events being noticed and interpreted increases when they take the form of extreme, striking events with radical consequences. For instance, the El Al Boeing crashing in Amsterdam, in October 1992, triggered the articulation of safety considerations in the policy process on the expansion of Schiphol Airport.

Social Variation

Social variation in policy debates is dependent upon a number of factors. First, actors who are included in more than one configuration provide one source of social variation. Owing to this multiple inclusion they are confronted with different values, ideas and assumptions which will influence their perceptions. For this reason they are able to take up the role of change agent in specific policy debates (Termeer, 1993).

Second, social variation is influenced by the entry or exclusion of actors in policy debates. The entry of a new actor may result in the introduction of new ideas. The exclusion of actors serves to reduce variation.

Third, social variation can be influenced by external pressures and threats. Without external pressure the inclination to adapt perceptions, objectives and strategies will be lessened (Cangelosi and Dill, 1965: 198; Hedberg, 1981: 8; Koppenjan and Hufen, 1991). Bargaining and communication within the context of policy processes often arise under the threat of regulation by government if parties are not successful in reaching agreement. Although external pressure may contribute to social variation, there are also risks. If the pressure becomes extreme, configurations may refuse to accommodate dissident ideas and actors. It may even be that they develop conspiracy theories and start eliminating variation within the configuration (Argyris and Schön, 1978; Janis, 1982).

Fourth, social variation depends upon the presence of independent 'third parties'. Third parties are actors who do not belong to one of the contending configurations and do not have a direct stake in the policy controversy (Van Twist and Termeer, 1991). If actors know there is an independent audience, they will be discouraged from forcing the issue. It may in fact encourage cooperation and influence the perception of risks connected with cooperative strategies. Furthermore, a third party may perform the role of broker or arbiter between the contesting parties (Kingdon, 1984; Sabatier, 1988).

Because the cognitive and social dimensions of policy processes are strongly interconnected, confrontation with cognitive variation may encourage reflection upon perceptions with regard to the cognitive aspects of interaction as well as to the social aspects. Reflection on new ideas may affect actors' willingness to accept the participation of new actors in the policy debate. Confronting actors with new participants may affect the values, assumptions and preferences of the contending parties.

5.5   Towards a Management of Perceptions

Managing Perceptions for Joint Action

The management of perceptions in policy controversies which evolve in policy networks is about creating a minimum of consensus in order to facilitate collective decision making and joint action. Managing perceptions is aimed at discovering win-win situations or, in the words of Agranoff (1986: 9), integrative, multi-beneficial solutions. These are possible courses of action which result in situations which are an improvement on existing or expected circumstances (Dery, 1984).

At this point, a possible misunderstanding needs to be rectified. By stating that the management of perceptions is aimed at creating a minimum of consensus, we do not mean that there must be an overall consensus between actors in order to solve societal problems. Actors do not need to agree on goals in order to act collectively. Partners in a collective structure share space, time and energy, but they need not share visions, aspirations or intentions. The idea of consensus building does not accord well with the mixed-motive nature of interaction processes in policy networks. As joint action begins to form, members converge first on common means, not on common goals. The most basic agreement involves the acceptance of interdependence (Weick, 1979).

Attempts to ensure that all actors have the same perceptions are unnecessary, undesirable, and doomed to failure. They are unnecessary because actors can cooperate without shared perceptions or consensus on common goals. They are undesirable because they lead to the suppression of legitimate aspirations. Such efforts prevent a variety of actors from accomplishing their objectives, which will in turn discourage them from investing their resources in joint actions. This is exactly why they are doomed to failure. In order to achieve consensus, at least some of the actors need to adapt their basic beliefs and values. This will serve to evoke conflict and block further interaction. For this reason, attempts to manage perceptions in networks are not aimed at the creation of an overall consensus, but at the minimum of agreement which allows for joint action.

Not a Planned Change in the Content of Perceptions . . .

In order to influence the perceptions of actors involved in a policy debate, several options may be implemented. These options can be classified according to the intentions on which they are based. A distinction can be made between *instrumental strategic options* which are intended to change the content of perceptions in order to create conditions favourable to the attainment of goals or policies promoted by the manager, and *procedural strategic options* which are aimed at managing the process in which perceptions are constructed and adapted. In the latter, the manager does not try to realize their own goals, but facilitates joint action by, for instance, preventing or resolving blockages or fixations in interaction processes.

An example of the first type of option is provided by the Dutch environmental policy. The internalization of ecological values by the population forms the cornerstone of this policy. Government tries to induce people to accept and internalize a particular perception of the nature of the problem and the preferred course of action. Such a strategy is often problematic because it presupposes that perceptions can be influenced in a particular direction. As we stated previously, perceptions are constructed in interactions. When a policy maker introduces a new perception, this perception will become part of the ongoing policy debate. The outcome of this interaction is uncertain. Furthermore, a prerequisite for such an approach is the existence of a well-defined policy problem. Often, however, such a consensus does not exist. This is all the more so if scientists also disagree about the true nature of the problem, which often tends to be the case. In such a situation, it is impossible to decide which perspective should form the point of departure for the management of perceptions (compare Rein and Schön, 1986: 6). Since problems are not objective entities, but social constructions, there is not one best problem definition, nor one ultimate solution.

. . . but Facilitating Processes in which Perceptions are Changed

The management of perceptions, should not, therefore, be directed towards convincing actors that one particular problem formulation is better or more likely to be true than another. Rather, *the management of perceptions is aimed at the direct or indirect adjustment of perceptions in order to improve the conditions for collective decision making and joint action.* The overall goal is to improve the mutual adjustment of perceptions in such a way that actors redefine the problem situation as an opportunity for improvement. If they do so, this will encourage them to undertake joint action.

As discussed earlier (section 5.4), interaction processes possess both a cognitive and a social dimension. These two dimensions provide points of intervention for managing the process in which perceptions are developed. The cognitive dimension refers to the perceptions which guide the strategic choices actors make. The social dimension refers to the kinds of actor who are participating and the way in which they are doing so. These aspects are interconnected. The perceptions of a problem situation affect participation: in the political debate regarding the regulation of abortion in the Netherlands at the end of the 1960s, the issue was defined as a medical question. As a result, representatives of the medical profession exerted a major influence on the process of legislation (Outshoorn, 1986). Conversely, developments in the social dimension affect the values, assumptions and preferences of those involved in the policy debate. When actors from different configurations enter the interaction arena, they introduce new ideas and contribute to the cognitive variation in the process.

As far as the management of perceptions is concerned, this means that strategies can address both the cognitive and the social dimensions of interaction. Strategies aimed at the cognitive dimensions of interaction try to influence perceptions directly, for instance by introducing new information about a problem. Note that these strategies do not try to manipulate perceptions, but to facilitate a process of reflection. Strategies aimed at the social dimension of interaction may involve the introduction of a new actor in the policy process. In this way perceptions may be influenced indirectly. Table 5.1 summarizes the strategies for influencing perceptions aimed at the cognitive and social dimension of interaction.

Table 5.1   *Strategies for influencing perceptions*

	Instrumental strategies	Procedural strategies
Cognitive dimension of interaction	Furthering particular goal or alternative	Facilitating reflection by creating cognitive variation
Social dimension of interaction	Indirectly furthering a goal or alternative	Indirectly creating cognitive variation by creating social variation

Strategies aimed at the cognitive and social dimensions of interaction may complement each other. Furthermore, in the case of a cognitive or social fixation, it is possible to direct management efforts towards that dimension of the process which is not fixed. For example, if actors are not willing to reflect on the content of their problem formulation, it may be a good idea to introduce a new, authoritative 'third party'. Variation in the social dimension may help to break cognitive fixations. Furthermore, if the existing actors are unwilling to interact with new actors, redefinition of the problem situation may prove useful. In the following two sections both types of strategy are examined. In section 5.6, strategies aimed at influencing perceptions indirectly by manipulating the social side of interaction are discussed. Strategies aimed at the cognitive dimension are dealt with in section 5.7.

5.6   Strategies Aimed at the Social Dimension of Interaction

Three indirect strategies to manage perceptions are identified: the development of new procedures, preventing the exclusion of parties, and the introduction of new actors.

The Development of New Procedures

Strategies aimed at the social dimension can be useful in situations of cognitive fixation. For example, when actors have different or even conflicting perceptions of values, problems, goals or solutions and they are unwilling to reflect on them, interaction becomes difficult. Offering new solutions will serve no useful purpose. Efforts to increase agreement on procedures may help to reduce the tensions resulting from conflict on substantive issues. Devoting attention to procedures can also prevent the development of cognitive fixations.

Procedures and Perceptions in the Case of Schiphol Airport

Until the mid-1980s, the development of the Dutch national airport, Schiphol, and the surrounding area took place in an uncoordinated way. As a result, municipalities encouraged the building of houses on sites which then increasingly experienced noise nuisance as a result of the expansion of the airport. In addition, the options for the continued expansion of Schiphol were further limited by the norms for acceptable noise levels which were laid down in legislation by national government. As the result of an initiative by the Ministry of Housing, Spatial Planning and Environment in the mid-1980s, a project group was set up to discuss the further development of Schiphol and the surrounding area. Schiphol Airport, the municipalities of Amsterdam and Haarlemmermeer, the Province of North Holland and several ministries all participated in this project group. From the start the various parties were rather sceptical about the perspective of the project. It seemed evident that economic and environmental objectives would never be reconciled. However, since no clear alternative existed they agreed to participate. The setting up of the project group was the first step in a process of interaction and bargaining which resulted, in 1990, in a joint Plan of Action, which was laid down in a covenant between parties involved in the project. This plan expressed the willingness to adapt strategic intentions to the interests and preferences of other parties. In this way, the environmental concerns became part of the strategic agenda of the management of Schiphol Airport.

Management strategies can address the negotiating of procedures (agreements, rules, contracts, organizations) which will guide further interaction. Such arrangements create stability and predictability in situations of uncertainty (Ostrom, 1986), and include agreements on conflict regulation mechanisms. Since actors have to commit themselves to these procedures, they also constitute an expression of actors' confidence in the success of the joint actions being undertaken.

This example provides a clear illustration of the idea that actors agree on procedures before they agree on content. At the beginning of an interaction process concerning a particular problem they commit themselves to a certain way of dealing with that situation, including time schedules and entry, exit, and arbitration rules. At that point, the costs and benefits of the joint action are not yet specified. Costs and benefits will become clear during the process of specifying and selecting possible solutions. By that time, actors will be willing to accept costs because they have participated in the policy debate, because they know that there are compensations, and because strategic uncertainties are reduced by the procedures they have agreed upon. Furthermore, since the costs will become evident only after a certain period, actors will not let their choices to be determined entirely by them. Moreover, agreements may include provisions to postpone the introduction of costly measures, in order to give parties time to adapt their internal processes and structures to these new developments. For instance, the covenant between the Dutch government and the packaging industry in which the industry committed itself to the introduction of sustainable packaging included a certain time period during which the industry could develop and introduce the appropriate technologies (In 't Veld et al., 1992).

Arrangements such as letters of intent, joint ventures, project groups and so on, may facilitate the interaction between actors with different or even conflicting goals. However, arrangements may also become dysfunctional. If actors experience existing procedures as unjust or inefficient, it will be necessary to devote attention to these problems because they may block communication about substantive matters.

Preventing the Exclusion of Actors

This strategy is aimed at maintaining social variation in the interaction process. If certain actors are systematically excluded from the policy process, this may result in social or cognitive fixations.

In order to ensure that policy processes remain open, the manager of perceptions should constantly be aware of the danger of fixations. Social variation can be promoted by preventing attempts to exclude actors by, for instance, initiating debates about entry rules. Special attention needs to be devoted to the tendency to exclude opponents, critics and 'bringers of bad news' from further interaction (Termeer, 1993).

Exclusion of Actors in the Case of the Dutch Passport

In 1983, the Dutch government decided to introduce a new passport system in order to combat the forgery of Dutch passports and to comply with European guidelines. The ministry responsible, Foreign Affairs, favoured a centralized system. This option was contested by the Ministry of Home Affairs and representatives of the municipalities. The Ministry of Foreign Affairs, however, succeeded in excluding its opponents from the decision making arena by giving the assignment to develop a centralized system to a consortium of private companies. In its haste to consolidate this bureaucratic political victory, Foreign Affairs took considerable risks. By reducing the variation of ideas and actors in the policy process, Foreign Affairs made itself dependent upon its new private partners. When these partners proved to be incapable of developing a passport system that could meet the standards set by the Dutch government, the project resulted in a complete failure. In 1989, after a parliamentary inquiry, the project was abolished. (Koppenjan, 1991)

The Introduction of New Actors

When the above-mentioned strategies fail and fixations arise then more radical strategies are needed. In the case of cognitive fixation, it is necessary that the actors involved learn to reflect on their perceptions. The problem is that attempting to force this process by introducing a new perception will be unsuccessful as long as actors are unwilling to reflect on their perceptions.

If the cognitive dimension of interaction does not tolerate any variation, then the social dimension becomes the sole accessible point of intervention. A solution can be found in organizing a confrontation with a 'third party'. A prerequisite for success of this strategy is the acceptance of this third party by the others. When this party is included in other configurations it is anticipated that it will introduce new perceptions into the interaction process. This may result in reflection on perceptions by the contesting parties. Note that the introduction of a third party does not force the contesting actors to accept new ideas. New perceptions are not introduced by force, but develop in the course of interaction.

The introduction of new actors resembles the well-known strategy of selective activation (Scharpf, 1978). The manager activates certain relations and deactivates others. However, there is a difference. Selective activation consists of involving actors who possess indispensable resources in interaction processes. This presupposes a well-defined goal or direction of action that accords with an instrumental strategy. In a procedural approach to the management of perceptions, the reason for activating a third party is not the availability of resources, but the creation of variation. The introduction of new actors can take many forms: the setting up or reorganization of a commission, the recruitment of new personnel, bringing in an adviser.

Introducing a New Actor into the Dutch Government's Major Cities Policy

In the mid-1980s, central government's policy with regard to the 'big four' Dutch cities, Amsterdam, Rotterdam, Utrecht and The Hague, consisted of developing measures to increase the discretionary powers of the cities by decentralizing funds and tasks. Due to a growing resistance to these measures at central government level and the prioritizing of the government deficit issue, support for the policy by the second Lubbers cabinet (1986–9) was reduced to a minimum. To proponents of the policy it was clear that if nothing was done, the policy would be terminated. They therefore persuaded the Secretary for Home Affairs to set up an advisory commission. Since the cabinet and, no less importantly, Prime Minister Lubbers were known to be responsive to the interests of the private sector, a 'captain of industry', Mr Montijn, president of the board of directors of Internatio B.V., was asked to chair the commission. In 1989, the commission published a report. When a representative of the private sector stated that the potential of the major cities for furthering the economic development of the Netherlands could only be utilized if their social, financial and administrative problems were tackled, the issue reappeared on the government's agenda. (Koppenjan, 1993)

The strategy of introducing new actors involves promoting certain roles within the interaction process. By introducing entrepreneurs, mediators, brokers or arbiters, the manager can help to break through fixations and stimulate interactions which may result in a mutual adjustment of perceptions. Moreover, an antidote to the tendency of actors to expel critics and opponents from the interaction process can be provided by consciously inviting these actors to participate.

5.7   Strategies Aimed at the Cognitive Dimension

In this section we will discuss four strategies directed towards the cognitive dimension of interactions. These four strategies are: furthering a common language, preventing exclusion of ideas, introducing new ideas, and stimulating reflection.

Furthering a Common Language

Actors tend to interact with other members of the same configuration. During these interactions they develop not only common perceptions, but also a common language. Interaction between members of different configurations is difficult partly due to conflicting perceptions, but also because even a common language may be lacking (Voogt, 1991). For instance, representatives of the agricultural sector discussing the environmental consequences of their activities will use different words, concepts and labels from actors who are part of the environmental configuration. These differences may result in misunderstandings and blockages in interaction.

When actors interact for the first time, they have to invest in getting to know each other, in understanding each other's interests and perceptions, and in developing a common language. To expect results in terms of policy outcomes in this phase is far too ambitious a target. Instead, the management of perceptions should be directed towards stimulating the development of a common language, for instance by creating settings in which representatives of different configurations meet. This activity can be regarded as a precondition for further interaction and negotiation.

Preventing the Exclusion of Ideas

If certain ideas are systematically excluded from the policy process, there is an increased chance that blockades will occur. In order to prevent cognitive fixations, therefore, the policy process should be open to new ideas. To ensure this, the process manager has to be constantly aware of the danger of the exclusion of ideas.

Exclusion can be prevented by efforts to maintain or introduce variation. Possible techniques include initiating research, organizing brainstorming sessions, initiating debates, et cetera. Special attention needs to be devoted to the formulation of criticism. As the passport project example illustrates, actors tend to exclude 'unwanted information' (compare also Majone, 1986; Dryzek and Ripley, 1988). One way to counteract this tendency is to institutionalize the input of critical notes within the policy process. For instance, in the Netherlands, as in many other countries, the initiator of a large physical project is required to carry out an Environmental Impact Assessment so that the assessment of environmental impact is assured a place in the decision making process.

The Introduction of New Ideas

Social fixation means that actors are not willing to reflect on their relations and strategies. In cases of fixation, more radical strategies are needed. Since the fixation is socially orientated it becomes very hard to introduce new actors or new procedures. Receptivity to these will be minimal. The only possibility is to introduce variation in the cognitive dimension. Organizing a confrontation with new ideas can offer good prospects. If these new perceptions are accepted it is possible that the actors will also wish to reflect on their relations with the actors who share these ideas. A prerequisite for the introduction and acceptance of new ideas is that they should not deviate too much from the dominant thinking of the participating actors, yet should deviate enough to shed new light on the subject.

Introducing New Ideas into the Dutch Manure Policy

The Dutch manure policy provides a good example of this. At the beginning of the 1980s the manure policy process was blocked. Actors from the agricultural configurations and actors from the environmental configuration were unwilling to interact with each other any more. Relations could be characterized as hostile and distrustful. Developing new procedures for contacting both configurations was no longer successful. The situation changed when a study was published in which it was proved that there were measures that could be implemented by farmers which improved both the environmental quality and economic results for the farmer. These research results were very positively received within the agricultural configuration. When it became clear that this research had been initiated by a new environmental pressure group, relations with the environmental actors were reopened. (Termeer, 1993)

A second technique is that of 'softening up'. The acceptance of new ideas takes time. Often a new idea only gains support after a considerable time (Kingdon, 1984: 134–7). Management strategies can be aimed at stimulating this process of 'softening up'.

The 'Softening Up' Strategy in the Field of Dutch Intergovernmental Relations

There was a long period during which interactions in the area of intergovernmental relations in the Netherlands were ruled by the principle of 'uniformity'. All the municipalities were to be treated as equal by central government. In 1983, the proponents of a special policy for the four big cities proposed the idea of differentiating between categories of municipalities. Their aim was, of course, to enable special arrangements to be made for Amsterdam, Rotterdam, Utrecht and The Hague. This proposal was rejected out of hand owing to the norm of uniformity. At various times after that, proposals for differentiation were put forward by different actors. It was not until 1990 that, as a result of 'softening-up' acitivities, the principle of differentiation was accepted as a cornerstone of the new Major Cities policy of the Centre-Left Lubbers administration. (Koppenjan, 1993)

Furthering Reflection

Variation alone is not sufficient to prevent the occurrence of fixations and blockages. Fixations can be prevented only if actors are prepared or willing to reflect on their perceptions. Reflection includes an openness to other ideas, but also a willingness to discuss one's own. It is the task of the process manager to create beneficial conditions for reflection. Strategies to foster such conditions include attempts to create a climate in which doubt, inconsistency and time for reflection are not valued negatively (March, 1988).

Another method for promoting reflection upon perceptions is 'reframing'. Levy and Merry describe this method as 'an intensive short intervention, focused on changing organization members' perceptions of reality by encouraging them to experience a new perspective on the problem at hand' (1986: 96). Reframing is not restricted to facilitating reflection processes, as the two previous strategies were. 'The approach results in changing perceptions, behaviour and relations' (ibid.). Such a change presupposes an irrational, illogical 'jump', which is described as a 'paradigmatic shift' (Rein and Schön, 1992; Hall, 1993). Reframing is a method which provides the incentive to go beyond existing frameworks and to view a problem, situation or relation from the perspective of others.

Reframing in the Case of the Development of the Canal Zone in Terneuzen

The technique of reframing was used in the project initiated by the Dutch province of Zeeland to solve the problems of land-use planning and environmental pollution in an industrial zone along the canal between Terneuzen and Ghent in Belgium. In this area, perspectives for the expansion of industrial activities were limited by the existing residential areas, with their norms with regard to acceptable levels of noise nuisance laid down by national environmental legislation. For the same reason, suitable locations for building housing in the area were scarce. It was thus proving difficult for actors to further their goals on their own. They were trapped in a zero-sum game: if industrial activities were expanded, residential building would become difficult and existing dwellings would have to be demolished. If the residential function were to be prioritized, the economic development of the area would become a problem. In both cases, everybody would lose, because both functions were essential for the area's future.

In order to coordinate the strategies of the different actors, the province set up a project group to discuss the development of the area. One of the techniques used to facilitate the mutual adjustment of perceptions was that of reframing. Sessions were organized in which the representatives of one organization had to defend the point of view of other participants. After an intensive process of exchanging information and points of view, participants committed themselves to a joint plan of action for the development of the area in which certain areas were marked out for industrial use and others for residential use.

Although this project can be viewed as a success story for the management of perceptions, it also illustrates that the possibilities for 'reframing' are not unlimited: because the environmental movement was not satisfied about the environmental impact of the interaction process, it refused to sign the joint plan of action.

Another reframing technique is the use of metaphors or powerful symbols in the policy debate, which may result in a shift in the way a situation or proposal is perceived and appraised. The Major Cities policy, for instance, was originally aimed at highlighting the social and financial problems of the 'big four'. In order to gain new support for the policy, its proponents tried to influence the government by adapting its perception of the major cities. They were presented as the driving force of the national economy. The course of obtaining money and discretionary powers from central government was no longer pursued by stressing the social and financial problems of the 'big four', but by underlining their economic potential.

5.8 Limits to the Management of Perceptions

This chapter has described a number of ways to influence perceptions. Such a manual for managing perceptions should not be presented without a word of caution to the user. These strategies are not without normative implications and risks.

First, managing perceptions involves a number of normative implications. To what extent should perceptions be influenced? If actors are free to adapt their views based on the available information, there would seem to be no problem. But to what extent are they free to do so? Can they check the reliability of the information presented? Are there organizational or social pressures which force them to adapt their views? Normative choices for the manager who provides information in an attempt to influence perceptions include the use of unreliable information or the exclusion of disagreeable information from the interaction process. If misinformation becomes part of the manager's repertoire, actors are then being misled. The management of perceptions in that case may take the form of manipulation and propaganda. The management of perceptions should comply with prevailing norms concerning good governance and proper and reliable conduct in inter-organizational relations.

Second, the management of perceptions is not without its risks. If attempts to force a collective decision or joint action result in the repression or exclusion of alternative perceptions, fixations will occur. The fixations may result in what Janis calls 'groupthink': an extreme form of consensus which may lead to inappropriate and high-risk behaviour. This will result not only in blocked interaction processes, but also in unbalanced decisions probably involving unforeseen and undesired impacts for the actors involved, but also for others (Janis, 1982; 't Hart, 1990).

For this reason we have stated here that the management of perceptions is not about creating consensus, and that strategies should be directed towards furthering and not eliminating variation. Managing perceptions is about creating a common ground for joint decision making and action, while accepting and respecting the autonomous positions and preferences of the actors involved.

5.9 Conclusions

In this chapter we have discussed the options for managing perceptions in policy networks. Cognitive and social fixations which are the result of actors' inability or reluctance to reflect on their perceptions, are assumed to be a main cause of blockages in interaction. Perceptions and fixations can obstruct interactions, but they can also be seen as points of intervention for influencing interaction processes. A prerequisite for the adjustment of perception is social and cognitive variation in terms of the availability of and receptivity to variation.

With regard to the management of perceptions it has been stated that there is no 'best' perception. The aim of management attempts to influence perceptions is to accomplish a mutual adjustment of perceptions which creates a common ground for collective decision making and joint action. The management of perceptions is successful if actors adapt their perceptions in such a way that they accept a common course of action as a promising perspective for the accomplishment of their goals. In order to do this, cognitive and social fixations have to be prevented or broken through by creating and/or maintaining conditions for an open debate.

Two types of strategy can be used: strategies directed towards the social dimensions and strategies aimed at the cognitive dimensions of interaction processes. The first category comprises the development of procedures, preventing the exclusion of actors and the introduction of new actors. The second group of strategies includes the creation of a common language, preventing the exclusion of ideas, the introduction of new ideas and furthering reflection. The management of perceptions is not without normative implications and risks: actors may be misled, and excluding variation may result in extreme forms of consensus. Attempts to influence perceptions should comply with the norms for proper and reliable governance and should respect the autonomous positions of the actors involved. The management of perceptions should therefore be about creating conditions for reflection by promoting, not eliminating, variation.

6

Strategies and Games in Networks

E.-H. Klijn and G.R. Teisman

6.1   Introduction

If policy making is the result of an interaction process between many actors
and if these actors all have their own goals and strategies, then policy making
can best be conceptualized as 'a complex process, that cannot be controlled
by one single actor'. In this chapter we discuss three questions which deal
with complex processes in networks, namely:

1   Which concepts can be used to analyse complex policy making processes?
2   What type of management strategies can be used to facilitate complex
      policy making processes?
3   What kind of evaluation criteria can be used to evaluate complex policy
      making processes?

In an attempt to answer the first question, in section 6.2 we will elaborate
upon four crucial concepts. The first of these, and the best metaphor for
depicting complex policy making processes, is that of 'the game'. The outcome of games depends upon the strategic behaviour of all the actors
involved. Therefore 'strategies' is our second concept. Actors choose game
strategies which seem rational to them in the context of the game they are in.
These strategies are based on the perceptions actors have of the game and
the important choices that are to be made in it. 'Perception' is the third concept we introduce. Perceptions are constructed by actors, but inspired by the
environment they are in. This environment, the 'network', is our fourth
concept.

  The third section of this chapter addresses the question of how complex
policy processes in networks can be managed. We will argue that the very
nature of networks demands specific network management skills. We will
specify the kind of skills that are necessary to deal with the interdependency
between actors and the management strategies that can be used by actors in
a network.

  In section 6.4 we deal with the question of how complex policy making
processes should be assessed. First, we explain why traditional evaluation
criteria such as goal achievement or the general/public interest are inadequate. We argue that the concept of the common interest might be a more
accurate criterion for evaluating policy results in networks. Furthermore we

present three criteria for evaluating the process of policy making which has led to the policy result.

This chapter will conclude with a summary of the ideas proposed for analysing, facilitating and evaluating complex policy making processes in networks.

6.2   Games as a Metaphor for Processes in Networks

If policy making is a complex interaction between several actors, this process can then best be analysed as if it were a game. Policy is not the domain of one actor but the result of interaction between several actors (Scharpf, 1978; Rhodes, 1981; Rogers and Whetten, 1982; Gage and Mandell, 1990). A characteristic feature of a game is that the result derives from the interaction between the strategies of all the actors involved (Elster, 1986; Koningsveld and Mertens, 1986). The games concept can help us to analyse complex policy processes. Games are characterized by an ever-changing set of players and their strategies. Since these are important sources for the dynamics of the game we will be examining the concept of strategies. Strategies are chosen by players, and since it is assumed that the choice of a strategy derives from the way the actor perceives their situation and their options, the concept of perception will also be elaborated on. We use this concept to emphasize that policy making processes are guided by reality constructions actors create for their situation and the choices they make within these constructions. We will complete our conceptual model by developing in detail the concept of networks. There are two reasons for this. First, because we assume that actors' perceptions are constructed within the institutional characteristics of the network. Second, because actors do not encounter each other only in one single game. Series of games evolve around policy issues. This means that the strategies in one game or the results of that game can be influenced by other games in the network (see Tsebelis, 1990). Game strategies and game outcomes are influenced not only by other games but also by the relation patterns that have developed in the network as a result of former interactions (Hanf and Scharpf, 1978; Aldrich, 1979; Milward and Wamsley, 1985; Rhodes, 1990).

Games as a Concept for Analysing Complex Policy Processes

The use of the concept of games to analyse policy processes was introduced some decades ago. Allison employed it in his famous book *Essence of Decisions* (1971) as an element of his 'Governmental Politics Model'. Before that, the concept was chiefly used by the theorists of rational choice models (Elster, 1986). These scholars attempted to analyse complex policy making by using highly formalized types of game, the best known of which is the prisoner's dilemma. In this tradition, game situations are analysed as strategies with fixed pay-offs. Different types of game (the prisoner's dilemma, the chicken game, the assurance game, the battle of the sexes; see Scharpf, 1989) are characterized by different pay-off matrices. Little attention was devoted to the context of the game, which renders the formal game models rather static.

One interesting and productive feature of Allison's model was that he used the concept to analyse the dynamics and complexity of the policy process. He argues that: 'The Governmental (or Bureaucratic) Politics Model sees no unitary actor but rather many actors as players – players who focus not on a single strategic issue but on many diverse intra-national problems as well; players who act not in terms of a consistent set of strategic objectives but rather according to various conceptions of national, organizational, and personal goals' (Allison, 1971: 144). The analysis should therefore focus on identifying the games, the players and their perceptions and interests, as well as on the coalitions which are formed and the compromises which are made in the game.

Games are not played at random. Allison argues that they are structured by action channels. Each specific policy has issues at stake and a unique set of action channels. 'Action channels structure the game by presenting the major players, determining their usual points of entrance into the game, and distributing particular advantages and disadvantages for each game' (Allison, 1971: 170). In addition to action channels, Allison also introduced the concept of 'rules' as the main characteristic of the structuring of the game. He identifies three types of rule:

- rules that specify the position of the players;
- rules that restrict the range of the game and the decisions that can be made in the game; and
- rules that secure sanctions on behaviour.

Since Allison is not quite clear about the relationship between action channels and rules, we propose some more specific definitions. In our view, action channels can best be defined as the organizational arrangements which regulate game interactions, for example project groups, consultation procedures and covenants. Rules structure these action channels, and are in that sense part of them, but cannot be reduced to action channels alone. The insights Allison has provided are helpful in our search for pivotal factors. He questions the unity of governments. Within government, policy making is a game in which several actors choose their own strategy. The characteristics of a strategy are of one's own devising, but both inspired and limited by existing rules.

Lynn (1981) uses the game metaphor in a slightly different way: 'Game is employed as a metaphor for ongoing, sequential chains of activity governed by both formal and informal rules, involving a high degree of interactive decision making, and with winning as an objective' (Lynn, 1981: 144). In Lynn's view, a game starts as soon as problems are discussed in public and governmental action is being called for. Games end when issues cease to be important. This can happen when players lose interest in the game (the issue remains attractive, but they do not envisage any chances of scoring in that specific game) or when they decide to invest their time in other issues. This introduces a new pivotal factor: network managers must not only play a game in the right way, but an important part of the job is also to choose the right game. 'Successful public management can be viewed as effective games-manship' (Lynn, 1981: 145).

Crozier and Friedberg (1980) have focused on organizational behaviour. An essential element in their analysis is the possessing of a margin of liberty to act. All the actors operating within the context of a multi-actor setting enjoy a certain freedom of action. The margin of liberty can be extended by the actor themselves if they are capable of developing strategic options which fit within the context of the game. Since resources are divided between several actors, they all have the opportunity to use this power balance in games. There is a good deal of uncertainty in games. No one actor controls this uncertainty, although several actors control parts of it. The zones of uncertainty which an actor controls constitute an important resource.

> A given organizational situation never completely constrains an actor. He always retains a margin of liberty and negotiation. This margin of liberty (signifying a source of uncertainty for his partners as well as for the organization as a whole) endows each actor with power over the others, which increases with the relevance for these others of the source of uncertainty controlled by the actor. (Crozier and Friedberg, 1980: 45)

One may anticipate that each actor will seek to constrain other actors while at the same time retaining a maximum of freedom for themselves. The margins of liberty can vary for different games depending on the rules of the game and the strategic choices of the actors. The rules of the game at any given moment constitute a constraint on the actors but are at the same time the product of interaction between them. 'They [i.e. rules] are provisional, always contingent institutionalizations of the solution to the problem of cooperation among relatively free actors' (Crozier and Friedberg, 1980: 53).

From Crozier and Friedberg we learn that strategies in games are a delicate combination of margins of liberty perceived by an actor based to a great extent upon the sources of uncertainty the actor controls, and the rules which are currently in force in the game, as well as in the ecology of games which are played in a network.

From our examination of existing literature on games we can conclude that a game is characterized by a set of players and their strategies. We define a game as *an ongoing, sequential chain of (strategic) actions between different players (actors), governed by the players' perceptions and by existing formal and informal rules, which develop around issues or decisions in which the actors are interested.*

Strategies and Perceptions Guiding Policy Making Processes

Behaviour is studied by all scholars of public administration and public management. But their analysis is not based on the same assumptions. Behaviour is often analysed as if it were instrumental in reaching a fixed goal. In our view, behaviour should be analysed in terms of its strategic characteristics. A strategy can be defined as the set of decisions taken by one actor which reflects the combination of resources and targets they bring into play. This means that the analyst is interested in the question of to what extent actors in games take into account the strategies of other actors and the structure of networks and games they are involved in. The analyst is interested in cohesiveness between the actions (defined as a combination of resources and targets) of one actor and those of other actors in a particular game. In other words, the analyst asks to what extent the actions of different actors are interconnected.

Some of the consequences of interactions and games are anticipated by actors, but many are not. If all the actors are operating strategically, not all the consequences of their actions can be envisaged in advance neither can all the consequences of former actions be acknowledged or recognized in current and future actions (Giddens, 1984). This means that there is a great deal of uncertainty about the consequences and impacts of actors' behaviour. Many of the insights into the nature of the game, the goals that are at stake in the game and the effectiveness of the strategies have to be developed during the game. Often, actors discover their targets (defined as goals suited to the game) during interaction, when they can discover what is to be gained and whether or not an attractive goal displacement is possible (March and Olsen, 1976b; March, 1978; Crozier and Friedberg, 1980).

What is involved in the game is a social construction between actors which takes shape during the process of interaction (Guba, 1990; Van Twist and Termeer, 1991). Relevant to the game are the perceived realities of the actors involved. Perceptions are the images or definitions that actors use in their game situations. Perceptions mediate between complex reality and behaviour. They provide an actor with an insight into their world and a method of selecting and evaluating outcomes of strategies and games. Since actors choose their strategies based on the way they perceive the game situation and the network, perceptions are important to the outcome of games. Perceptions are linked to three important aspects of the game situation (Klijn and Teisman, 1992):

- the interdependencies between the actors arising from the division of the resources needed to fulfil their ambitions;
- the ambitions and 'stakes of the game' of the actors;
- the policy game and the importance of the policy problem being addressed in the game, compared with the policy problems being addressed in other games.

Perceptions have a certain stability in that many of the assumptions about reality are not subject to rapid, drastic fluctuations. In most cases, actors' perceptions undergo an incremental change during the games as a result of interactions or of confronting other actors' perceptions. In most cases, the policy outcome will then also undergo an incremental change. Sometimes, however, interactions cause major changes in the perceptions of several actors. Such an event can be termed 'a paradigmatic change' (Rein and Schön, 1986; Hajer, 1989; Van der Wouden, 1990). It will lead to substantial changes in policies.

In order to understand policy making, therefore, we need to obtain insights into the sources of changes in perceptions. Analytically, four sources of such changes can be identified:

1   interactions within a game, or in allied games which are played simultaneously, can cause changes;
2   the entrance of new players into the game introduces other perceptions and can cause changes in game interactions and game patterns;
3   perceptions can be changed by the (un)foreseen consequences of former games which bring about a change in the game situation and subsequently lead actors to interpret their situation differently;
4   the consequences of other games outside the policy network can change perceptions and game patterns within the network. Thus, the games within the housing policy network can be influenced by games in infrastructure networks (e.g. Klijn and Van der Pennen, 1992).

Policy making can thus best be conceptualized as a game. A game is an interaction between the strategies of interdependent actors. These strategies are inspired by the way actors perceive their reality. Their perceptions create the margins of liberty an actor has in a game and can be changed in an attempt to extend the actor's margins. These changes can be caused by new insights reached in the course of the game itself, but also by developments in allied games that take place in the policy network or in other networks.

Games and Networks: Institutionalization and Innovation

If we assume that the network is the context for games, then we must tackle the question of the relationship between networks and games. In fact this raises one of the classic questions in social science: the relation between action and structure. Generally speaking, this thorny problem has been only cursorily treated in the literature on networks. In most cases, the term 'structure' has been reserved for the relation patterns between actors, but the question of how these patterns are created and sustained in action has not been addressed fully (see Cohen, 1989).

Networks, seen as relation patterns between actors, are the context in which separate games take place. On the other hand, these games change and influence the interaction pattern within which they take place. For this reason, networks have been defined as '*changing patterns of social relationships between interdependent actors which take shape around policy problems and/or policy programs, and that are being formed, reproduced and changed by an ecology of games between these actors*' (Klijn, 1993: 231). A network is an interaction system reproduced by concrete games. At the same time, the network shapes the context of new games (Giddens, 1979, 1984).

In this conceptualization of policy networks a mutual causation of action and structure can be found. This 'duality of structure' has already been proposed by Giddens. 'The essential recursiveness of social life as constituted in social practices; structure is both medium and outcome of the reproduction of practices' (Giddens, 1979: 5). Social systems plainly would not exist without human agency. On the other hand, it is not to be expected that actors create new social systems every time they play a game. In fact, 'they reproduce or transform them, making what is already made in the continuity of praxis' (Giddens, 1984: 171). Structure is conceptualized here as 'rules and resources recursively implicated in the reproduction of social systems' (Giddens, 1984: 377). It exists only as memory traces and manifests itself in games. In order to illustrate his thesis, Giddens refers to the use of language: human beings can only communicate verbally and in writing if they employ grammatical rules. Structures are thus a precondition for action: without rules and resources no meaningful interlinked interactions would be possible. At the same time, these rules can only be studied in the course of a concrete game. In this way, the action–structure problem is solved. Structure enables action, but is also reinterpreted and changed during concrete action.

Thus, by repeatedly playing the same types of game time after time, actors develop social relations between each other and structural characteristics that belong to those patterns (Giddens, 1979, 1984). They create a meaningful structure which represents both a necessary precondition for further interactions and games and at the same time is reproduced, sustained and changed in the course of the concrete games actors play. So the network, as a more or less stable pattern of relations, is constantly being (re)produced in concrete games. In the ecology of games, actors develop mutual expectations of each other's behaviour and they create resource divisions between actors that set the stage for further interactions. During interaction actors try to figure out which rules are appropriate for the game situation they are in (March and Olsen, 1989) and they draw upon resources in the network to achieve their ends or to participate in current game situations or create new ones. In this way, processes in concrete games are connected to the structure of the network, that is, the rules and resources that are involved in the (re)production of games.

Both rules and resources, together forming the structure of a network, are important to the constitution and recreation of games. *Rules, understood as generalizable procedures applied in the enactment and/or reproduction of games* constitute meaning and provide sanctioning modes in games. They establish 'agreement concerning what is real and what is illusory' (Weick, 1979: 3). Resources are a necessary factor in producing social practices: like rules, they are creations of the actors in the game. This becomes quite clear if we consider know-how, a resource which is only relevant in specific circumstances. Know-how about housing is only important within the housing network. The same can be said of a resource such as money. Money is something which is based on trust. The difference between resources and rules is that some resources, such as money, are, as Giddens indicates, 'disembedded', that is, they are lifted out of social relations and made independent of a specific context and time. But these resources are still based on trust, as illustrated by the breakdown of economies and the depreciation of money.

Actors draw on these resources in their transactions to achieve their desired goals and when they try to influence other actors.

6.3   Management Strategies in Networks

If policy is the result of actors' interactions in games, improvements in policy can be achieved by the effective management of those games. In this section we will describe in more detail ways in which this can be done. First, however, some differences between network management and management in apparently hierarchical situations need to be elucidated.

Network Management

An essential feature of network management is the assumption that all the actors involved possess a margin of liberty which they will use in the game. It is therefore highly inaccurate to expect that one actor's policy proposal will be implemented by others. Network management not only has to deal with the environmental dynamics and uncertainties described in the classical approach (see Chapter 1, pp. 10–11), but also with the uncertainty of actors' behaviour in the network and in the game.

Network management takes effect from the moment it helps to create games in which all the necessary resources are available. This is not self-evident, however. In networks many actors are operating strategically. They have differing goals and perceptions. This factor, combined with the absence of a central actor who commands enough resources and steering power to determine the strategic actions of the other actors, renders network management quite different from a more classical view of management. Network management is the managing of interactions (Mandell, 1990). The absence of a central steering point means that network management cannot, or cannot only, be oriented towards the a priori stated, fixed and unquestioned goals of one of the actors involved. Network management has to deal with the uncertainties resulting from the interactions between different actors' strategies.

Network management is further complicated by the absence of an official appointed exclusively to manage the network. It is possible that more than one actor functions as a manager in a specific game. In fact one should probably consider network management rather as an activity which can be performed by any of the actors taking part than as something which is exclusively carried out by one actor.

Network management can be divided into game management and network constitution. These categories comply with the analytical distinction between game and network developed in the preceding section. Game management is directed at influencing and facilitating interaction processes in games. Network constitution is aimed at changing the network (and thus changing the context for separate games). Both types of management have to deal with questions of content, players (and their strategies) and institutional arrangements. Game management can target the perceptions of actors involved in a game, the number and type of actors taking part in it, and the arrangements according to which the players try to play it. Network constitution can be directed at the fundamental reframing of perceptions, but it can also be aimed at influencing either the actors in networks or the more permanent institutional arrangements. Table 6.1 gives an overview of the categories of network management.

Table 6.1   *Management strategies in networks*

	Perceptions	Actors	Institutions
Game management to improve the game	Covenanting: exploring similarities and differences in actors' perceptions and the opportunities that exist for goal convergence	Selective (de)activation: (de) mobilizing actors who possess resources (to block a game)	Arranging: creating, sustaining and changing ad hoc provisions which suit groups of interactions
Network constitution changes to improve the network	Reframing: changing actors' perceptions of the network (which games to play, which professional values matter, etc.)	Network (de)activation: bringing in new actors or changing positions of existing actors	Constitutional reform: changing rules and resources in networks or trying to fundamentally change the ecology of games

Covenanting: Improving Social Knowledge and Learning Processes

As already mentioned in this chapter, policy is the outcome of interaction between several actors with different perceptions. This implies that the quality of policy making is not a result of the consistent nature of the decisions taken by one participant, but results from the consistent nature of the decisions of all those involved in decision making. In such situations, consistency cannot be improved by management activities aimed at increasing the cognitive knowledge of one participant in an attempt to cause that participant to make rational decisions. Consistency has to be improved through social knowledge. All the participants taking important decisions about the object of policy making have to reach some kind of congruent definition of what they are doing and of the place of their decisions in the series of decisions that result in complex policy making. The term 'covenanting' refers to a management strategy aimed at improving the consistency of the decisions made in the game by exploring and consolidating the perceptions of different actors in the game.

Ostrom (1980) has used the concept of covenanting to address the problem of creating congruency between perceptions of what needs to be done, which resources can be used and under which conditions. Covenanting is not synonymous with attempting to formulate a compromise. This can constitute one element of the covenanting process, but need not, however, form the most important part. One might even argue that this is rather a poor definition of the covenanting task of a network manager. Covenanting is a concept used above all to emphasize the potential for enriching particular initiatives through interaction, the underlying idea being that initiatives for new policies are always taken by specialized actors in a network. They are specialized because highly developed societies are characterized by structural differentiation. They even have to be specialized because such units in a highly developed society are the source of innovative initiatives.

Thus, an effective network manager will accept specialized initiatives and will try to interlink them in order to improve the policy initiative around which a game is constructed. In order to achieve this, it is important to identify the motives which have led to the initiative, the resources which are needed to transform the initiative into a policy in action, the actors who possess these resources and the conditions on which they are prepared to provide them.

A manager needs to make a twofold analysis. First they need to reconstruct the perceptions of the initiator and the actors in terms of the conditions under which these actors will support an initiative. The second step in the analysis concerns the problem of how the different perceptions can be modified and operationalized in such a way that the content of a proposal is considered satisfactory by a coalition of actors powerful enough to transform the proposal into policy in action. This second step is partly a cognitive activity (replying to the question of what the different actors have in common) and partly a strategic one (the question of which actors have to be activated to create coalitions). The latter question will be dealt with in the next section. First, however, we cite an example to illustrate that covenanting is a widely known and successful strategy used in many routine situations (the example is taken from Teisman, 1992: 131–67).

In the Netherlands, the railway system is a monopoly owned by the Dutch Railway Company (NS). Several years ago, this company decided that either a new bridge or a new tunnel was needed in Rotterdam. There were no advantages for the municipality in this project. As far as they were concerned, the construction of a tunnel would turn the inner city into a building site for several years, creating a negative impact on businesses and residents. Nevertheless, the municipality's cooperation was essential since they owned the land and were also the authority responsible for physical planning and issuing the permits necessary to commence construction on the project.

The decision making took several years, chiefly because the railway company wanted to talk about the project only as they had defined it. They assumed that the municipality would recognize the company's legitimate motives and would therefore cooperate. For the municipality, however, there was no incentive to cooperate. The managers of the company continued to repeat their proposal, without adding any elements which might make the project more attractive to the owner of important resources needed for the project. In fact, it was the municipality which formulated some additional proposals. It was prepared to cooperate on condition that the railway company was willing to sell them a certain area in another part of the city. Initially, the railway company refused this package deal. They did not want to combine themes from two separate games. The decision making process was blocked.

There followed an extended period of blocked policy making after which the railway company appointed a new manager for the project. He was less preoccupied with the motives of his own organization, and understood that successful policy making would require special management skills in order to achieve a win-win situation for both his company and the municipality. So he reformulated the project in such a way that it became interesting for the municipality and included a compensation fund for residents and businesses.

From that moment, several participants perceived the project as an interesting one, and the decision making process was consequently accelerated.

Selective (De)activation: The Creating and Influencing of (New) Games

Games are played by a minimum of two actors. If an actor wants to achieve an objective in a network they have to initiate new games or participate in existing games in such a way that their targets come within reach. Whether or not they will achieve their targets depends on the presence of indispensable resources (represented by certain actors) and on the absence of threats (represented by opponents) (see Scharpf, 1978). Since resources and threats become relevant as soon as they are represented by actors, it may be concluded that the question of which players are participating in the game is a matter of some importance. In prescriptive terms this means that policy making processes can be improved by means of the selective (de)activation of participants.

The formation of any game is not merely a question of allowing entry to certain actors, however. It also involves timing and promotional activities. These are crucial, since although every actor has a limited attention span, there are nevertheless many games to be played (March and Olsen, 1976a). As long as an actor (who, from a particular point of view, possesses indispensable resources) is playing other games which fill up their agenda, it will cost more effort to involve them in games where they are needed. Once one or more of the games they are involved in are concluded or are demanding less attention it becomes easier for them to participate in new games or in other existing games. Thus, one of the skills of management is the ability to attract attention to a new game, especially on the part of those actors who are considered to have indispensable resources. Many policy making processes have turned into a fiasco because the initiator neglected to include a number of such players (e.g. the passport affair in the Netherlands: Ringeling and Koppenjan, 1987–8).

In addition, management skills are needed if a manager is to become involved in new games started by others or in a new set of games which appear interesting (Lynn, 1981). When an actor wishes to participate in an existing game, they first need to examine who the other players are and what the game is about. Furthermore, they need to discover the rules of the game, especially the rules of entry. Some methods of entering the game will be more effective than others, depending on the rules the existing players have in mind. For our purposes, we shall assume that all potential participants are capable of employing entry methods. The combination of all the selective activation strategies leads to a frequently unforeseen set of bi- and trilateral relationships, which together form the activated network (ecology of games) during any specific period in the policy making process. In these activated networks it is particularly those participants who have the skills to activate potential partners in a selective way who increase their influence on the policy making process. This can lead to situations in which an actor with a relatively small amount of resources wields more influence than an actor who has many resources but lacks the necessary skills.

Selective (de)activation skills can be learned. An important factor is the awareness that policy making is a game and that selective (de)activation is an important part of it. Network managers are not dealing with one participant, nor with one process. They have to deal with several games being played at the same time and a series of games played over time. The following are some concrete examples of selective activation taken from the railway tunnel case study.

Decision making about a railway tunnel consists of more than just a covenanting process between the railway company and the municipality. In order to succeed, a wide variety of actors need to be activated. In this case, the game was played by members of the municipality, the railway company and national government. None of these organizations, however, can be seen as a cohesive actor. Within the municipality, different roles were played by the chairman of the council executive, the council, the land development department, the Port of Rotterdam Authority and the Department of Public Works. Within national government, different roles were played by the Ministry of Transport, the cabinet and parliament.

In the course of the game played by these actors a number of more or less conscious attempts to activate certain actors can be identified. For instance, during the difficult negotiations between the railway company and the municipality the configuration of actors was changed several times. At times, departments from both organizations were negotiating, at others, the chairman of the council executive and a representative of top management from the railway company were carrying out the negotiations. When blocked decision making occurred, one of the two parties activated the Ministry of Transport to function as a mediator.

On another occasion, the Minister of Transport took a decision which was not accepted by the railway company nor by the municipality. They managed to activate parliament. Parliament invited all the actors involved to present their version of the situation and subsequently urged the Minister of Transport to reconsider her decision.

A third example concerns the activation of the Port of Rotterdam Authority. This organization was activated by those in favour of a tunnel because they anticipated that the Port Authority would also welcome a tunnel: the existing bridge caused major delays to large vessels. Building a railway tunnel would reduce delays, thereby improving Rotterdam's position as number one port. The Port Authority activated the shipbuilding industry, whose representative then wrote a letter to the minister informing her that a new tunnel would prevent the loss of several billions of guilders caused by these delays.

Two important lessons which can be drawn from this case are:

- that selective activation is not the monopoly of one actor; and
- that selective activation involves not only the question of which organization has to be activated, but, more importantly, which actor within the organization has to be activated.

Arranging: The Constitution of the Game

If policy is the result of interactions in games, the manager is confronted with a specific coordination problem. How can the different strategies of the various actors be linked together? In the classical perspective on management (see Chapter 1) this problem is solved by hierarchical control. In a network, however, hierarchical control does not exist, which means that the network manager has to deal with the problem in another way. In fact, they have to create organizational provisions to achieve effectively linked games. At the same time they have to take into account the negative impact of the arrangements on actors with conflicting interests. Arrangements are *ad hoc* organizational platforms for interaction and procedures for solving conflicts. 'Arranging' as a management activity is the art of linking interdependent actors in such a way that the arrangement costs are low and do not result in high transaction costs. In principle, many different arrangements are possible (project groups, covenants, etc.). Some of them are highly formalized while others are not (see Rogers and Whetten, 1982). The network manager has to choose the simplest arrangement which is accepted by all the participants, and yet one which is sophisticated enough to deal with the existing conflict of interests. For this reason it is not possible to select the most effective arrangement in advance. It is more important to find arrangements which are accepted by the players in the specific game which is being played, and to change arrangements which become obsolete in the game.

The creative manager tries to develop sets of arrangements which are tailored to the game situation and the actors, and which effectively facilitate the interaction process between actors. Generally, they will try more than one arrangement and will set up the construction in such a way that the different arrangements support each other.

A good example of arranging decision making is the development of an old, dilapidated area of the port in Rotterdam (for a more extensive case study, see Teisman, 1992: 224–43). This project, the Kop van Zuid, was started in 1986. Redevelopment of this kind of area often proves very difficult because so many parties are involved. An integrated tackling of the problem, in which all parties participate, is often not possible. In the case of the Kop van Zuid this integrated approach has proved successful. Within a decade, the concept of a waterfront development has been transformed into real life plans and real life projects. A major part of this successful start is the result of effective arrangements by the local council and the Ministry of Spatial Planning. The local council has entered into bilateral arrangements with both the residents of adjoining neighbourhoods and with private investment banks and building companies. Furthermore, in order to achieve effective internal policy making games, the municipality has created an internal project organization to integrate the different disciplines needed for the development of an inner city area. In addition to these three arrangements, the Ministry of Spatial Planning has created a platform for joint decision making at national level, between the Ministries of Housing and Spatial Planning, and the Ministry of Transport. These ministries decided on a joint financing arrangement. In order to link local and national decision making, a fifth arrangement was developed, formalized in an agreement signed by the Ministry of Spatial Planning and the local council.

All these arrangements were facilitating specific games between unique sets of actors. They were able to facilitate the policy making process to an important extent, not because of any specific characteristics, but because the participants agreed upon the type of arrangements used. This resulted in more interaction patterns. In the various arrangements, effective links in the interactions were provided by four intermediaries (three network managers appointed by the local council and one by the Ministry of Spatial Planning).

Network Constitution: Setting the Stage for Games

In the previous three subsections, attention has been focused on strategies to facilitate the playing of policy making games. However, games are initiated and take place in a network and are influenced by the characteristics of that network. Here we will address the question of how to influence the interactions in games through influencing the network as a whole.

As with games, three pivotal factors can be discerned: perceptions, actors and institutions. When strategies are aimed at the perceptions of actors regarding the nature and functioning of the network this is termed 'reframing'. An example of this is when one tries to redefine the image of the task of the network as perceived by its members. Policy documents are a favourite way of trying to change the perceptions of the participants in a network: perceptions of the goals which need to be attained or the relevance of other actors in the network. Numerous similar attempts can be found in practice. A good example is the redefining of the tasks of the networks of military organizations after the fall of the Berlin Wall. In order to legitimize the existence of these networks, a paradigmatic change in their reasons for being were needed. Key actors in these networks tried to redefine the tasks of the participants. Instead of providing a defence against communism, intervention in war zones was now their mission. From the moment this paradigmatic redefinition is accepted it may be assumed that several games will henceforth be played in a different way.

The second pivotal factor is provided by the actors in a network: for example, the introduction or the abolition of an actor in a network. A good example of the first of these can be found in the Netherlands where there are proposals to set up a governmental body at regional level. It is to be expected that many games played in, for instance, the physical planning network or the housing network will be influenced by this. An example of the second can be seen in the UK where the Thatcher government abolished regional governmental bodies such as the Greater London Council.

A third pivotal factor is the institutional provisions on the network level: these are the more permanent organizational provisions and procedures which channel interactions between actors. These management strategies are aimed at changing the structure of the network by the introduction of new rules, the abrogation of existing rules, and the reallocation of resources. In fact, this can be seen as an indirect method of managing policy making processes. This management activity is not directed towards producing a particular outcome to the game but towards a procedure which in principle affects all the current and future games in the network. By changing the rules and procedures for interaction which are used in the network, the incentive structure of the network is in effect being changed. One example of this type of management is the creation of a conflict regulation mechanism. Actors in a network can agree upon certain procedures to be followed when intense conflicts occur. They can, for instance, appoint a referee who can arbitrate in the event of a conflict occurring between parties. The importance of such a referee will depend upon the abilities of players to solve conflicts themselves, and the outcome of arbitration will depend upon the positions of the players involved in a conflict. Referees also have a margin of liberty.

Management strategies to change the network are often lengthy, which renders them less suitable when fast changes are needed. Network constitution strategies are not exclusive to public actors. It is possible, for instance, for all the actors to introduce new actors into the network and to try to give those actors a solid position within it. For some of these strategies, however, legal resources are necessary. This gives public actors more opportunities to adopt this type of management strategy.

One example of an institutional modification of the network can be found in the decision making on new railway tracks. As already mentioned, the Dutch Railway Company is a monopoly, responsible for railway investment as well as the transport of passengers and goods. It was owing to this specific constitutional arrangement that the Dutch Railway Company could act as it did in the case of a new railway tunnel. In 1993, central government decided to split the railway company into three divisions. The division responsible for infrastructure may possibly become a part of the Ministry of Transport. Clearly, this modifying of the division of resources and rules will change the way new games on investment in railway infrastructure are played.

6.4   Criteria for the Evaluation of Complex Decision Making

If we analyse a policy making process as if it were a game, we also have to address the question of how to evaluate this process and its outcomes.

In the context of this chapter it is not very useful to evaluate such processes as if they only existed in order to achieve the goals of one of the actors involved. For this reason, traditional evaluation criteria such as goal attainment and general/public interest are inadequate. We will argue that the concept of 'common interest' would be a more accurate criterion by which to evaluate policy results in networks. When policy is the result of a decision making process, then the quality of the policy depends upon the quality of the interaction. Therefore, we will present three additional criteria by which to evaluate the process of policy making which has led to the policy result. First, in order to evaluate the contents of the process the question has to be addressed of to what extent it has enriched the target set at the beginning. Second, in order to evaluate the quality of the interaction we will focus on linking activities. Interaction in networks often takes place between a changing configuration of actors, and therefore has to be organized. Third, in order to evaluate the quality of the structure of a policy making process the question has to be addressed of to what extent the actors involved have developed effective arrangements to organize their mutual interaction.

From Public Interest and Self-interest to Joint Interest as the
Keystone for Evaluation

If one wants to make a distinction between good and bad policy making, one has to establish a standard. In the mainstream of evaluation, research analysts are interested in the question of whether or not the result of a decision making process is in accordance with the a priori expectations of the key participants involved. These a priori expectations are postulated as the standard for evaluation.

The choice of this specific standard is based on the philosophy that something called public interest exists, that this public interest can be identified and that the key participant, usually a governmental agency, is the one who is able to define what it is. Even though we have known for a long time why great expectations in Washington, or any other capital in the world, can be dashed in Oakland or any other city in the world (Pressman and Wildavsky, 1983), one may still assume that the key participant knows what is best from the *public interest* point of view. From this standpoint the problem is perceived as a control problem. It focuses on the lack of cooperation from those who ought to obey the wishes of the central organization.

This perspective, however, is under heavy criticism. Partly owing to the poor results of central planning and partly owing to more ideological arguments, many repudiate the possibility of making decisions at one central locus about what ought to be done. For instance, due to a dearth of information the decision makers at the central locus will always choose solutions which are far from optimal. It is for this reason that some have advocated that *self-interest* should be the standard for the evaluation of good and bad policy making. They argue that a society will do well as long as all its members are pursuing their own interest (the normative argument), and that the quality of the outcome of public decision making can be measured against the standard of the sum of the participants' self-interest. This second perspective on evaluation has also been criticized. The most important argument against self-interest as the standard for evaluation concerns the anticipated conservatism of this standard. When self-interest alone is being pursued, nobody will invest in the necessary innovations, with the result that decision making will become myopic.

We think it is possible to overcome the shortcomings of both approaches by introducing a third perspective on evaluation which employs *joint interest* as a standard for evaluation. Actors who refer to public interest will often be important innovators in our society because they take initiatives in order to solve societal problems, but at the same time they will take a selective view regarding problems and solutions. Therefore the initiative they take is only the first step in a series of decisions made while putting policy into action. In order to enrich the initiative it is important that a range of participants should express their views on the proposal. Their views will often be based upon their perception of self-interest. During the process of initiating, accommodating and selecting, all the participants involved in decision making can try to discover what they really consider worth aiming for. From the moment when a policy process is formed that is able to gain the support of a powerful coalition, a joint interest is created. We consider this a useful standard for evaluation. Using joint interest as the most effective evaluation criterion for policy making will drastically change the evaluation outcome.

Of course, it remains possible to evaluate the process in terms of *democratic quality, effectiveness and efficiency*, but the way these criteria are operationalized will change. Effectiveness, for instance, will no longer refer to the a priori goal of one of the actors involved. This would not be consistent with our own postulates. Effectiveness has to be dealt with in a multi-actor setting in which a number of actors achieve different targets. Policy making can be seen as effective when it has led to a policy result which the players of the game consider satisfactory in the light of the goals they have prioritized at the moment when they determine the policy result. Goal displacement is no longer seen as one of the worst sins of decision making. We consider it far more interesting to know whether or not a project or policy process is fulfilling present (and future) goals than whether or not it is fulfilling goals from the past. If a result of decision making is to be satisfactory, irrespective of whether it was foreseen or not, irrespective of whether it was pursued from the beginning of the process or adopted only in the last round of decision making, the evaluation has to lead to a positive outcome. As long as the redefining of targets during the game leads to a result which satisfies the actor more than the result they would have been able to achieve in a situation in which they stick to their a priori goals, it can be argued that the policy making process is satisfactory. Results which satisfy many actors and as a consequence accommodate several goals are characterized in our evaluation as a rich result. The process is defined as enriching and therefore effective.

The more the quality of the result differs from the target which was formulated at the start of the game, the more efficient policy making processes are. Quality is as important as velocity. An evaluation based on joint interest and measured in terms of satisfaction, multi-goal achievement and enrichment, will give a good indication of the quality of decision making.

The democratic quality does not, as with more traditional evaluations, depend only on the activity of elected bodies. Of course it is important for policy proposals to receive support by democratically elected councils. But the democratic quality of decisions can also be evaluated by assessing the degree to which the decision process is open to new ideas and actors (see Van Twist and Termeer, 1991; Termeer, 1993) and the way these various interests and goals are weighed against each other. In order to evaluate policy making in this way a great deal of data has to be gathered. First of all, the evaluation by the individual actors involved is an important standard against which to measure whether or not the result is satisfactory. Second, a reconstruction has to be made of the reasons for actors' satisfaction or dissatisfaction with the result. We have to challenge the dangers of cognitive resonance. There has to be a traceable gain for players who define the result as satisfactory. Third, an evaluation has to be made of the amount of enrichment the policy making process has generated. This has a direct impact on the efficiency of the process. Thus, by introducing the criterion of joint interest we can evaluate the quality of the result of complex policy making processes. This evaluation, however, does not include the policy making process itself. Therefore we suggest three additional criteria which refer to the quality of the context, the interaction and the structure of the process.

Three Criteria for Evaluating Complex Policy Making Processes

Just as someone using a more top-down perspective on management would ask whether the goals are clearly stated and whether the intended measures have been taken, an analyst who uses the network perspective wants to know whether and in what way interactions between actors are linked, covenanting takes place and actors were selected for interaction processes. The standard against which to measure good activation and linking, covenanting and arranging is the extent to which these activities contribute towards the various players' satisfaction with the outcome of the process and enrich the original policy proposal. The standard for 'good' network constitution is determined by the extent to which it improves the interaction within these networks. Good network constitution aims at creating organizational arrangements for interaction which do not become obsolete; creating meaningful standards and rules to which actors can turn but which at the same time maintain enough flexibility to enable network arrangements to adapt to changing situations. In addition, network constitution obviously has to take into account the more fundamental principles of the social order. Most important in this respect are the fundamental rules of democracy and the rules of law.

In order to achieve positive outcomes in situations of interdependency, participants in a game must have covenanting capability. A participant anxious to attain their a priori goals, unconcerned about the goals others formulate and unable to detect changes in the decision making process which enable the attaining of unforeseen, but nevertheless important goals, will not be capable of covenanting. As soon as they doubt the possibility of reaching their a priori goals they will refuse to bring in the resources they possess. The result will be a blocked decision making process.

Thus, by looking at the ability of the participants to interlink their own a priori goals, or their targets discovered during decision making, with the goals and targets of other participants, one can draw conclusions about the quality of the content of the decision making process. If participants have been unable to formulate their goals and targets, to communicate these to others in the game, to reconstruct the goals and targets of those others, and, furthermore, have been unable (and this is the most important part of covenanting) to interlink their own more or less congruent goals/targets with those of others, they will not be able to reach a satisfactory outcome because they are unable to obtain a coalition of participants who can raise enough resources to enable realization of the joint proposal.

In addition to the covenanting criterion we propose the linking criterion for evaluating the quality of the process. In order to facilitate the covenanting process, effective interaction between the parties involved is needed. These links often do not exist, because the decision making comprises several participants who may be part of several formal organizations. Thus, complex decision making is not only about policy content but also about who needs to be involved. Managers have to focus to a large extent on the question of which actors possess important resources and on creating and sustaining relations between those actors. It is not the planning of the responsibilities and tasks in advance, but the recognition of significant others and the ability to set up links, which are important indications of an effective process. Linking activities are neither the responsibility nor the monopoly of one of the participants. Every player in the game can conduct such activities. It is also possible for a third party to enter the game, not in an attempt to reach private goals with respect to the theme under discussion in the game, but in order to mediate between the parties already involved in decision making (the intermediary).

Paying a good deal of attention to linking activities (which indicate the recognition of interdependency in the game) improves the quality of the process. The introduction of brokers, for instance, is an indication of the fact that the participants recognize that they have different points of view and that they want to resolve the deadlock (Termeer, 1993).

In addition, we propose a criterion for evaluating the structure of decision making. Complex decision making often takes place in a context which comprises several actors from different formal organizations. This means that the game they are playing has no organizational platform of its own. All the participants bring in expectations drawn from their own organizations. These expectations can vary considerably. This incongruence regarding the rules of action can create conflicts which will not make decision making any easier. It is for this reason that the participants in decision making need to create arrangements to facilitate their linking and covenanting activities. In contrast to the structure of a single organization, the arrangements for joint decision making cannot be decided in advance, nor can one of the participants decide which arrangement will be most effective.

An important part of complex decision making is concerned with the question of which participants are playing the game and how the playing of the game can be structured in an effective way. Thus, the number of arrangements, and the consistency and links between the various arrangements which coexist in time, will give us an indication of the quality of the structuring process. The quality of arrangements can be measured in terms of the way participants use them. Arrangements are an indication of the wish of participants to achieve results (for a more detailed discussion of the different arrangements and their uses, see Teisman, 1992).

6.5   Conclusions

Conceptualizing policy areas as if they are networks of interdependent actors involved in an ecology of games in which they take decisions on interrelated themes, is a very productive method for describing and analysing the policy reality we are facing today.

Policy is the result of the interaction between actors in games: games in which actors use perceptions to interpret their reality and to choose their strategies. Games are conditioned by the rules and resource divisions of the network in which they take place. Managing policy processes in networks means managing the interactions in games and the setting of the game. The manager has to understand the network structure of the policy area and develop management skills which take interdependency into account. The availability of these skills will obviously improve the results of policy making.

A participant who accepts the reality of interdependency and who tries to deal with this concept can be a very successful network manager. A smart manager will understand that dealing with the network structure will give them a very powerful instrument with which to increase their influence in the interorganizational decision making process. Dealing with the network structure means, in the first place, that the manager has the capability to enter into all kinds of bilateral or trilateral links with potential partners who will sustain the line of decision making proposed by the network manager. We have dealt with this insight by using the concepts of covenanting, selective activation and adjustment in an attempt to illustrate what in our view must be seen as effective network management.

We propose to evaluate policy making processes from this standpoint using the criterion of joint interest. Joint interest is defined as the contribution the policy result makes towards the targets players aspire to at the moment the result is reached. It is an evaluation based on a posteriori goals developed during the game and inspired by the a priori goals which started the game. We assume that the result will be better or achieved faster if the strategies of important actors target an effective interlinking between a priori rationality and a posteriori rationality, as Crozier and Friedberg demonstrated ten years ago. Joint interest must be created by means of interaction. The criteria for evaluation can no longer be the a priori goals set at the beginning of a decision making process. The most important factor is that they should produce a satisfactory solution for the initiator as well as any other participants who entered the game at a later stage. It is possible that one or more participants will, in evaluating the result, refer to their a priori goals. However, it is also possible that they will refer to the more attractive new goals which were discovered in the course of the process.

Using this open method of evaluating complex decision making processes means that we reconstruct how participants themselves evaluate the process and the result, what they see as important gains (and losses) and to what extent the inter-organizational decision making process has been helpful in realizing surplus value, above and beyond the initial proposal of the participants who started that particular decision making process. By this means, the scholar gains a clear insight into the covenanting quality of the decision making process. Thus, the first criterion for evaluation deals with the content of the decision making process and was originally conceptualized as covenanting by Ostrom. In addition to this criterion for the content of decision making we have also identified two other evaluating criteria: arranging and linking. Arranging refers to the capacity of the participants involved to develop platforms on which games can be played and to the capability of the participants to develop or use rules for interaction. Linking refers to the quality of the network management performed by the different participants involved.

We consider that the analysis, prescription and evaluation of policy processes according to the insights dealt with in this chapter will improve our understanding of these processes considerably and will guide us towards practical advice which will prove to be productive.

7

Instruments for Network Management

J. A. de Bruijn and E. F. ten Heuvelhof

7.1 Background and Problem Definition

This chapter explores the options for managing networks. One of these, which will be discussed in greater depth, concerns the opportunities for network management stemming from the use of governance instruments. This is not a straightforward task. Governance instruments perform their function on the level on which governance is taking place, that is, the operational level. It remains to be seen whether, and to what extent, it is possible to transfer instruments that are active on the operational level to the level on which network management is used, that is, the institutional level. The question of whether, and to what extent, it is possible to utilize elements from one activity for the other activity will be dealt with in this chapter.

Governance is an activity which takes place on the operational level. The most important characteristic of this level is that the context is given and immutable. Two aspects of this context are of great importance in any discussion on governance and network management. The first aspect concerns the targets. On the operational level, governance assumes targets which are fixed, and is aimed at achieving these targets by influencing the behaviour of the actors to be governed in such a manner that it becomes more goal-driven (Derksen, 1989). The governing actor brings governance instruments into play. These instruments are effective if they result in furthering the targets set. The second aspect relates to the features of the field of influence within which the governing actor operates. These features concern the characteristics of the policy network, including the actors taking part in it and the relations between them. On the level of governance the characteristics of the network are considered invariable.

In a discussion of what is possible and what impossible for governance to achieve on the operational level, context plays an important role, since the nature of the context renders governance difficult or impossible, or, on the contrary, serves to facilitate it. Once it has been ascertained that governance is problematic, therefore, the next logical step is to explore the possibilities for changing the context and to do so in such a way that governance is facilitated. Interventions aimed at changing the context of governance are part of network management.

This area of network management is the institutional level. Network management focuses on the characteristics of the policy network. The features of the context need to be such that they facilitate goal-seeking processes. This is the primary task of network management and involves its ability to modify the characteristics of the governance context in such a way that more options for governance on the operational level are created.

Activities and interventions on the operational level are often described in terms derived from the 'governance' metaphor. Goals, direction, routing and instruments are all concepts which form part of this metaphor and which fit into discussions and reflections concerning this level. This chapter explores the options for applying elements derived from this metaphor to the institutional level. In other words: to what extent is it useful to consider instruments in terms of their potential for managing a complex policy network? Which instruments have an inherent potential for managing networks? What are the possibilities and dangers associated with the construction and use of instruments on the institutional level? These questions are explored from the perspective of a public actor.

In section 7.2 we deal with the concept of instruments. The concept is defined and families of instruments are identified. In order to be able to deploy instruments on an institutional level, two sets of conditions must be met. Section 7.3 deals with the first of these sets, which arises from the fact that authorities operate within horizontal structures. This imposes certain restrictions with regard to the way in which they can deploy instruments. This group of conditions applies similarly to the operational level. The second group of conditions is specific to the institutional level. Section 7.4 illustrates that the linking factors for instruments on the institutional level differ widely from those on the operational level. Obviously, these differences have an impact on the selection and deployment of instruments for network management. Section 7.5 forms the central focus of this contribution, and deals with the instruments used for network management. Section 7.6 describes the considerable hazards associated with applying the concept of instruments on the institutional level. If instrumentalism constitutes a real threat on the operational level, it presents an even greater one on the institutional level.

7.2   The Tools of Government: Three Families of Instruments

Discussions about governance have frequently focused on the concept of governance instruments. Both narrow and broad definitions of this concept have been evaluated for their usefulness (De Bruijn and ten Heuvelhof, 1991: 4). The crux of these definitions is that instruments are the means to attain particular goals (Ringeling, 1983: 1). A conflict within network management is made manifest here. Network management, namely, is aimed at creating conditions under which goal-oriented processes can take place. The question is whether and to what extent instruments can be used both to influence goal-oriented processes (governance) and to create the conditions which facilitate the mutual formulation of targets (network management).

This chapter builds on a broad distinction between instruments, referred to here as 'families of instruments' (Van der Doelen, 1993: 1). The members of a family of instruments are clearly seen to be interrelated without there being one single attribute which is shared by all (De Bruijn and ten Heuvelhof, 1991: 5). Three of these families will be discussed here. First there is the legal family, consisting of orders and prohibitions; second, the family of economic instruments, which mainly consists of financial incentives; finally, the family of communicative instruments which focuses on the transfer of information.

Instruments are closely linked with other elements of policy processes. It has been argued that actors choose from a 'toolkit' of instruments by comparing instruments in terms of their ability to contribute to the realization of previously determined goals. Empirical research has qualified this simplistic view of policy processes: the relation between goals and the means used to achieve them is quite different. Instruments are more than the final element in a policy process. A more realistic view of policy processes is to consider actors, goals and means as interacting with each other. Instruments, for their part, facilitate the formulation of goals. The accessibility of instruments can itself provide reason enough for actors to become involved with a problem and to become active in a network. Goals are also realized on the basis of the means available. Actors are not as free in their choice and use of instruments as they might seem. There are three important limitations which actors should bear in mind when selecting and deploying instruments. The first of these is that actors are, to some extent, committed to particular instruments. They are used to working with them and possess the relevant knowledge and expertise to use them. They are interwoven into the fabric of their culture. This first limitation is found at the intraorganizational level, and consequently will not be further discussed here. The second limitation is that the characteristics of the network also serve to determine the effectiveness of an instrument: one context requires different instruments from another. Since these characteristics determine the choice and use of instruments on the operational level, they should also determine the selection of instruments on the institutional level. These characteristics therefore deserve attention when considering the potential of instruments for aiding network management (see section 7.3).

The third limitation is that instruments need linking factors in order to be effective. Linking factors at the institutional level differ significantly from those at the operational level. The question that arises, therefore, is to what extent instruments can be tailored to the linking factors that typically occur on the institutional level (see section 7.4). The characteristics typical of this level necessitate a specially adapted form of deployment. The linking factors for instruments on the institutional level differ so radically from those on the operational level that the question arises of whether the instruments also need to be adapted.

7.3 Policy Networks and the Choice and Use of Instruments

It has been argued elsewhere that applying the instrument metaphor carries the connotation that the governing actor is able to set their course and can bring instruments into play to attain their goal (De Bruijn and Ten Heuvelhof, 1991). The underlying hypothesis is that the governing actor has an overview and is able to analyse the effect of the instruments at his disposal, and to select from among them. A necessary precondition for this is that the governing actor needs to be situated above the actors to be governed. Only within such a vertical structure does the governing actor command a proper overview and the power to substantiate this hypothesis. The chief characteristics of traditional governance instruments such as regulation and central planning render them suitable for use in a vertical structure. These 'first generation instruments' are mostly compulsory, unilateral and have a generic effect.

The Characteristics of Policy Networks

On the whole, however, reality bears no resemblance to such a vertical structure. A far more realistic image is that of the horizontal structure. In this structure, the relations between actors are substantially different from those found in a vertical structure. In a horizontal structure, all the actors are considered to have justified interests and goals and all of them utilize governance interventions. All the actors, including the public actors, are equal in terms of the governance capability they possess. Admittedly, public actors have access to unique sources of power, but private actors have other, also unique sources of power. This horizontal structure with all its governing actors, including the governing public actors, is referred to by the term 'network'. Networks are characterized by pluriformity, self-referentiality, interdependency and dynamics.

One of the chief characteristics of a network is *pluriformity*. Pluriformity is a dominant presence in networks on several levels and in various ways. Individual actors can be pluriform: large organizations are composed of sharply differing suborganizations open to a variety of governance signals. The network as a whole can also be pluriform: the power of the various actors in the network can vary as can the extent to which they are open to their environment. One effect of the pluriform nature of networks is that the degree to which actors are receptive to governance signals may vary greatly. Each actor will have a governance signal which is most suited to them.

Furthermore, networks are often characterized by *self-referentiality*. The actors in a network have a certain autonomy and, partly as a consequence of this, are relatively closed off from their environment. They each have their own frame of reference and are receptive to signals which fit within this frame of reference. Moreover, actors are often oriented towards themselves or towards actors with similar frames of reference. As far as any government with ambitions for governance is concerned, this means that its instruments must be tailored to this frame of reference. For example, legislation and regulations have little chance of success if the actor to be governed has not adopted the norms on which the rules are based.

A third characteristic of networks is *interdependence*: actors in a network are dependent on each other. These dependencies can be expressed in different ways (finances, powers, political support, land, etc.). The relations of dependence may be simple, but can also be very complex. For example, relations can be both asymmetrical and asynchronous. Asymmetrical, because actor A is dependent on actor B, B on C and C on A: this means that simple 'duologues' are not always possible. Asynchronous because these dependencies are not all present at the same time: the actors realize that they are dependent on each other at different times. This rules out any simple exchange agreements on an equal basis.

Dynamics constitutes the fourth characteristic of a network. How variable are the pluriformity, self-containment and interdependencies within the network? Rapid changes in these features can present opportunities for governance to some actors, and yet block them off from others. Actors who are alert and capable of interpreting changes in their environment, who have the ability to take advantage of emergent opportunities, can secure new options for governance; for other actors, the same dynamics may appear as simply chaotic and they are unable to perceive any opportunities for themselves.

The above four characteristics may be described 'from the outside' and understood in 'objective' terms, but actors also perceive these characteristics in their own way. It is possible for their perceptions of the interdependencies, for example, to change without any variation occurring in the 'objective' dependencies. These changes in perception alone, regardless of any underlying variations, can affect the opportunities for governance.

Second Generation Instruments

Within a network, traditional governance instruments are often not very effective. Instruments suitable for use in a network context are the so-called second generation governance instruments, such as covenants, contracts, communicative planning, parameters and incentives. These instruments are suitable for dealing with the pluriformity, self-referentiality, interdependency and dynamics of networks. They comply with what is termed the condition of contingency, that is, instruments need to fit into the structure within which they have to function.

One of the reasons why governance often proves so difficult is that traditional or 'first generation' instruments appropriate to a vertical structure are used in a context which is relatively horizontal. Such a horizontally structured context is most likely to be found in a situation in which the governing actor takes account of the options for network management. After all, an inability to govern effectively is one of the chief reasons for engaging in network management. In so far as instruments are suitable for use in network management, they will be second generation instruments.

The Use of Second Generation Instruments

A necessary precondition for being able to achieve a successful deployment of instruments is that the requirements of the quasi-network context should be met. This is important not only to governance, but especially to network management. The horizontal context requires actors who govern and function as managers to deploy instruments in a way which differs from the traditional approach. Four points are of particular importance (De Bruijn and Ten Heuvelhof, 1991: 59–66):

Indirect use of instruments   Since the governing actor no longer occupies a position above that of the actors to be governed, it is not always possible for them to realize their goals directly. Where direct options are not available, indirect ways may still be open. One option is for the actors to be governed to be approached via other actors. A second option is that governance does not directly focus on the behaviour, that is, the output, of the actors to be governed, but instead focuses on the input they need. The deployment of instruments in a network requires both the governing actor and the actor operating as manager to take account of the options for using instruments indirectly.

Fine tuning   Actors to be governed in a vertically structured context have one feature in common which is of the utmost importance to the governing actor, and that is, that they are subordinate to the governing actor. This subordination makes it possible to govern generically: all the actors to be governed are approached in an identical manner. However, this form of governance is not suited to a network. The position the public actor occupies within the horizontal structure, where they are on a par with the other actors, serves to deprive the actor who both governs and functions as manager of the option of treating the actors to be governed as one another's equals. If these actors wish to effect changes, these will have to be based on the differences between the actors and tailored to the specific sensitivities of these actors. Fine tuning then replaces generic forms of governance.

Serendipity   It is only in exceptionally simple situations that a policy theory which is consolidated to any extent will be available to the governing actor. Such a theory shows them which instruments should be deployed to attain particular goals, and will not be available in a more complex situation. Consequently, the governing actor does not know in advance which interventions will cause which effects. Instruments deployed with a view to attaining a specific goal may have effects other than those anticipated. These effects may contribute towards the realization of entirely different goals, however. The governing actors must therefore be aware of unexpected and unanticipated opportunities which present themselves in governance, even when such opportunities arise in other situations than those for which governance was originally set in motion.

Multilaterality Since governing actors and those to be governed each attempt to govern the other, and since each has comparable governance capability at their disposal, this means that each needs the support of the other in order to be able to govern. There is no longer any question of unilateral directives: multilaterality has superseded them. It is necessary for governing actors and the target group to reach agreement on the nature and direction of the governance interventions.

The quasi-network context of governance affects the choice of instruments and the method of their deployment. If instruments are to serve a useful purpose in network management, they will need to be deployed in a similar manner.

7.4 Linking Factors for Network Management

The leap from the operational level to the institutional level entails a number of consequences for the deployment of governance instruments. The linking factors for the instruments on the operational level differ from those on the institutional level, and consequently the instruments on each level also have a different shape. On the operational level, the instruments are tailored to the behaviour of the actors to be governed, while on the institutional level other factors are important. The question arises as to whether instruments which are appropriate for influencing behaviour are also capable of changing the characteristics of the governance context which are essential for governance. The problem is how the network characteristics relevant to governance can be influenced. Which linking factors can be used to influence these characteristics?

Two linking factors are available to network management. The first is found in the actors who are part of the network: their number, their variety, their internal organization, their interests, their size and their ability to learn constitute those features of actors through which the characteristics relevant to governance can be influenced.

The second linking factor is found in the relations which exist between the actors in a network. What pattern do these relationships have? Is it egalitarian in the sense that all the actors are associated with each other to the same extent or are there, in addition to highly involved actors, also actors who are relatively isolated? Are the relations such that the dependent actors can actually be linked to each other? Do the relations leave enough room for competition? How permanent are the established relations? Instruments which are effective on the institutional level will have to focus on the actors in a network and the relations between them. By using these two linking factors, the actor functioning as manager is then able to modify the network characteristics relevant to governance.

7.5   Instruments for Network Management

Instruments can influence the governance-relevant context in two ways. First, instruments designed and deployed for governance, and which are tailored to the actors' behaviour, exert an indirect, possibly unintended effect on the governance context (De Bruijn, 1990). On the institutional level this effect may be far-reaching. At worst, it is possible that instruments which influence behaviour effectively and efficiently simultaneously influence the context within which they are used in such a manner that they are no longer able to produce this effect at a later stage. This unintended form of network management is not dealt with here.

The second form of influence derives from the fact that instruments are consciously designed for managing networks. They may exert an indirect and unintended impact on a different level than that for which they were intended, subsequently influencing behaviour indirectly and often unintentionally.

For each family of instruments, examples of those instruments which are tailored to actors will first be described followed by examples of instruments which transform the relations between actors.

Regulatory Instruments

A number of regulatory instruments are designed to be effective on the institutional level. This category of instruments influences characteristics of the governance context which are relevant for governance via the actors and/or the relations between them.

Regulatory instruments Aimed at actors   There is a wide range of regulatory instruments which are tailored to the actors in a network. There are regulatory instruments which influence the number of actors in a network, the power they wield and the intraorganizational pluriformity.

Regulatory instruments affecting the number of actors in a network can operate in two ways: directly or indirectly. The most direct way is when a public actor creates a new actor by means of allocating them a place in a particular regulation. The regulation might stipulate that the new actor has certain powers and responsibilities, is empowered to collect money, and so on. Utility companies were created in this way, for example. Again, the current trend of placing government agencies which meet certain conditions at a distance from the government may be seen as a form of network management which falls into the category of 'adding actors to the network'. In the indirect variant, government acting as manager establishes rules which enable the creation of new actors and which describe the conditions which the new actor has to meet. They provide the 'barriers of entry' and the 'facilities of entry'. The rules may offer the opportunity for actors other than the regulating public actor to create the actors desired. The housing associations in the Netherlands, for instance, were set up on the basis of such rules (Gerrichhauzen, 1990: 20). The law stipulates which conditions an association or foundation has to meet in order to qualify as a housing association.

However, it is up to other actors to take the actual initiative to found the association.

Regulatory instruments can also serve to bring about a reduction in the number of actors. An argument frequently used in favour of such reduction is that with the present number of actors the execution of tasks is too fragmented: increasing the number of tasks allotted to each actor would result in improved performance. This argument may be specified in a regulation: for instance, the government might formulate norms incorporating thresholds which affect the continued existence of actors (e.g. the minimum number of pupils at a school, the minimum number of inhabitants in a municipality).

Another way in which regulatory instruments on the institutional level can be tailored to the actors is to change the balance of power among the actors concerned by means of rules. Rules can impair or, conversely, extend actors' sources of power. Powers, information, prestige, funds and so forth can be allocated to actors or taken away from them. Such shifts can substantially alter the balance of power in the network.

A third form of regulation on the institutional level concerns the internal structure of the actors in the network. Regulation can influence the intra-organizational differentiation and thus the manner in which actors behave in interorganizational transactions. A traditional form of network management which falls into this category is the separation of powers. Many regulations are based on the principle that the legislative, executive and judicial powers are discrete. Individual actors are allowed to hold a position in only one of these spheres. If one actor were to perform two roles, the chances of an abuse of power would be too great.

Rules aimed at introducing certain internal checks and balances into organizations fall under this form of network management. Rules can be used to bring the various rationalities into some kind of balance within one organization. Legislation has contributed towards a balance between the interests of financiers and those of employees within a company. The law furnishes diverse options for various legal persons to meet the needs of both groups of interests.

This same category includes the rules and regulations that make councils of employers a statutory requirement for certain types of companies, the premise being that in company policy social interests are too likely to lose out to other interests. By making works councils compulsory and granting them certain consultation powers and the power of veto, the social interests within the company will be more adequately represented and its subsequent behaviour will be more socially oriented.

The argument for effecting a certain internal pluriformity is that this will influence, from within, the company's decision making and behaviour. Once it has implemented this form of network management, the authorities will be in a better position to influence the behaviour of the company, since its instruments on the operational level can be tailored to the internal rationality which it has first helped to create.

Regulatory instruments aimed at relations   A second linking factor for regulatory instruments concerns the relations which exist among actors. One category of these regulatory instruments is tailored to the relations which the governing and public actor functioning as manager maintains with other actors, including the target group. A second category of regulatory instruments focuses on the relations between the actors in the network which bypass the public actor. The first category includes the many statutory processes of rights of consultation and the power of veto. Regulatory instruments can establish relations between actors and create dependencies which were previously absent. Actors can, for example, be placed under the supervision of public actors or of other actors. Actors who were previously allowed to do as they pleased now need the consent of the actor designated as their supervisor. A less tightly controlled relation concerns the duty of consultation. Actors must not proceed before they have consulted with an actor named in a regulation. Many public actors are subject to such a duty. They must obtain advice and subsequently make this public. A comparison between such advice and what is actually done would be a good starting point for a political debate. Obviously, regulatory instruments can also be used to free actors from these kinds of dependencies. The processes of rights of consultation and the power of veto are then relaxed or dispensed with altogether. An argument used in favour of this is that decision making will proceed faster and will be less likely to reach a deadlock.

The following are two examples of the second category, that of regulatory instruments affecting the relations between actors in the target group. The first example relates to regulations intended to strengthen weak ties and create new ones between actors. In the Netherlands, a set of environmental acts covering each of the environmental media has been established over the last decades. Until recently, companies often needed several licences under various of these acts. Each licence had to be applied for from the proper (and separate) authorities. This body, whether in consultation with the applicant or not, imposed the conditions to be met in order to qualify for the licence. There was no need for any cooperation between the various bodies concerned and they could stipulate their conditions independently. At worst, this arrangement resulted in the competent authorities being intent on keeping the backyard of their own sector of the environment clean (air, water, etc.), and consequently the licence applicant was forced to transfer their environmental loading to another sector of the environment where a licence was not yet needed. A new environmental act intends to put an end to this practice. In future, the applicant will deal with one competent authority which issues an integrated environmental licence. It is the intention that the authorities consider the licence applicant's total environmental loading and that a balanced decision then be taken as to which environmental compartment is best able to bear this burden. The point being made here is that the government, which is acting as manager and which has established this act, is forcing the public actors who grant the licences to enter into mutual consultation regarding the issuing of the licence. Public actors, between whom no relation previously existed, become linked to one another as a result of this act.

The second example deals with regulations that serve to extend already existing relations between actors. For companies that stand in a competitive relationship to one another, it may be highly advantageous to cooperate and even to reach price agreements. Governments try to oppose such agreements, which counteract the advantages of the free market and competition, by means of anti-cartel regulations forbidding certain forms of cooperation.

Financial Instruments

Like regulatory instruments, not all financial instruments are aimed at changing behaviour. There are financial instruments which are intended to be effective on the institutional level.

Financial instruments aimed at actors   The first group of instruments is tailored to the actors in the arena. Governments can stimulate the creation of new actors, for example by utilizing the forces that are inherent in the market. The government creates a particular demand for goods/services or ensures that a particular supply exists. New actors will then rush to fill the 'vacuum' thus created. From the moment the government adopts a policy of separate waste collection, companies that want to process the separated waste will come into being.

In creating new actors, regulatory instruments and financial instruments make a very good combination. The government creates a demand and at the same time formulates rules specifying the conditions which actors have to meet to be able to take advantage of this demand. Education in the Netherlands provides one example of such a combination. By introducing compulsory education, the government created a demand for educational agencies and at the same time issued rules on the requirements which must be met by actors desirous of providing the education needed.

Financial instruments can be useful in strengthening the autonomy of actors, so that they will be in a better position to function in the policy arena. This category of instruments includes unconditional, general tax relief for actors. The government that introduces this tax relief reasons that concrete behaviour is better left to the actor. After all, they have more know-how and is in a better position to judge their own strength than the government is. What is involved here is that actors are given the financial leeway which enables them to decide for themselves without being dependent at least on financial aid from others.

Financial instruments aimed at relations   A second group of financial instruments is aimed at the relations between actors. A public actor can bind other actors to them with financial cords. This is possible, for example, where a public body shares in the venture capital of the actor concerned and is given a certain amount of authority in exchange for it. Combinations of regulatory instruments and financial instruments are prevalent. The authorities then issue rules on which financial relations are permissible and which are not.

Financial instruments can also serve to induce actors who have always functioned independently to cooperate. Municipal environmental agencies are responsible for the implementation and enforcement of environmental policy in the Netherlands. Since the municipalities in the Netherlands have widely differing numbers of inhabitants, the options for expanding their workforce of civil servants differ widely. The larger the municipality, the more civil servants it can employ, of a higher calibre and at higher salaries. This has resulted in the municipal environmental units also differing greatly in size and quality. Large municipalities had large, high-quality agencies run by specialized and highly qualified officials, while small municipalities had units that were too small to employ staff of this calibre. Due to this high degree of pluriformity, municipalities as a target group for the national government were difficult to govern. Governance signals suited to one municipal agency proved not to fit within the frame of reference of the others. In response to this, the government created a scheme whereby agencies which entered into cooperative links would qualify for the allocation of additional positions. This financial instrument implemented on the institutional level had a dual impact: all agencies acquired staff of a certain calibre, and the pluriformity of the target group decreased – the differences in size and levels of expertise were reduced – which made it easier for the state to deploy instruments relevant for every agency.

Communicative Instruments

Similarly, communicative instruments can be deployed on the institutional level, and can be tailored both to the actors in a network and to the relations between them.

Communicative instruments aimed at actors   The first example of this category focuses on the actors. Communication on the institutional level is not directly aimed at modifying behaviour, but is intended to bring about a change in the perception of problems, a change in people's values and norms and even a transformation in the 'belief systems' (Donaldson and Lorsch, 1983) of organizations. Communicative instruments which operate strategically can be content oriented. Environmental policy in the Netherlands is aimed at stimulating the population and the target group to internalize the values which underlie it: once this has been effected, it is anticipated that it will be easier to deploy instruments on the operational level which encourage them to modify their behaviour, in this case towards more environmentally friendly behaviour. Other instruments on this level lack substance: they are simply aimed at putting procedural values into practice, e.g. formal procedures that stimulate private enterprises to take environmental interest into consideration when taking investment decisions (Termeer, 1993).

Communicative instruments aimed at relations   The following examples of strategic instruments concern the relations between actors. One such instrument is the design of the concepts actors choose for formulating their problems and the solutions they devise for them; in other words, the terms which actors use to formulate a problem, and into which existing problem category a new problem is placed. 'Management of meaning' is therefore an important strategically operative instrument (Pool, 1990: 233).

The concepts a public actor uses to formulate a problem may determine the options for governance which will later be available to them. It is worthwhile to examine the impact which the introduction of a number of concepts has had on Dutch environmental policy. One example is that of the target group policy. The government formulates norms for and consults with a particular target group regarding the way in which the target group is to realize these norms. The consultations can result in diverse instruments on the operational level, such as a number of variants on regulations and covenants. The importance of designing and choosing a concept such as that of the target group is that the members of this target group, prior to the creation of this concept, may have been functioning completely independently, but have become interlinked simply because they belong to the same category or target group. A government that enters into a covenant with the target group calls relations into existence that were not there before. The members of the target group are suddenly mutually dependent, in that they have jointly committed themselves to the covenant. It is highly likely that default on the part of one of the members of the target group will have a negative impact on the other members.

The 'chain-linked life cycle' concept introduced into Dutch environmental policy is a similar strategic instrument. The life cycle of a product is the aggregate of actors who have to deal with it at different times during its life. The chain begins with the companies that mine the raw materials of which the product is composed. Subsequent links in the chain consist of the processors of the raw materials, the manufacturers of semi-finished products, the manufacturers, the retailers and the waste processors. Until recently, these actors were not associated in any way other than through the economic relations of supply and demand and through the flow of funds and materials passing between them. By interlinking these actors via the chain concept and subsequently assessing the environmental impact of materials and products during their entire life cycle, the government creates new interdependencies between the actors in the chain. The environment-related performance of a product is as weak as the weakest link in the chain. If one of the actors behaves irresponsibly, the product will come under attack, which could result, for example, in restrictive regulations and levies which might be detrimental to all the links in the chain. Thus, the manufacturer of the semi-finished product may benefit from the retailers ensuring forms of selling which minimize the environmental impact. This manufacturer might, for instance, urge the retail trade to organize a system of returnable deposits on packagings which would reduce the problem of waste disposal. Another notion closely associated with that of the chain is that of product liability: one link in the chain remains liable for any damage caused to the environment by their product, even after this actor has transferred the product to other links in the chain. The environmental damage resulting from another actor's default may be substantial, thus putting pressure on this actor, if necessary via the insurance company that covers them against such liability, to manufacture the product in such a way as to minimize the possibility of damage and, subsequently, to contribute to similar measures on the part of the other links so as to minimize any further damage.

7.6   Instrumentalism on the Institutional Level

The concept of instruments has been applied in a productive way on the operational level up to a point, with the emphasis on 'up to a point', for even on that level the image is not wholly applicable. In complex networks in particular this metaphor has limited validity. Too radical an implementation of this concept results in the instrumentalism that has been criticized elsewhere (Schuyt, 1985: 114–18).

The Dangers of Instrumentalism

Instrumentalism means that the actors responsible for the deployment of instruments evaluate the success of deployment merely on the basis of whether the targets set are achieved effectively and efficiently. Other values which public actors should be striving for and which are connected with the constitutional state are then neglected.

On the institutional level, apparently, the limits of instrumentalism are reached even sooner than on the operational level. Two parts of the instrument metaphor, in particular, have only very limited validity on the institutional level. The first part of the metaphor concerns the suggestion that problem strategy lends itself to the deployment of an instrument. The metaphor suggests that it is possible to reach a diagnosis of the roots of the problem (the 'policy theory'), after which the governing actor can select their instruments and deploy them with 'surgical precision'. Even on the operational level this part of the metaphor is not valid or only so to a limited extent, while on the institutional level the dynamics are such that this part of the metaphor is hardly productive at all.

The second part of the metaphor, which is of little value on the institutional level, concerns the instruments' success indicators. The metaphor illustrates that instruments are successful once the problem has been effectively and efficiently remedied. As far as the operational level is concerned, it is worthwhile to retain this part of the metaphor, but on the institutional level other values are relevant besides considerations of effectiveness and efficiency. Consequently, transplanting the normative parts of the instrument metaphor to the institutional level is not without its problems and might even be dangerous.

The Dynamics of Network Management

It is almost impossible for network management as an institutional activity to be evaluated ex ante in terms of its ability to tackle a concrete problem of governance. Starting from a concrete problem, it is not possible to devise how and in what way the characteristics of the network need to be adapted in order to reach a solution to that problem. The precision and certainty required for such an operation are not found in network management. The problems that arise in governing on the operational level in a network are also relevant in this context to interventions on the institutional level. Even in situations where it is possible to modify the governance-relevant characteristics of the network, the implications for the creation of options for governance and the creation of new problems remain hard to predict. The complexity of the structures involved and of the processes, both current and those yet to be initiated, is far too great. If this is the case, why is network management necessary? The point is that network management will change the structure of the network. It is indeed impossible to precisely predict the content of such changes and their consequences, but in any event there will be some movement. These changes will offer opportunities for governance, although governance on the operational level may become even more difficult. Network management is a strategy for situations in which governance on the operational level is problematic. It brings about movement within the network and as a result of this opportunities arise although these are not without risk. Network management will change the network and thus lead to new problems and opportunities which are hard to predict owing to their complexity and interrelated nature. It is productive to consider such reorganizing processes as 'garbage cans': 'highly contextual combinations of people, choice opportunities, problems and solutions' (March and Olsen, 1989: 80). The reshuffling of the network and the surprising dynamics which then emerge will offer opportunities for tackling entirely different problems than those originally anticipated. However, the actors to whom these opportunities are of interest must then be in a position to identify these new opportunities and utilize them. This demands actors who not only meet these changes with an open mind but are also able to decide swiftly and skilfully on any institutional changes of course which may be necessary, utilizing the new opportunities which come forward. Three processes, both individually but even more so in combination, are responsible for these dynamics and their limited predictability.

The first group concerns intraorganizational change processes. The effect of institutional changes which actors initiate, such as the creation of new actors and changes in the intraorganizational pluriformity of actors, will carry over into these actors' internal organization. For example, newly created organizations may initially be rather informal. After a time, however, processes of bureaucratization and formalization will occur even in organizations set up by private initiative (Kramer, 1981: 4). These internal change processes will affect these actors' options for functioning as governance intermediaries. Similarly, the pattern of relations within which an actor functions and the changes within that pattern will affect the actor's internal organization. Ever since the Dutch Ministry of Housing, Spatial Planning and Environment (VROM) identified agriculture as an environmentally relevant target group, this ministry has had a division which deals with this group. The task of this division is to carry out an assessment of this target group in order to facilitate better governance by the ministry. However, through its contact with the target group, the Ministry of Agriculture and intermediary organizations within agriculture, this division will gain some affinity with agriculture's interests and thus could become an actor who serves to inhibit the VROM's vigorous approach to this target group.

A second process is that of 'discolouring'. In the course of time, actors may change their 'colour' or affiliation. Network management can accelerate this process and maximize its uncontrollability. Examples can be seen in the changes which occur in actors who have been created to occupy a position between the governing actor and their target group. An intermediary organization of this kind may adopt the colour of its creator or, on the contrary, that of the target group. Organizations created by the government come to resemble it (Couwenberg, 1988: 42). In the course of time, the new actor loses some of their independence and begins to take on the shape of an implementing organization or even resembles a part of the government. The confidence of the target group initially enjoyed by these organizations may diminish and their original capacity to contribute governance-relevant information to the governing actor decreases.

A third form of unanticipated dynamics arising as a result of network management is that the changes effected in the actors and their relations with a view to governance may in themselves stimulate other actors to initiate changes on the institutional level. The housing associations referred to earlier, the creation of which is a form of network management, have, over the years, created umbrella associations, thus changing the make-up of the network once again (Couwenberg, 1988: 23).

These dynamics are the result of the fact that the actor functioning as manager is situated in a horizontal structure where they are not elevated above the other actors but is in the midst of them. This serves to encourage other actors to engage in network management. All the actors in the network are given the opportunity to manage the relevant network. The various actors' strategies will interfere with each other, with surprising results.

Network management will lead to dynamics from which an alert actor, focused on identifying emergent strategies, can benefit. However, modifying the make-up of actors and relations, which at first glance appeared to enhance the options for governance, may also have the reverse effect. This is particularly likely where changes in policy are concerned. Actors and/or relations created with a view to a particular policy may become obstacles to a policy shift. A change in policy may turn actors who were loyal under the former policy into formidable obstacles during the implementation phase. The General Inspectorate (Algemene Inspectie Dienst, AID), for example, was able to remain loyal both to its parent organization, the Ministry of

Agriculture and Fisheries, and to its clientele, i.e. farmers and fishermen. The interests of all three were analogous. From the moment when Agriculture and Fisheries started to steer a slightly different course, the AID proved to have adopted the colour of its clientele to a significant extent, thus rendering impossible a rapid U-turn in implementation (Bekke and De Vries, 1991). This role applies even more in the case of terminating policy. Specially created implementing organizations will oppose the terminating of a policy with whose implementation they have been entrusted.

Normative Aspects of Network Management

It has been argued that in areas where governance on the instrumental level has proved problematic, interventions on the institutional level may be worth considering, because they may enhance the chances of success of interventions on the operational level. This approach is attractive because it may enhance the authorities' governance capabilities. At the same time, dangers also threaten if this approach is taken to its logical conclusion. If all interventions, including those on the institutional level, were deployed simply on the basis of the need to realize formulated goals as effectively and as efficiently as possible, then it would become instrumentalism. All interventions, including those on the institutional level, would then be evaluated on the basis of their ability to contribute to the realization of goals.

It is of great importance that the set of values on one level should differ from that on the other level. Individual values which are of paramount importance on one level will carry less weight on the other. Thus, 'good governance' is interpreted somewhat differently on the operational level than on the institutional level (Hood, 1991: 3–19; Lehning, 1991; Toonen and Ten Heuvelhof, 1993). On the operational level, considerations of effectiveness and efficiency play a major role. On this level, the goals are fixed. Governance is considered to be 'good' if it succeeds in deploying instruments which help achieve goals with a minimum of effort.

On the institutional level, the targets are not fixed, since the aim here is precisely to formulate goals. Structures and processes on this level are satisfactory if they contribute to goal formulation. There is good governance on this level if the procedures according to which goals are formulated are authoritative and the goals as formulated can expect broad endorsement from the actors concerned. Instruments which are effective on the institutional level must be evaluated primarily in terms of their contribution to the realization of the values relevant to this level, i.e. goals which are fair, balanced and reasonable.

The fact that values and norms on the operational level and the institutional level are not by their very nature analogous, carries a great risk. The pressure from managers to deal with the problems of the hour may contribute to instruments designed for the institutional level being deployed for realizing goals. There are numerous examples which illustrate this. The difficulties experienced in getting certain definite infrastructure projects off the ground has been claimed as a reason for changing appeal and advice procedures. Administrative reorganizations are set in motion with the argument that certain concrete problems cannot otherwise be solved. Instruments on the institutional level are being deployed here to tackle operational problems. A question which has wrongly been neglected is to what extent these interventions are harmful to the values that are at issue on the institutional level. In other words, an administrative reorganization which might indeed expedite the advent of certain infrastructure projects may well be at the expense of the ability to arrive at a balanced, fair and broadly supported policy. Short-term gain will later turn out to have been dearly bought.

7.7 Concluding Observations

Just as the instrument metaphor proved productive for the reflections on governance on the operational level, it is also worthwhile to carry the analogy through for network management on the institutional level. It proves possible to indicate links between the construction and deployment of instruments on the one hand and effects on the institutional level on the other. Instruments enable network management to take place.

The metaphor clearly has its limitations, however, and four of these have been discussed. The first is that the public actor who functions as manager and deploys instruments needs to realize that they are operating in a network, that is, in a horizontal structure. This imposes specific requirements on the way in which they can deploy instruments. The second limitation is that network management has its own linking factors which differ from those for governance. Instruments for network management must be constructed in such a way that they can be geared towards these linking factors. The third limitation is that it is by no means always possible to tackle a specific problem using instruments for network management. The deployment of such instruments involves such far-reaching and long-lasting consequences that their impact is difficult to predict. These instruments possess their own dynamics which are unpredictable and uncontrollable. However, the processes which will be set in motion by these instruments will offer new and unanticipated opportunities for governance. The fourth limitation, finally, is that the criteria applicable to the functioning of instruments on the operational level need to be allotted a different degree of importance on the institutional level. Criteria of effectiveness and efficiency are important on the operational level, but on the institutional level their role is secondary.

8

Managing Implementation Processes in Networks

L.J. O'Toole Jr., K.I. Hanf and P.L. Hupe

8.1 Introduction

Central Question

Policy making involves efforts by governments to solve public problems. As earlier chapters have suggested, effective public problem-solving in late welfare states requires the cooperative efforts of a variety of individuals and organizations. Often, no institution of government possesses sufficient authority, resources and knowledge to enact – let alone achieve – policy intentions. Instead, policies require the concerted efforts of multiple actors all possessing some capabilities for action but each dependent on others to solidify policy intention and to seek its conversion into action (Scharpf et al., 1976, 1978; Hanf and Scharpf, 1978; Hanf and O'Toole, 1992). The kinds of circumstances in which no single actor can solve a problem alone nor compel others to seek effective solutions are precisely the sort which propel networks to centre stage.

With complex network arrangements now standard features of contemporary policy settings, conventional public problem-solving approaches – visible, for instance, in the typical injunctions of public management – are of little practical help in understanding and dealing with situations where the challenge is one of managing across the boundaries of single organizations. Accordingly, new perspectives are now needed to address the problem solving requirements of such policy settings.

This chapter focuses on the management of the networks involved in the implementation of public policy at the local level, the point of immediate impact of governmental activity on the target groups. Against the background of the issues discussed in earlier chapters, we attempt to highlight some of the features of the context within which this management activity takes place and to indicate some of the strategies available to these managers for putting together and using networks for the implementation of policy at this level.

One difference between the use of networks in the management of implementation compared with other phases of the policy process lies in the fact that during the implementation phase the tasks to be performed – oriented as they are to more specific objectives or problem-solving activities – will tend to be more narrow and concrete. Furthermore these tasks will involve a number of functionally specified networks. And although there may be an officially mandated, or self-selected 'overall manager' of these implementation activities, the management of implementation involves the sharing and coordination of 'management' between multiple parties, often located at different levels of government. Given the more specific goal orientation of network activity during this phase, the management of implementation will also rely more on the search for and development of common purpose among the participants than is the case with the use of networks during other phases. Nevertheless, despite these differences, we will see that several of the lessons regarding network management, discussed elsewhere in this book, also bear on the management of implementation. In this chapter we attempt to integrate these different strands of network management in an examination of the management of policy implementation at the local level.

Contents

In the following section we define the terms 'implementation', 'networks' and 'management'. Next, we sketch the characteristics of managing implementation from the perspective of actors charged with public programme responsibilities at 'the bottom'. Although implementation may involve the joint efforts of various organizational actors, linked by a sense of shared, common purpose, there are situations where the cooperation required must be sought and effected in the face of divergent or even conflicting objectives. We examine some management strategies for local implementation under these contrasting sets of conditions.

Although the analysis that follows is based on a bottom-up consciousness, this does not mean that we ignore insights culled from the so-called 'top-down' implementation perspective. The importance of variables putatively influenced from the centre thus also forms a consideration in the coverage that follows.

We draw from the literature on both sides of the Atlantic. While authors in both North America and Europe have contributed much to our understanding of implementation networks, they have done so from somewhat different perspectives. European policy and implementation research has been especially influential in focusing attention on policy networks and some of the deeper systemic causes of the gaps between governmental steering efforts and actual impacts. The Americans, on the other hand, have contributed in manifold ways to the literature on public management generally, as well as to the still small but growing tradition of scholarship dealing with the practicalities of managing policy implementation in complex networks.

8.2   Concepts

Implementation

By policy implementation we mean problem-solving efforts stimulated by government and ordered into programmes. The actors involved in implementation are not only drawn from governmental units; they may also include others whose efforts are required for the success of the implementation. Indeed, the bottom-up perspective employed here draws attention to the point that for some implementation endeavours the target groups (as they are often called) of official efforts must be counted among the necessary participants and incorporated in network analysis, rather than ignored or treated as passive objects populating the implementation landscape. In empirical terms, the degree of problem-solving success often varies greatly depending on the extent and type of involvement of targeted individuals and organizations in 'co-producing' the cooperative effort (see Hanf, 1993; Hupe, 1993). Therefore, when we refer to those involved in implementation using the term 'networks', we are referring to actors extending beyond those included in the conventional style of delivery system which operates from the centre.

Networks

An implementation network, like any other policy network, is the pattern of linkages traced between organizational actors who are in some way interdependent. It is also a socially constructed vehicle for purposive action. Like organizations themselves, implementation networks are intended to be used as instruments for mobilizing the energies and efforts of individual actors to deal with the problem at hand. The image of the 'policy implementation network' can be used to convey the idea of the highly differentiated and complex array of public and private organizations that are involved in the translation of the policy intentions of the national political community into appropriate measures or actions for the realization of these objectives at the 'level of the consumer'. In this sense it represents the organizational infrastructure required for the application of policy instruments intended to bring about the changes in social behaviour or conditions sought by national policy makers. Used in this way, the concept of an implementation network denotes more than a contextual factor to be taken into account by policy makers when designing their programmes.

The characteristics of the context imply an important challenge for those seeking to manage implementation at the local level. A part of the practical task that the manager of implementation performs is to encourage the coalignment of network action among diverse parties. Some of them, such as national authorities committed to the policy, are bound to the execution of a central mandate. Others may be actors whose assistance is technically required for success but who are largely uninterested in the policy agenda. Still others – local problem solvers, for example – may be committed to dealing with the practical issues involved yet may view any central policy as just one tool in their set for solving the problem(s) within, and sometimes even despite, the constraints of the action space marked out by the broader constitutional and policy system. The nature of the 'management' activities themselves thus becomes a relevant issue.

Managing

Although it does not make sense to speak of 'the network manager', there may at times be someone or some subgroup of actors trying to bring together a set of individual actors who will support and be able to move towards resolution of a particular problem or will work to implement a certain policy or programme. More importantly, it needs to be emphasized that these network managers cannot always assume that a common purpose can be defined around which the different actors will voluntarily coordinate their individual actions in terms of some overarching jointly shared interest or objective. Other measures are therefore required to coordinate the contributions of these separate actors when the integrating focus of common purpose is lacking. In this sense, managing policy implementation involves more than the crafting and use of common purpose. An effective manager must have a wider range of strategies at his or her disposal with which to achieve cooperation under conditions of conflict and disagreement.

There is, then, a general recognition of the potential importance of the linking, mediating and coordinating function in networks, even if there is little agreement regarding the precise activities being embraced, or the requisites for their successful fulfilment. In this chapter, the term 'management' refers to all these functions, but especially to activities aimed at effecting cooperative problem-solving from the bottom.

8.3   Managing Implementation

It may seem that we are dealing with one single network structure encompassing the different functional activities connected with a particular programme or problem. In fact, in functional terms, we can distinguish a number of subnetworks through which different sets of actors, drawn from different levels of government and from different phases of the policy process, are interlinked. As Hjern and Porter have pointed out: 'There is no single implementation structure for a national program; rather there is a collection of localized implementation structures, each comprising a distinctive array of public and private actors' (Hjern and Porter, 1981: 222–3). Furthermore, if we look at the clusters of functional roles performed by subgroups of actors, we find that there are networks for 'policy making, planning and intelligence, resource provision, intermediary coordinating roles, service provision and evaluation' (Hjern and Porter, 1981: 223). The degree and form of coordination within and between these substructures, will, of course, vary from one situation to another.

Separate networks can, therefore, be constructed, at least analytically, around basic management activities such as goal setting, programme development and operational implementation. It is the task of empirical analysis to determine, in any given case, to what extent and in what form individual network structures can be found for these activities. A limiting factor would be a situation where the same actors are involved in doing all of these things;

in other circumstances, the same organizations could be involved, but with individuals drawn from different organizational levels performing different functions; and yet another possibility would see different sets of actors involved in each separate function, drawn from different levels of government and/or hierarchical positions within the organizations concerned. Consequently, both the analyst and the practitioner of network management need to recognize that implementation comprises managing across and through different functional subnetworks.

Such structural differentiation compounds the complexity of the context within which the implementation manager must operate. They will often need to juggle different groups of actors, depending on the functional activity in progress, and will also need to address questions of coordination between these sets of network participants. At the same time, making these functional distinctions provides a way of linking decision processes within these interorganizational networks back to the organizations with which individual network actors are affiliated. Re-establishing the position of organizations in the analysis of network management offers, furthermore, a method of integrating a number of questions that have traditionally occupied implementation analysis.

Various Activities

In his discussion of what he calls 'the management of transorganizational structures for the integrated delivery of social services', Agranoff distinguishes three interdependent management activities and links participation in the separate functional networks to different hierarchical levels in the organizations involved (Agranoff, 1990a, 1990b). First of all, there is the need to develop policies or strategies that will support integration at the service and programme implementation levels. In order to come up with shared problem definitions and to develop agreed-upon courses of action, public programme interface must take place at the executive decision level. Officials with authority to commit their organizations must guide the process by framing the parameters of the integrated effort. For example, heads of independent human services departments or the top staff at the apex of a combined agency must meet on an equal footing and decide which organizational commitments – money, information and people – will be made to support integrated effort. Admittedly, the people at the top may have to consult with their next-level operational managers for the details of operations, but it is the executives who need to make the decisions. This is an important point: the kind of commitment you can enter into – or deliver on – will depend on the hierarchical position you occupy in the organization. In this sense, network participants are valuable initially not as 'free-floating' individuals but as 'representatives' of an organization that controls part of the programmatic action or relevant resources. The fact that interactions within and through the resulting network may take on another dynamic of their own is another matter.

The second step involves the creation of operating plans and programmes that provide the framework for the case-by-case service-level integration.

These programming decisions are the result of the strategic choices of the executives, as top staff (defined as the managers just below the top: programme heads, planning directors, budget deputies and agency programme directors) work out key details and agency domain problems relating to how each integrated policy element is to be executed. These managers possess a high degree of programme knowledge and sufficient delegated authority from those at the top to enable them to make organizational commitments to the aspects they are responsible for. Nevertheless, it is important that they also have 'real world' input from those who will actually be carrying out interactive activities at the operational level.

Finally, there is the development of the system of local contacts and interfaces, at the level where the client potentially receives services. Interaction among services then unfolds at the delivery level through the creation of various systemic linkages – the most common of these linkages appears to be those between case management, information and referral, interagency agreements, access to other needed services, and client monitoring. These procedures and routines serve to link and coordinate the daily operational decisions of individual actors within the separate service agencies.

It is at this local, operating level that the agency's commitment to the networked service or activity must be asserted and successfully defended in the face of competing claims from other organizational actors for a share of the organization's resources. Furthermore, it is at the level of the participating organizations that the network commitment must be translated into concrete operational activities aimed at (or carried out in conjunction with) the ultimate target groups of the joint programme effort. While the structural relations in the network define the parameters within which each member will operate, with regard to the programme or problem in question, the actual provision of services will usually be handled by the 'street-level bureaucrats' working within the network-relevant subdivision of the organization. Thus, while network analysis focuses upon the performance of the network as a whole, the agencies involved (or the relevant parts of these agencies) 'remain autonomous entities concentrating on manageable pieces of the full service that best fit their specific area of expertise' (Provan and Milward, 1991: 394-5).

The increasing importance of networks as vehicles for joint problem-solving and policy implementation does not, by any means, cause formal organizational, jurisdictional or governmental boundaries to disappear or to become inoperative and irrelevant. By breaking down or 'decomposing' a given network into a number of separate but related functional subnetworks, it is possible to lay bare the variety of organizational actors as well as the patterns of relationships between them. By anchoring networks in the organizations from which their members are drawn, we gain analytical access to the dynamic interaction between decision processes at the inter-, intra- and organizational levels. At the same time, we can better avoid the danger of 'reifying' networks as actors by recognizing that in the final analysis the implementation of networked programmes involves the effective management of 'street-level bureaucracy' as the ultimate carrier of service delivery (Lipsky, 1980).

Various Levels

It is an unavoidable fact of political life that those who are responsible for the front line delivery of public policy to the citizen-consumer or target population are in different organizations from those who set broad policy directives. It is at the local level that prior commitments unfold and operational responsibilities are translated into concrete actions; it is here that daily routines are worked out and applied, and where decisions are taken regarding the factual allocation of programme outputs.

Thus, policy problems take on tangible significance in the municipalities, in the field, at the points where the array of activities encouraged by the apparatus of governance makes contact on a large scale with those who are the targets of the organized effort: unemployed clients in need of retraining, firms subject to environmental regulation, and so forth. Consequently, the implementation network will encompass the set of relationships between actors involved in solving or dealing with a problem or set of problems, such as implementing a particular programme. For those seeking to manage by bringing about the necessary degree of collaboration at the local level, the possibilities available for mobilizing such joint efforts are sometimes so tightly circumscribed that repeated interactions can even produce results that are perverse for all concerned – creating an implementation version of a repeated prisoner's dilemma (Lynn, 1993).

However, as the network insights emphasize, this set of relationships is not the only constraint or influence on implementation management at the 'bottom'. Although the analysis of the management of such implementation networks starts out from the local level, and our initial task is to describe how the activities in which we are interested are organized and managed at that level, we can neither exclude national actors or higher level actors as participants in these activities nor neglect non-local factors shaping both constraints on and opportunities for action. In trying to account for what happens locally, we need to examine national level factors in so far as they appear to be relevant.

The full range of networked links must be mapped and analysed, from the point of street level impact 'backwards' (Elmore, 1979) within the core implementing organization(s) and through the set of interdependent actors that – taken together – constitute the structure of interdependence for problem-solving. In this respect, the local implementation network encompasses government and societal actors from the same (horizontal) and 'higher' (vertical) levels of action. It is here, of course, that the network management activities of national decision makers can be of importance in defining the constraints and opportunities that shape the action space within which local policy implementation takes place.

There would seem to be two ways in which actors from higher levels of decision making can make an appearance in these local networks. First, they

are involved in the prior policy decisions that are intended to structure subsequent phases of the decision process by defining formal roles on allocating
resources, including authority for initiating action, and laying down the
rules and procedures to be followed. These decisions can be perceived as network management actions that set conditions under which implementation
games at the bottom will be constituted and played. Formal policy specifies
the mandates of certain actors and, at the same time, defines the formal
occasion for action around which interactions form. It can become a
resource available to actors seeking to deal with their own problems and it
lays down the conditions under which these problems can be addressed, that
is, it spells out the constraints and opportunities for problem-solving efforts
by local actors. The action space for local problem-solving activities is delimited by both the rules that have been determined by higher levels of decision
making and the implementation field defined by the locally relevant
constellation of political forces.

There is a second way in which actors from higher levels of government
may be involved (either by choice or as a result of contacts initiated from
below) and that is as active participants in different phases of the implementation game itself. The rules and the conditions of the local game are not
unchanging constants but potentially manipulable variables. In the course of
fitting national programmes to local conditions, there will be occasion for
negotiations between local and national actors regarding mutually acceptable
adaptations of policy programmes. In this sense, the constraints within which
local managers work undergo modification as general programmes are
adapted to local conditions.

Resources and Constraints

Here the bottom-up perspective is helpful in reconsidering the management
challenge in local implementation settings. If one keeps in mind the practical
need to solve policy problems in a local context and the constraints faced by
managers of networks at this level in applying policy to targets (and, in various forms of co-production, 'with' these targets), what can be said about the
challenge facing the bottom-up managers in their efforts at implementation?

As those seeking to manage the implementation efforts from municipal or
field locations look 'up' and 'out' from street level, they are likely to see an
array of instruments and resources (organizational and financial, for
instance) in their environment. Some of these elements are central policies
promulgated with the idea of local or field enforcement. From the bottom-
managerial point of view, they are likely to seem less like priorities and more
like complex combinations of constraints and opportunities. A central policy
may be couched in informal language and offer financial resources, but will
also contain clientele restrictions, reporting requirements, and priorities that
do not neatly mesh with the problem as experienced locally. Managers near
the bottom, then, are likely to find themselves attracted to the idea of assembling pieces of such resources/constraints into a larger whole that might offer
at least partial solutions to the locally defined problems.

The packages of resources and constraints, furthermore, do not figure in any abstract sense, but are attached to various organizations, or portions of organizations – these variously distributed across layers of government, across specialized agencies, and across public, private and non-profit sectors (see Hjern and Porter, 1981). Each piece of the problem-solving solution thus implies a networking imperative, a set of joint decision making requirements, that add further to the constraints of the task. The restrictions of joint decision making derive from the structure of the policy instruments, and also from the necessary sharing of the decision making effort among the parties who hold keys to partial resolution. Adding participants during the assembly process, then, increases potential problem-solving capacity but also decreases the space within which bargaining solutions can be explored.

The implications of this sketch are several. From the managerial bottom, the implementation task is framed by a need to assemble pieces of policy programmes to address a problem as defined in a bottom-up way. The implementation manager at this level is likely to look for, or press for, synthetic combinations of instruments and resources that may not have been consciously designed or even foreseen at the centre. Furthermore, the difference in perspective between top and bottom inevitably fuels some tension: for those managing near the bottom, the central mandates are instrumental, at best, to community problem-solving; for central actors, the concerns of consistent and fair governance are primary and local problem definition in any particular case is somewhat peripheral. This means that the process of assembling the requisite networked-actors-cum-instruments-and-resources for dealing with locally defined priorities, while also building or maintaining sufficient space for jointly decided action, lies at the heart of the implementation management task at the bottom. Strategies to fulfil this task are thus the focus of the following analysis.

8.4   Strategies

Voluntary Cooperation

Implementation managers reviewing the possibilities for assembling parts of several organizations, to be linked from the bottom in complex ways to form a problem-solving network, have a number of options for meeting the cooperative challenge. One possibility, indeed the one which has been most strongly emphasized in recent American discussions of 'network management', is to work towards inducing voluntary conscious collaboration to help achieve a problem-solving programme. The emphasis on commonality of purpose, latent or manifest, occupies a central position in the work of innovative researchers such as Agranoff (1990a, 1990b). Agranoff has investigated the management of integrated service delivery at the local level and found numerous cases of local efforts to assemble and integrate complexes of potentially interested parties on behalf of bottom-up objectives. Mandell, too, has focused on the normative 'glue' of commitment to joint problem-solving – the 'program rationale', as she terms it – observed in numerous cases at the local level (see Mandell, 1990, 1992).

Mixed-motive and Multi-level

It is clear that purposiveness as the primary option for implementation management at the bottom is a possibility identified in a number of empirical cases. When present, it is likely to provide powerful assistance in meeting the implementation challenge. However, there are many situations in which common purpose is not present and cannot be generated as the basis for effective joint action. Under such conditions, we argue, there are other options available for the management of implementation networks. Indeed, the range of variation in the types of network and thus in the types of challenge to be found in implementation settings is a point that needs to be emphasized. Networks in which implementation managers operate from the bottom may differ markedly in terms of both structure and inducements towards cooperative effort. Therefore, specific management strategies are needed.

How can implementation managers induce cooperative action on behalf of bottom-up problem solving? The range of network circumstances is wide and different interunit arrangements offer different degrees of challenge to the field manager seeking implementation success. One reason for this is the interunit pattern itself and the opportunities and constraints it presents. A related complication is the orientations of the set of actors who collectively constitute the 'raw material' for joint decision making and action. Of course, structure influences orientation. There is more than a grain of truth in 'Miles's Law', which states 'Where you stand depends on where you sit.' However, the actors that need to be mobilized into networks for policy implementation are likely to have complex sets of overall preferences and agendas for action. These can be only imperfectly predicted by their positions in an interunit structure.

While it is sometimes possible to find a sense of common purpose among the constituent units of a network, or at least a level of commonality sufficient to stimulate voluntary cooperation on behalf of the problem-solving effort, circumstances often dictate otherwise. Despite the best efforts of a manager and the good faith of the various actors, solving a policy problem may require more cooperative capacity than is available. What then?

Occasionally, the absence of sufficient common purpose among the interdependent actors can be finessed during implementation if they are bound, or potentially able to be bound, by authority. However, the kinds of network settings under analysis here are unlikely loci for authoritative direction, especially for management from the bottom. This point is even more apropos when implementation managers seek influence at other levels of action: shifting and linking the games (see p. 149 below) and altering the structure of the networks, rather than merely operating within the limits of the games.

A standard circumstance, then, is one of limited common purpose, restricted authority through the network, and a range of perspectives across the multi-unit structure through which implementation is to develop. This set of conditions fits the criteria for the classic mixed-motive game, albeit of the multi-level variety.

Strategy A: Bargaining and Compromise

One mode of seeking to stimulate agreement – regarding problem-solving from the bottom, or indeed anything else – is to encourage bargaining leading to compromises in which all parties get some but not all of their concerns met in the programme. Bottom-up managers of implementation processes can assist by identifying bargaining points and potential agreements, as well as by brokering bargaining processes and monitoring to encourage the maintaining of commitments over time.

Thus, managing implementation consists in part of assisting efforts at conflict resolution and compromise in functionally specific implementation networks. In fact, those aiming to help manage implementation from the bottom may be well positioned to work on behalf of exchanges leading to compromise. These positions are typically occupied by individuals with detailed understanding both of programme requirements 'on the ground' (and thus of the priorities among issues that may be proposed for compromise during conflict resolution processes), as well as of the perspectives and interests of the other parties – again, individuals and parts of organizations functionally important for the task at hand – whose cooperation is needed. One obvious implication is that, while the ability to induce and help sustain commonality of perspective is a crucial attribute for implementation managers, bottom-up managers also have to exhibit diplomatic and negotiation skills. Interestingly, these two roles can sometimes conflict.

Strategy B: Changing Perspectives

Serious difficulties can create further complications in mixed-motive network settings. The most significant challenge is that conflict resolution produced by a series of compromises may threaten to vitiate the problem-solving effort – the core of implementation in practice – at least in the eyes of some key actors in the process. Thus, for instance, the literature on the implementation of many intergovernmental programmes in the United States emphasizes how often the impact of even broad policy goals becomes attenuated as programmes wend their way through the networked context. The consequence, it is often argued, is that an initiative with the formal approval of all key players satisfies the priorities of no one. The two dangers of exchange processes then, seen from this perspective, are deadlock (impasse) or ineffectiveness.

One rider to this pessimistic interpretation of mixed-motive network settings is to stress a point typically omitted in formal analyses of mixed-motive circumstances: the perspectives and preferences of actors linked in networked patterns of interdependence are not constants, but variables. Part of the challenge of implementation management is to recognize the circumstances in which apparent deadlock or unproductive compromise can be moved towards a more favourable outcome. Here, once again, the notion of multiple levels of managerial moves is apropos. Implementation managers can both encourage the choice of cooperative and effective solutions to a particular network game and also (sometimes even simultaneously) seek to shift the views of the actors and also the structure of their interdependence so as to create the possibility of cooperative outcomes where these did not exist before.

Outstanding examples of how apparently perverse circumstances can sometimes be altered from the bottom to produce cooperative solutions – some exceedingly stable even over generations – are provided by Ostrom (1990). In her tentative explanations, the author emphasizes properties of communities (size, diversity, stability, perspective towards the future, constitutional-level understandings, levels of trust, norms of reciprocity) and characteristics of the problem at hand (in these cases, the nature of the common pool resource), rather than management efforts. However, there is no reason to expect management efforts at problem-solving to be inappropriate or ineffectual, provided that 'management' is interpreted broadly. Indeed, several community characteristics are themselves subject to managerial influence, as we use the term.

Strategy C: Managing the Context

Another point may be just as important. It is sometimes possible to induce cooperative action in mixed-motive situations not only by encouraging exchange towards compromise or by inducing changes in the perspectives of the networked actors, but also by encouraging cooperation without resolving conflicts. Stoker offers a provocative analysis of this point:

> Theories of conflict resolution link the extent of conflict in collective decision making to the likelihood of cooperation. . . . However, the two are conceptually separate. Cooperation is more properly seen as a response to conflict, not the absence of it. . . . Beyond this, outcomes to strategic interactions are only unambiguously predicted in the relatively rare cases of Harmony and Deadlock. The outcome of the more likely strategic context – any one of many possible mixed motive games – is viewed as ambiguous.
>
> This implies that while the strategic context is important, it is often not the determining factor in decisions to cooperate. Although there is a wide range of ambiguity regarding the effect of conflict upon the likelihood of cooperation in a mixed motive context, theories of cooperation suggest that the likelihood of cooperation can be altered even when the amount of conflict is held constant. This implies that the problem is not to eliminate all conflict . . . but instead to create conditions in which participants are more likely to respond to conflict with cooperation.
>
> . . . [I]t may be possible to manipulate the conditions of the implementation process to encourage cooperative responses to conflicts of interest. (Stoker, 1991: 50)

One important but relatively straightforward fashion in which such encouragement may be possible, albeit from the 'top' rather than the bottom, is via the implicitly coercive hand of governmental authority. Earlier, we asserted that in the network settings under consideration in this analysis, authority is weak or absent. Here we can insert a limited rider. Even if the weight of central governance institutions is not sufficient to compel compliance during implementation among diverse network participants, government neverthe-less remains a distinctive party in joint decision making. Central actors do control, at least formally, certain unique resources. And should central gov-ernment actors determine that an implementation issue is of sufficient priority, they can be particularly influential. Those at the top cannot attend to all issues, and their monitoring and enforcement reach is also finite. Still, any anticipation of their potential intervention in an implementation effort is likely to alter the character of the bargaining. A 'default option' in the event of deadlock, for instance, may be a set of governmental moves unattractive enough to encourage cooperative efforts among the interdependent parties. Such a form of influence is likely to be relatively invisible. Thus, an initial point on the subject of inducing cooperation in the presence of persistent con-flict is that governmental action in the 'shadow' of ostensibly multilateral implementation bargaining cannot be discounted and is undoubtedly more important than can be demonstrated in behavioural research. Technically, this class of cases can be analysed as a subset of the array of nested or linked games (see Alt et al., 1988; Tsebelis, 1990). One game is the implementation bargaining effort. Another to be taken into account is the game of potential central government intervention; the latter is linked to the former via a dead-lock default option. There may also be more than one implementation game in the network. The fact that the form and style of governmental intervention is not precisely known is a part of the structure of the implicitly linked inter-vention game but does not alter the conclusion of its strategic connection to the implementation effort. Indeed, the uncertainty may actually increase the leverage.

Another set of possibilities may be available for seeking to induce net-worked agreement in the face of conflict. The context of bargaining is an object of management influence accessible to managers at the bottom as well as to others. In earlier work we focused especially on some of the contextual features that can be subject to alteration by implementation managers (see, for example, O'Toole, 1988, 1995). Stoker has also recently considered this general strategy. At the core of what he calls 'regime analysis', he attempts to identify

> contextual conditions that facilitate the development of cooperation between autonomous actors. Cooperation is more likely when participants are engaged in an ongoing relationship that creates a record of constructive interaction and expecta-tions for the future. When these conditions are absent, unilateral actions may be undertaken by implementation participants to enhance the possibilities for coop-eration. Possible actions include issue linkage, establishing rules of conduct, boosting the rewards of cooperation, and dividing programs into a series of smaller exchanges. (Stoker, 1991: 54–5)

While such moves may be taken from structural loci closer to the centre, they are also available to implementation managers working near the local level. Indeed, certain of these possibilities may be especially attractive to bottom-up managers, depending on the context. One instance is the idea of issue linkage. Earlier in our discussion, we pointed out that a number of functionally dis-crete tasks are necessary parts of the solution of any significant public problem at the local level, and these are typically executed through overlapping but partially distinct networks: for planning, resource mobilization, operations and so forth (see Hanf et al., 1978). These multiple but interdependent tasks, proceeding through several overlapping networks, provide some opportunity for issue linkage even in technically specialized issue contexts and even when the actors have not already developed a history of cooperation.

The general point here regarding implementation management is that those seeking to influence networks towards cooperation often need to attend to their strategic contexts and not merely seek a common rationale to unite disparate actors. They will need to look for acceptable compromises, convince participants to alter their perspectives and invoke the shadow of governmental intervention. They must also attend to the context of the network settings to determine what potentially manipulable factors can alter the set of achievable outcomes towards effective problem-solving.

At an abstract level, this discussion of managing context to encourage cooperation despite continuing conflict can be seen as an implementation analogue of the classic discussion by scholars such as Lindblom regarding policy making in pluralistic political systems. Building a majority legislative coalition in favour of any particular piece of legislation does not necessarily require agreement among all the cooperating parties on the purpose of the policy in question. In the appropriate context, it may be possible to attract support for a single programme from individuals of very diverse perspectives and persuasions. For the implementation setting, and in the language of formal theory, the point can be restated. Bottom-up managers can look for opportunities to influence the set of strategically interdependent choices available to network actors so that at least some Nash equilibria consistent with cooperative problem-solving are present in the matrix of options. The trick is then to encourage movement towards such points of stability.

8.5   Conclusions

Managing implementation from the bottom is both similar to and different from network management in the other phases of the policy process. Perhaps the most important difference is related to the need to attend to the developing, maintaining and utilizing of common purpose within and across functionally specific clusters of interrelated actors. This involves particular management challenges that we believe distinguish the management of implementation from other phases of the policy process. At the same time, managing implementation requires attention to be paid to the other points of leverage for bringing together and coordinating the activities of interdependent actors. We have also analysed a number of the strategies available to network managers at the bottom for effecting the concerted action needed when common purpose is not sufficient – or not available – to integrate the activities of the actors involved. These strategies are also available to network managers operating at other levels and phases of the policy process.

These different types of strategy, and the circumstances in which they can be used, have been analysed here seriatim. However, within the context of a single implementation setting and at a particular time more than one of these approaches can be indicated. The various parties are likely to differ in the degree of their commitment to the common policy task. Some can be expected to be solidly in support of the problem-solving effort and ready to assist the efforts of a bottom-up network manager, while others may be drawn to emphasize the common task – through or even despite the constraints of their 'home' organizational setting – by virtue of the efforts of skilled managers in the problem-solving setting. Some are likely to be relatively indifferent to the policy problem itself but may be induced into cooperation via any of the following: an alteration in their perspectives, an exchange-based compromise in which the *quid* of problem-solving cooperation is elicited for the *quo* of side payment, the potential for central government intervention in street level settings, or a managerially induced alteration in the context of implementation to render cooperation a more attractive possibility among the options available.

In pursuing these approaches, furthermore, managerial efforts at the bottom are likely to involve moves in games in multiple spheres of action. Implementation managers can be expected simultaneously to conduct their problem-solving efforts within the constraints set by central policies and the understandings and priorities reached between network actors; to influence the redirection of these instruments and constraints over time towards greater problem-solving capacity; and to seek opportunities to couple and decouple functionally specific games and networks, as well as to alter the structure of network interdependence itself in ways that are likely to favour systematic increases in problem-solving ability.

Managers of implementation, furthermore, must often address these challenges without the leveraging advantages available to those operating entirely through a formal organization. From the centre it may even be suspected that these managers at the bottom are utilizing mandates to mobilize unacceptable efforts or to pursue a contrary agenda. The density of the policy spaces in late welfare state settings, after all, injects the priorities of the centre into the manifold bargaining efforts in the field. It also enhances the prospects for centrally unanticipated inter-programme or inter-instrument effects, and creates new field coordination options for public managers who operate in the interstices of networked institutions.

Managing complex implementation processes in network settings, then, is an exceptionally daunting responsibility. For reasons sketched at the very outset of this chapter, however, the problem-solving capacity and the legitimacy of late welfare states may depend on its success.

9

Normative Notes:
Perspectives on Networks

J.A. de Bruijn and A.B. Ringeling

9.1   Introduction: A Fool May Ask More Questions in an Hour . . .

In a democratic constitutional state public organizations have a special status. This position is accompanied by normative postulates which in a parliamentary democracy are often broadly based. In network analyses, public actors are ascribed a different position than their usual one. A public organization is seen as one of the actors in a network which it forms together with other, social actors. This may cause a change in the norms for public sector performance while the concept of networks may be criticized from existing normative perspectives. The latter forms the focus of this chapter. A tension may occur between the norms to which public organizations in a democratic constitutional state are bound and the norms which are employed in networks. How, for example, does the decision making within networks relate to the principles of democratic legitimacy to which public organizations are subject? Does the decision making within networks reinforce this legitimacy or does it in fact damage it? Not all the products of a network are by definition 'good'. They may differ significantly from what public actors want or from the dominant political preferences. From a normative viewpoint questions need to be asked regarding the functioning of public bodies in networks.

There is a well-known Dutch saying that a fool may ask more questions in an hour than a wise man can answer in seven years. This maxim also applies here. It is easy to formulate any number of questions about the position of public organizations in networks: answering them is more difficult. The primary explanation for this is that normative problems usually create a dilemma focused on the tension between effective and functional behaviour on the one hand, and normalized behaviour (normalized in the sense of norms which serve as the accepted standard for public organizations in a democratic constitutional state) on the other. This tension is reinforced by the often diffuse nature of the relevant norms.

In the following sections, a number of these problems are discussed in the light of the norms to which a public organization in a democratic constitutional state is bound. At the conclusion of each section, an area of tension relating to a public actor in networks is formulated. Consideration is given to the special status of the public sector (section 9.2), the relationship between process norms and substantive norms (section 9.3), the structuring of networks (section 9.4) and issues of responsibility and control (section 9.5). The chapter concludes with a final summary in section 9.6.

9.2 The Special Status of Public Actors

In the criticism levelled at thinking in terms of networks, the key issue is the devaluing of the status of the public sector to that of one actor among many (cf. Nelissen, 1992). This position could have a seriously adverse impact on the achievements of the democratic constitutional state. A public body has a special status, to which special norms apply. These can result in public sector behaviour which is incompatible with behaviour prompted exclusively by considerations of effectiveness. In this section, a number of traditional objections to devaluing the status of the public sector are summarized. These objections are subsequently worked out in more detail and conclusions are drawn.

Public Organizations are Special!

The central function of a public body, according to Easton (1965), is to allocate values. A public body which is no longer in a position to allocate values ceases to be a public body. It becomes indistinguishable from other social groupings. Given this function and the tasks flowing from it, public sector performance is expected to meet high moral standards which are more important than considerations of effectiveness and functionality. According to Barry and Rae (1975: 382–94) these standards include items such as serving the public interest, justice, equality and parity, freedom and democracy. These may be concretized by setting a number of standards for public actors which could prove incompatible with the assertion that a public body in a network is an actor like any other.

First of all, the public sector guarantees the protection of the constitutional rights of the people. This can conflict with the development of governance processes in networks. Network management may take shape, for example, through selective activation and exclusion: for reasons of effectiveness, certain actors will be involved in realizing goals while others are excluded. Civil rights such as the principle of non-discrimination, however, can impose limits on this kind of selective activation. The special status of a public body implies here that its limitations are imposed by network management. It is equally important that its special status can imply that it should correct network management through other (non-governmental) actors, for example, by prohibiting certain forms of selective activation and exclusion.

Second, public organizations can be called to account when certain social problems arise. They are supposed to solve problems which have not been and often cannot be solved by other organizations within society. The public sector has special tasks or special responsibilities for certain tasks. This view contrasts with others in which the equal status of the public sector and the actors to be managed is emphasized. It might imply in the long run that the public sector's special tasks could be given equal status with its powers and become a medium of exchange for meeting the objectives of other actors. The result of this might even be that, in common with other actors, public organizations become free to carry out tasks or reject them. However, a characteristic feature of a public body in a democratic constitutional state is that it cannot and may not back out of its responsibilities. In a number of ways, the public sector in a democratic constitutional state should adopt a different stance from that of other actors.

Third, governmental organizations have at their disposal a number of instruments which may not be used by other social actors, for example, the use of unilateral instruments (legislation and regulations) or the use of violence. The special nature of these instruments often involves special (legal) norms for implementation. The result of this can be that sometimes a public body is compelled, on the basis of normative considerations, to steer using instruments or procedures which restrict its freedom of movement and give it little chance of success.

Fourth, public sector performance is the subject of political and democratic legitimation. This can give a public sector decision a special status. Here, too, a tension can arise between considerations of effectiveness and functionality. The latter take great account of existing positions of power. Democratic decision making is particularly aimed at breaking down such positions of power.

Special?

The provisional conclusion that may be drawn here is that a public body in a democratic constitutional state has a special status. This special status implies that a public body sometimes decides to intervene for normative reasons, although the effectiveness and functionality of these interventions may be doubted from the outset. At the same time it implies that a public body's performance in networks can be subject to special norms as well. However, this provisional conclusion needs clarification on two points.

The scope of the objections is limited, constantly shifting and not directive for the choice of instruments   The truth of the normative objections referred to may be acknowledged, but the scope of these objections is limited. Certain public organizations have a special status and are then subject to special norms. However, a public actor can also function as an 'ordinary' actor – from a normative point of view as well – and is then either not subject to special norms at all, or to a lesser extent. In those situations they can be considered as being on an equal footing with non-governmental actors. There is no difference between a public actor wishing to purchase computers, and an insurance company. Especially where equipping its own organization is concerned, the public sector is a player like any other in the market. Yet this statement also has its limitations. As a buyer of fighter planes, the public sector's status is already rather special since there are few other actors with such preferences. As a purchaser of land the public sector is unique because in certain situations it can push through a sale even when the owner does not wish to sell.

Furthermore, the dividing line between a special and an ordinary public actor is constantly shifting. In certain areas where the public sector still has special status today, it may find that tomorrow its role has been taken over by, for example, banks (student grants), private companies (security), or public–private cooperation (infrastructure). Normative perspectives on the position of the public sector within the hierarchy are also in flux. The fight against organized crime (where the status of the public sector is special) takes place in a quasi-network situation. In certain countries, negotiating with organized crime is illegal. In other countries, certain legal arrangements are made which indicate negotiation: in Italy a *pentito* will be given protection if he breaks *omertà*. In countries where the issue of organized crime is becoming increasingly serious, tolerance of such arrangements appears to be increasing (Falcone and Padovani, 1992).

Given the supposedly special status of public organizations, what is ultimately important is that there should be no linear correlation between special status and special instruments. Whenever special, fundamental powers are at issue, quasi-network forms of governance are also often present. The primary factor is that the exercise of special powers often involves negotiations with non-governmental actors. These negotiations can have a bearing on, for example, the setting of norms by public organizations or on the process of enforcement. When a public body issues environmental licences, for example, these form the subject of extensive consultations between representatives of the public sector and the company involved (cf. Mayntz et al., 1978; Van der Tak, 1988). Similarly, from a normative point of view, too, there is scope for horizontal steering when special powers are at issue. Thus there are legal options for deploying these powers as a medium of exchange in negotiations with social actors. Two examples of this are policy agreements and agreements regarding executive powers.

Ineffective public sector performance undermines legitimacy   The second point which needs clarification also starts out by recognizing that there is a tension between the public sector's normative considerations referred to earlier and its actual position. Prioritizing normative considerations might take place at the expense of the effectiveness of public sector performance. This also has normative implications. The ineffectiveness of public sector performance may, in the long term, undermine its legitimacy. A public actor who continually fails to achieve their targets suffers an increasing loss of credibility.

A public body which finds itself faced with such a loss of legitimacy will make efforts to reduce the gap between the goals it has set itself and their realization. Given the special status of the public sector, this is a hazardous undertaking.

A major risk is that a public body may be tempted to strongly relativize its special status and the norms linked to it. It may deny its special status and thus lower the level of its aspirations. The gap between its aims and its actual capacities is then narrowed. Due to its negotiations with interest groups it becomes handicapped and consequently forfeits its freedom to pursue certain courses of action which are closed off during the negotiation process (Stever, 1988). Its legitimacy may suffer as a result.

Another risk is that a public body may use the pretext of its special status to narrow the gap between aims and performance. Its special status is then brought to bear as a justification for backing out of certain responsibilities. Ten Heuvelhof (1993) describes how it frequently occurs that a public actor will enter into contractual agreements with non-governmental actors and subsequently realize that these agreements prevent them from achieving their objectives. They will then try to back out of these agreements, pleading their special status as an excuse. Such an opportunistic use of special status naturally results in a loss of legitimacy.

Thus, a complex interweaving of effectiveness, legitimacy and the special status of the public sector takes place. Ineffective public sector performance can result in a loss of legitimacy. A public body which attempts to remedy this situation runs the risk of undermining its special status, which can also lead to a loss of legitimacy. It could be argued, freely based on Ettore Scola ('A king who flees is that much less a king': from the film *La nuit de la Varennes*), that a public body which does not abide by its normative principles is that much less a public body. An opportunistic public sector invites opportunistic behaviour from individuals and organizations, thus getting a taste of its own medicine. For a public actor it is essential to adopt a position as regards the three core elements of effectiveness, legitimacy and special status, which harmonizes these competing values as far as possible.

Conclusion

It may be concluded that a complex interdependency exists between effectiveness, legitimacy and the special status of a public body. A unilateral emphasis on only one of these competing values is risky. Both ineffective public sector performance resulting from its special status and effective public sector performance achieved by undermining its special status may lead to a loss of legitimacy. Effective interventions tend to promote the legitimacy of public sector performance. Ineffective interventions, however, may also be functional since they can prevent the erosion of one of the public sector's most important power bases: its legitimacy.

A public body is a special actor and this can lead to conduct which conflicts with considerations of effectiveness, but which yet promotes legitimacy. A unilateral emphasis on the special status of the public sector can also undermine its legitimacy. Not all public actors are special; their special status is not constant and there is no unambiguous correlation between special status and the use of special instruments. A unilateral emphasis on the special status of a public body may thus be normatively undesirable, particularly where public bodies are concerned which no longer enjoy a special status. This kind of emphasis on special status can stem from considerations of effectiveness, which, however, lack legitimacy: thus, a public actor may define themselves as special – although they are not – in order to be able to disregard rules which apply to non-governmental actors.

9.3   Process Norms and Substantive Norms for Steering

Discussions on policy networks often draw attention to the importance of implementing process norms: the assessment of what takes place within networks is based on the way in which management processes develop. This section describes how process norms tend to promote both policy effectiveness and the more normative hypothesis that policy must be legitimized.

Process Norms: Effectiveness and Legitimacy . . .

Some authors are of the opinion that in networks the significance of interaction between actors should be emphasized. The idea is that intensive interaction will ultimately affect actors' substantive image building and thus their behaviour. If parties are not in agreement, then *continuous interaction* is important (cf. Termeer, 1993). *Procedural prudence* is also sometimes cited as a process norm (In 't Veld et al., 1992). It is important that decision making in a network should proceed according to a previously determined procedural structure. If the most important actors in a network are committed to this structure, there is a likelihood that they will also be committed to the (sometimes difficult to predict) substantive outcome of this procedure. Two additional norms have a bearing on the outcome of the procedure, quite apart from the decision making process itself. Thus for some authors their main concern is whether actors are satisfied with the outcome of steering processes and to a lesser extent with what this outcome involves. This can be termed the *satisficing* principle (Crozier and Friedberg, 1980; Teisman, 1992). Other authors emphasize *consensus* building (Ten Heuvelhof, 1993). Intervention processes should result in actors in a network reaching agreement. The task of the public sector is to promote consensus building. This minimizes the potential for conflict within society.

  Such proposals for implementing procedural measures can stem from considerations of effectiveness as well as from normative considerations. The effectiveness considerations are that steering processes and process norms generate less resistance among actors to be managed. Goals, information, resources and implementation scenarios, however, are the result of interaction and are not unilaterally imposed. Thus, process steering is attractive for the actors to be managed, and at the same time the steering actor – the process manager – is able, by means of procedural measures, to direct to some extent the substantive element of the policy to be developed. The normative considerations are that process management offers various actors the opportunity to be involved in policy development, a factor which tends to promote policy legitimacy.

Though Nevertheless with Some Reservations

First, the emphasis on process norms can conflict with the pursuit of 'good public policy' (Kelman, 1987). However, process norms in no way guarantee that the outcome will satisfy the ideal of 'good policy'. Thus it is clear that there is disagreement within networks concerning the question of precisely what that involves. However, it is important that the preference for process norms, which are not linked in any way to substantive norms, can lead to indifference regarding the substantive outcome of interaction processes. This is problematic, since everyone will acknowledge – whatever their values and norms may be – that there may be normative objections to the outcome of certain interaction processes. Thus, according to Arentsen et al. (1994), however frequently consultations with target groups take place (process norm) it is unlikely that these will lead to solutions to environmental issues (substantive norm).

Second, there is a likelihood that process norms will display significant flaws (Kelman, 1987: 213–22). Process management can entail the necessity for introducing ever more radical refinements to the procedures used in interaction. This increases the chances of a very complicated process finally emerging in which the participants lose track of the situation and become entangled in the procedures they themselves developed. To put it another way, those who put their sole trust in procedures may in certain situations only reach decisions through the 'law of the jungle' (ibid.). Process management degenerates into proceduralism, and hence to uncontrolled decision making in which ruthless competition and self-interest prevail. A similar trend can be seen in the 'consensus' norm. In Dutch, the term *stroperigheid* (treacliness) is employed to describe how process-driven and consensus-seeking behaviour becomes so extreme that it degenerates into sluggish decision making which is not results-oriented, where the same ground is gone over again and again and actors' substantive input becomes bogged down in the 'treacle' of the consensus machine. As Barry and Rae argue (1975: 344), the process steering norm is not always a rational one, 'because big opportunities to increase profits are perhaps being missed'.

Third, there is the question of when 'satisficing' and/or consensus have been reached. Is this when everyone endorses an outcome with no reservations? When one of the actors is prepared to do this only if a gun is held to their head? When one of the actors has a number of reservations? Furthermore, there is the question of which actors are needed for consensus building. All the actors? All the actors concerned? All the relevant actors concerned? How and by whom is the selection of actors made? The 'satisficing' criterion is used by Simon (1957) to characterize individual decision making processes. Lindblom (1979), who has transposed Simon's ideas to group decision making in the public sector, demonstrates that evaluating trends is a tricky business given the shifting political-administrative preferences; an argument that seems to be tailor-made for describing decision making within networks. The process norms 'satisficing' and 'consensus' therefore need to be defined in more detail, which entails a number of risks.

Fourth – and linking up with the previous point – it is important that process norms should result in the relativizing of an actor's responsibility for certain substantive choices. The decision has after all been a joint one. The various actors reached agreement on the decision. They participated in the decision making but none of them determined the decision. They cannot be held responsible for the content of the decision and although they do not hold themselves responsible for the outcome, they do consider themselves responsible for agreeing to the decision. At the same time it is true that certain actors might have been excluded from the decision making. The consequences of that are discussed in section 9.5.

Fifth, many process norms simultaneously contain a substantive element. Freedom of speech is not only a process norm but also a substantive norm with an intrinsic value. Furthermore, process norms are not value-free; substantive choices underlie them. Lehning argues that, fundamentally, the preference for process norms lies in a sharp division between (substantive) norms and facts. Such a division is rooted in positivism which preaches a value-free approach thus rendering it not only naive but also misleading and dangerous (Lehning, 1991).

Conclusion

The above criticism illustrates that a normative approach to network management requires more than process standardization. It must be admitted that employing substantive norms in a network is unlikely to succeed unless the actors are in agreement regarding those norms. However, a unilateral emphasis on process norms also entails great risk. Process norms are sometimes able to mitigate the disadvantages of the use of substantive norms. Substantive norms, on the other hand, are no less essential in controlling the disadvantages of process steering.

A public body should be aware of the risks of process norms. This is not a simple dichotomy between a normative and a de facto desirable pattern of behaviour. Process management can enhance both effectiveness and legitimacy, but can also clash with normative perceptions of the position of the public sector. Such a diffuse image offers ample scope for a public actor wishing to behave in an opportunistic way: they can confine themselves to a process role. Should they allot themselves a special role, then they will also be alert to the negative aspects already mentioned.

9.4 The Structuring of Networks: Plurality of Values

Whereas traditional approaches view the public sector as the guardian of the public interest, in a network approach this is highly problematic. First, because 'the public interest' is difficult to identify in a quasi-network context in which subsidiary interests are constantly being put forward. The public interest has become a vague norm and any attempts to concretize it tend to be resisted. On the concept of 'the public interest' Stillman notes the following:

> The Public Interest became the public interest: i.e., clouded, more fragmented, less easy to know or to act upon and hence, it became a subject few administrative theorists addressed or even tried to assert as an important or worthy guide for administrators' action. . . . Indeed the subject was something of an embarrassment for serious students of the field to 'take seriously'. (Stillman, 1991: 114–15)

The second problem is that the values which a public actor looks after – and which can be defined as the public interest – are partly complementary, but also partly in conflict with each other. The complementary elements cause no problems. The values can be represented with no adverse effects on individual or group values. It is, however, a different matter when there is a conflict of values, which is a characteristic feature of a public authority operating in networks. Governments attempt to achieve mutually contradictory objectives. They build more roads while attempting to reduce the carbon monoxide levels in the air; and while advocating the freedom of the individual, they put people in prison.

Structuring and the Dual Role of the Authorities

What is the best way to deal with these problems? A number of authors have pointed out the importance of institutionalizing divergent values within the governmental organizations (cf. Ringeling, 1993: 161–6). This means that within those organizations diverse and mutually contradictory values are represented by different parts of the organization. The subsequent clash of incompatible values generates a conflict of interest within the organization. This can be functional both for concretizing vague norms and for assessing alternative values. When vague norms are concretized by actors with divergent views, the confrontation between these actors can produce a definition of a vague norm such as 'the public interest'. Such a confrontation, furthermore, can enhance the final choice between divergent values.

In connection with this, the importance of institutionalizing the various values in a network may be pointed out, since this provides an important normative dimension to network structuring. For a public body it can be essential to structure a network in such a way (e.g. involved actors, operational rules) that the most important and relevant values are represented.

Thus, public actors play a dual role in a network. On the one hand they are one of the actors, trying to maximize their own interests. From this perspective they may attempt to structure a network in such a way that scope is provided for maximizing their own values, with considerations of effectiveness primarily underlying this. On the other hand, in their special role they should ensure that the most important values are incorporated into policy formation. From this perspective, a public actor will try to structure a network in such a way that essential values are represented.

This is an important normative factor which might thus conflict with structuring networks from the viewpoint of effectiveness. A public actor who is prepared to play such a dual role neutralizes a number of risk factors in networks (cf. Nelissen, in Koppenjan et al., 1993: 171–3):

- The power of the actors already present is called into question. A public actor can endeavour to break down existing power relations or use them to serve their own interests.
- The public sector's dual role does not imply that it automatically goes along with the existing demarcation of the network. Public organizations have to make choices about the actors they wish to see operating in the network, and those they do not. The complexity of the problem is increased by the interdependency of interorganizational networks, whereby the boundary between actors who participate and those who do not becomes blurred.
- In networks, processes of attracting and repulsing various organizations are constantly taking place. Each of the actors in the network will try to strengthen their position by eliminating certain organizations from the network and allowing others to participate. Thus, coalitions of actors are continually forming within the network. Given the conflicting values which are present in any one network, public organizations have the task of maintaining an equilibrium between participating organizations.
- In a network territoriality occurs. For dominant coalitions there is a temptation to extend the relevant issues to related areas, close to the domain of a particular network. This not only leads to infighting between networks, but the assessment of values in these related areas may also differ from that within the network itself. Here, too, on the basis of normative considerations a public body can play a structuring role.
- A primary risk factor is that formal decision making in networks is increasingly replaced by informal decision making by representatives of the dominant coalition. The public authority has the task of safeguarding the nature of public decision making.

Network structuring can be tantamount to extending the number of conflicts within a network. This is an important observation since in the literature it is argued that public sector performance should be assessed in terms of the reduction of conflict within society (Kirlin, 1984) and the building of consensus (Ten Heuvelhof, 1993). In section 9.3 the criticism was voiced that process norms are inadequate for an appraisal of public sector performance in networks. It can now be added here that the 'consensus' norm inadequately defines the mission of the public sector to – in the above-mentioned circumstances – generate conflict in order to reach a decision in the case of conflicting values.

Conclusion

As a result of the development of networks, the status of the public sector is sometimes devalued, which from a normative perspective can be problematic. If the public sector wishes to fulfil its central function – allocating values in society – then it might be necessary for it to actively support the proliferation of networks. The public sector can ensure that the high moral values it represents are introduced into networks or are generated within them by a clash of values. If Stillman is correct in his assumption that 'the public interest' has become fragmented and less easy to know, it may be essential for a public actor to institutionalize values in a network as much as possible. The interaction processes between these values or between the actors who represent them might help to reveal part of the public interest. However, this may clash with structuring activities based on considerations of effectiveness.

9.5   Responsibility, Liability and Control

Finally we will deal with the tension between networks and responsibility. In any network a need will be felt for certain actors to be held responsible for certain operations. The outcome of the steering process, however, may be damaging to other actors.

Who is Responsible, Who Regulates?

Determining responsibilities and powers in a quasi-network situation can be problematic since, owing to the diversity of actors in a complex network, it is not always possible to establish a causal connection between damage done and culpable behaviour on the part of one or more actors. Often responsibility is shared by a large number of actors: each has contributed in a minor way to the harmful outcome of the interaction process. The dynamics and divergent perceptions in a network imply that there are various possible answers to the question of who contributed what to the harmful outcome. It will be the contention of many an actor in a network that their own role in the interaction process was not a *sine qua non* for the ultimate damage. Any number of environmental problems could be called upon to illustrate this: many minor misdemeanours can add up to major damage to the environment.

Owing to the complex interdependencies within networks, it may prove impossible to trace the person responsible for the damage. This exacerbates the problem of establishing liability: recovering damages can be seriously hampered by this complexity and may cause far more substantial damage than the behaviour of one individual actor is likely to do. This also raises the question of political responsibility: why hold one actor politically responsible for the outcome of processes in networks when this actor was only one of the players?

Following on from this, attention is sometimes drawn to the lack of transparency of decision making processes in networks. Ill-defined decision making, or decision making in which it is unclear which actor bears which responsibilities, limits the options for democratic control. A public body which adopts forms of network management hampers the political control of its performance. An example of this can be found in the criticism that the use of covenants (network instruments *par excellence*) is undemocratic. In such a situation a public actor is negotiating with non-governmental actors, and consequently political regulatory bodies often have limited options for correcting the outcome of these negotiations. On balance, the public sector's negotiating partner may thus exert more influence on the final policy than the democratically chosen regulatory bodies or other relevant public actors (Damen, 1993: 101ff.).

Actors in networks may exploit these diffuse responsibilities and hampered attempts at control. They may present them as offering opportunities for effective steering and they may even foster them. By dint of such opportunistic behaviour they create for themselves extra room to manoeuvre. Normatively speaking it is more desirable that responsibilities should be allocated in as clear a manner as possible, that these responsibilities should be met and that network management should take shape in such a way that (parliamentary) control remains possible.

Responsibility: Between Fiction and Fine Tuning

The options for dealing with the tension between actual and legal or political responsibilities can be seen as a continuum, with the creating of fictitious responsibilities at one extreme and the fine tuning of responsibilities at the other.

Since discovering a causal connection between culpable behaviour and damage in a network is not always easy, the public sector resorts to legal fictions. Fictional responsibility implies that an actor is formally considered to be both fully competent and responsible, whereas in fact they only play a limited role in the network. Thus, the situation can arise whereby the blame for the damaging outcome of interaction processes in a network is shifted to one actor. In the Netherlands, a classic example of this is the political responsibility of a minister. Parliament may call for a minister's resignation if something has occurred in his or her department of which Parliament does not approve. It is unimportant whether the minister participated in the proceedings in question or whether he or she had any knowledge of them (cf. Scheltema Commission Report, 1993). The fiction of ministerial responsibility makes it possible for the executive power to be accountable to parliament. In addition, it affects the behaviour of the civil servants involved, since it is impressed upon them that the minister will be held responsible for their actions. Berg (1991) terms this necessary fiction a whip for keeping bureaucracy in line.

Legal fictions also play a role in liability issues in the private sphere. A well-known example is that of the Soil Cleanup (Interim Measures) Act of 1982, in which the liability for heavily contaminated land is laid at the door of the actor who is the owner of the land at the time when contamination is ascertained. A legal fiction enables liability to devolve upon one actor who was only a link in the chain of actors who actually caused the contamination. Thus, the situation can occur where one actor is held formally liable, although in fact they may be only one of those responsible for the damage or may even have played no part in it at all.

Conversely, fine tuning implies that an attempt is made to harmonize factual and normative responsibility as far as possible. This is not easy. Loth, in an argument on responsibility within groups and organizations, points out that determining liability is a kind of balancing act. In the recent past, unilateral arrangements were made in the case of collective liability whereby those responsible managed to get off scot free: the director of a company was able to hide behind its legal status. On the other hand, arrangements have been made whereby those not responsible were called to account by extending the group liability (Loth, 1991: 25–36). In practice, fine tuning will never be wholly successful, chiefly because networks are constantly shifting: each fine-tuned allocation of responsibility may be superseded at any time. The constant modifying of responsibilities is not possible, of course, mainly owing to the inertia of legal instruments.

The purpose of this normative discussion is not primarily to catalogue the arrangements which may be made to allocate responsibility. What is more important is that each arrangement creates a tension between factual responsibilities on the one hand and political or legal responsibilities on the other. The tension referred to earlier between opportunistic behaviour (exploiting the opportunities offered by diffuse responsibilities and hampered control) and prudent behaviour is not affected. Moreover, each new division of responsibilities will generate new opportunities for opportunistic behaviour and new norms for restraint and prudence. A minister may be put under extra pressure during negotiations by the fiction of ministerial responsibility; a prudent approach in this case may imply showing restraint.

Parliamentary Control

Reference was made earlier to the fact that a public body may exploit problematic parliamentary control. Parliament's existing instruments will often fail to provide effective parliamentary control. In addition to this opportunistic attitude, however, a more prudent attitude is also possible. These alternative patterns of behaviour may be expressed as follows (De Bruijn and Ten Heuvelhof, 1995):

- Is the outcome of negotiation presented as a *fait accompli* or is parliament informed during negotiations and given the opportunity for intervention?
- Is the outcome of negotiation a package that can only be rejected or accepted, or may parliament submit amendments at its own discretion?
- Is there substantive accountability only regarding the outcome of negotiation or also regarding the process itself?
- Is parliament given an opportunity in advance to formulate the key issues for negotiation or not?
- Does the negotiating minister intimate that an agreement with him is an agreement with the government, or does he clearly state that parliament can determine its own viewpoint?

In the first of the two scenarios in each of the above, parliament is offered the scope to monitor the negotiating governmental actor. If the latter adopts a prudent attitude, he will attempt to maximize parliament's opportunities for monitoring and control, whereas an opportunistic governmental actor will exploit every opportunity to hinder them.

Conclusion

It is possible to derive two patterns of behaviour for public organizations from this. If they behave according to the first, prudent pattern of behaviour, public organizations will attempt to clearly formulate responsibilities, and to maximize the regulatory opportunities for elected bodies. If they behave according to the second, opportunistic behavioural pattern, public actors will exploit the problematic nature of responsibility and control in a network.

9.6 Normative Risks

A complicated picture of the status of a public body in a network emerges from this. A public body finds itself faced with a number of serious dilemmas. These manifest themselves particularly when, in the course of steering activities, a tension is created between normative considerations and considerations of effectiveness. A public body in a network will often be faced with a choice between two patterns of behaviour, one of which is primarily motivated by considerations of effectiveness and the other by normative considerations. The matrix shown in Table 9.1 gives an overview of this choice.

Table 9.1 *Normative choices of steering*

	Normatively desirable	Normatively undesirable
Special status	Harmonize competing values: effectiveness, legitimacy and special status	Unilateral choice of one of these values
Process steering	Process steering and substantive steering	Process steering
Network structuring	Partly based on normative considerations: everyone must be heard	Based solely on considerations of effectiveness
Responsibility and control	Defining responsibilities as clearly as possible and meeting them; offering scope for control	Exploiting opportunities to hamper responsibility and control

Considerations of effectiveness usually underlie the normatively undesirable pattern of behaviour. Such a behavioural pattern offers a public organization short-term gains but may in the long term – given the interdependencies in a network – adversely affect the sustainability of the relationships in a network (De Bruijn and Ten Heuvelhof, 1995).

This chapter began with a reference to the special status of public actors in a democratic constitutional state. The table illustrates the ways in which a public body is special: with regard to the four variables mentioned, it should not let itself be led exclusively by considerations of effectiveness. If it does choose to pursue such a course, however, the consequences in the long term will be that it acquires an untrustworthy image.

PART III
CONCLUSION: STRATEGIES FOR NETWORK MANAGEMENT

10

Managing Networks in the Public Sector: Findings and Reflections

W.J.M. Kickert, E.-H. Klijn and J.F.M. Koppenjan

10.1 Introduction

In this book, the consequences of policy networks for governance and public management have been investigated and discussed. The result is a series of contributions on (various aspects of) network management in the public sector. Chapters 2 and 3 presented an overview of the literature on networks and governance in networks and showed that, although there is conceptual variation in the field, a common ground emerges on what policy networks are and what possible network strategies can be. This book has taken this common ground as a point of departure to exlore and develop the issue of network management

In this final chapter, the following issues will be examined: the problem of defining network management; the conceptual frameworks used in its development; the possible strategies for network management; the problem of evaluation; and the role of government in managing networks. The chapter concludes by observing that much of the theoretical and conceptual diversity can be explained by the existence of three different perspectives on network steering which also have implications for the use of network management strategies: an instrumental, an interactive and an institutional perspective. It is argued that explication of these approaches results in better conceptualization and sounder analysis and prescriptions. The chapter, and the book, close with a brief reflection on the significance of further academic research on network management for future developments in policy practice and for theory formation on governance and public management in complex societies.

10.2 Network Management: Finding a Common Purpose

Network management has been defined in this volume as a form of coordination of strategies of actors with different goals with regard to a certain problem or policy measure within an existing framework of interorganizational relations. In general this description fits well with what the different chapters describe as ways to manage processes in complex networks. There is also a clear consensus in the chapters on what network management is not and how it differs from more classical views on management.

Most of the authors in this book emphasize that network management takes place in a context where there is no shared opinion on which way to go. There is no clear goal or set of goals from one actor which can be taken as a guideline for managing activities for interaction processes within policy networks. Nor is there a clear hierarchy in which the manager stands at the top and can profit from a clear authority line. Last but not least, network management is not characterized by clear decision procedures on which the manager can rely. As shown in the preceding chapters, management in networks is about creating strategic consensus for joint action within a given setting. The authors show that in fact finding a common purpose is one of the main tasks of network management (see Chapters 5, 6 and 8). Characteristic of network management, if one compares the different chapters, is a strong orientation towards facilitating interaction processes, mediating between different actors and an orientation to goal searching rather than goal setting.

It is also clear that most authors agree on network management as a 'weak' form of steering or at least as a form of steering in which uncertainties are 'built in'. Because network management is an indirect form of steering which tries to influence the strategic actions of other actors, unexpected effects, resulting from different strategies of actors, are possible. Termeer and Koppenjan point out that stimuli are interpreted by the actors according to their own frame of reference. Klijn and Teisman stress the unpredictable possibilities of strategic interaction of the actors and the interactions between these different strategies. O'Toole et al. also address the complexity of the context in which the implementation manager must operate. This complexity is the result of the presence of different actors, often acting on different levels, the existence of different relevant policy programmes and the lack of an encompassing, formal organizational context.

The point about perceptions of actors is expressed even more emphatically by Schaap and Van Twist, who argue that within the network certain frames of reference are produced and reproduced. This means that actors not only make their own interpretations, but they do not 'recognize' stimuli which do not 'fit' in these shared reference systems. The 'closed character' of reference systems reduces complexity within organizations, advocacy coalitions, and networks, while at the same time increasing the complexity of their mutual interaction. Within networks only a 'limited' number of problem definitions, solutions, etc. are taken seriously in discussions. Communication with others will, however, be complicated by this relatively closed set of references.

Who is this network manager the authors talk about? In principle every actor who is active in the policy process can fulfil the role of manager. The reader may get the impression that a choice is implicitly made for a governmental actor. This, however, is not our point of view. The role of manager can, in principle, be fulfilled by public as well as private actors. Nevertheless our specific interest in this book is network management as a possible steering strategy for government. An even more interesting possibility is that we should not attribute network management to one single actor, but first analyse management strategies and then look at which actor is responsible. In this view complex policy processes need some guidance, though which actor provides this guidance is not crucial (traces of this point of view can be found in Chapters 6 and 8). Nevertheless it is plausible that some strategies, especially those aimed at changing the network, can be implemented most easily by governmental actors. There are normative arguments why it is preferable that government perform this role. We will return to this issue in sections 10.4 and 10.5.

10.3 Strategies for Network Management

In the literature on policy networks, as in this volume, a great diversity of management strategies are mentioned. Although the network manager operates from a relatively weak position, with little hierarchical means at their disposal, they are by no means deprived of strategic alternatives.

We can distinguish two levels on which strategies are applied: the game and the network levels. In addition it is possible to make a distinction according to the aim of the strategies. On the one hand strategies may aim to influence the interactions between actors; on the other hand they may focus on the ideas or, as discussed in earlier chapters, the perceptions of actors (Chapters 4 and 5). These two conceptual distinctions, which, as we will show, can be found either implicitly or explicitly in the contributions of all authors, can help us come to grips with the diversity of possible strategic activities.

Games and Networks: Two Levels of Network Management

Strategies applied at the level of the game are aimed at influencing the specific interaction process with regard to one issue or one problem area. These strategies are part of what is called 'game management', which can be distinguished from 'network structuring'. Network structuring refers to strategies aimed at the context of a specific game – the rules, perceptions, values, the ecology of games arena, the ecology of games, the distribution of resources and the patterns of relations that are characteristic of the policy network as a whole. The common denominator of all these variables is that they are more encompassing and more enduring than one single game or one interaction process (although games can be protracted as well).

Kickert and Koppenjan (Chapter 3), as well as Klijn and Teisman (Chapter

6) explicitly use the concepts of game and network, but the underlying reasoning can also be found in the contributions of other authors. In Chapter 8 O'Toole et al. mention three strategies: bargaining and conflict resolution, influencing perceptions, and influencing the context of the game. The first two refer to game management, the last to the level of the network and perhaps to the macro context. In Chapter 4 Schaap and Van Twist deal with three levels of closedness that lie at the root of governing problems: conscious use of veto power by actors, their frames of references and the culture of a network as a whole. It is clear that these three levels correspond to the strategies mentioned by O'Toole et al. Termeer and Koppenjan in Chapter 5 focus on influencing perceptions in processes, in games. However, some of the strategies they discuss also have a bearing on policy networks. Since the levels are interconnected, this makes sense: games can be influenced indirectly, by strategies aimed at the level of the network. In Chapter 7 De Bruijn and Ten Heuvelhof distinguish between the operational and the institutional level. The operational level is the level of goal-driven behaviour in which the context is considered given and immutable. The institutional level is that of the network.

Interactions and Ideas: Two Points of Intervention

In addition to these two levels, several authors use other ways of ordering strategies, for instance by referring to 'points of intervention'. Klijn and Teisman (Chapter 6) distinguish between cognitions, actors and institutions; De Bruijn and Ten Heuvelhof (Chapter 7) between actors and their relations. Termeer and Koppenjan (Chapter 5) refer to the cognitive and social dimensions of interaction.

From the reasoning that processes in networks consist of interactions between actors and the ideas that are being exchanged, the distinction between interactions and ideas as the targets for network management seems a useful one. Strategies like covenanting, influencing perceptions, reticulist judgements with regard to information, furtherance of a common language, reframing and so on, are all concerned with the ideas or perceptions of actors. Strategies aimed at the interactions between actors include selective (de-activation, arranging, introducing certain roles, development of procedures and rules, and changing resource distributions. Table 10.1 gives an overview of the types of strategies discussed in this volume.

The Choice of Strategies for Network Management

Of course the point in making these distinctions is that they matter: not all strategies are equally effective in every situation. Because of the complex character of interaction, due to the variety in strategies and perceptions of different actors, we do not believe in the fruitfulness of suggesting a contingency scheme with regard to which strategy is appropriate in which situation. We believe network management is about making intelligent choices with regard to these strategic possibilities, taking the specific need for governance

Table 10.1   *Strategies for network management: an overview*

	Game level	Network level
Strategies aimed at ideas/ perceptions of actors	Covenanting Influencing perceptions Bargaining Development of common language Prevention of/introduction of ideas Furtherance of reflection	Reframing Changing formal policy
Strategies aimed at the interaction between actors	Selective (de-)activating Arranging Organizing confrontations Development of procedures Furtherance of facilitation, brokerage, mediation and arbitration	Network (de-)activating Constitutional reform: changing rules and resources (De-)coupling games Changing incentives Changing internal structure and position of actors Changing relations Management by chaos

into account. This means that in each situation the nature of the governance need has to be considered in order to determine the appropriate level and dimension of intervention. And of course, because levels and dimensions are interconnected, it is possible to solve certain blockages or governance problems which occur on one level or dimension by using strategies which are aimed at other points of intervention. So, closed networks may be opened up by initiating new games, just as games may be affected by influencing rules on the network level. Cognitive fixations may be influenced by introducing new actors, just as strategies aimed at perceptions may help break through social blockages. Furthermore, strategies may be used in combination, a strategical mix, in order to reinforce their impact. It is important that the network strategies fit with the nature of the problems and blockages that occur in the interaction.

10.4   Evaluating Network Management

Evaluating networks, the outcomes of processes in networks and strategies of network management elicits intense discussion. Widely differing opinions exist on the desirability and inevitability of networks, the way outcomes of processes in these networks should be evaluated and on what good management is. In this section we will address these three questions.

Opinions about Networks

Some authors consider policy networks to be closed subsystems dominated by established interest groups which lead to institutional sclerosis within the public sector (Ripley and Franklin, 1987; Marin and Mayntz, 1991; Marsh and Rhodes, 1992; Nelissen, 1993). Networks are condemned because, according to critics, they result in:

1   neglect of common interests by governments. Governments need to perform certain tasks. Participating in networks results in bargaining and compromises, as a result of which goals are not always accomplished. For instance in the field of environmental policies, the risks that environmental interests are not adequately promoted by government in networks is mentioned as one of the main objections to policy networks;

2   hindrance of policy innovations. Established procedures and vested interests will block the solution of new problems and the acceptance and implementation of new policy measures. This results not only in non-decision making and ineffective policy outcomes, but also in enduring and costly decision making processes;

3   non-transparent policy processes. Informal interaction, complex consultancy structures and overlapping administrative positions make it impossible to determine who is responsible for what decision. Collective responsibility for joint decisions will result in a situation in which nobody is accountable. Control by representative fora becomes very difficult;

4   insufficient democratic legitimacy. Interaction between civil servants and representatives of private interest groups, other governmental layers and implementing organizations makes it very hard for representative bodies to influence policy. It is not unlikely that they will be confronted with compromises that can no longer be altered.

In short, networks produce ineffective, inefficient and insufficiently legitimized policies. However, there are also arguments in their favour:

1   because of networks, interest groups and implementing organizations are involved in policy making. As a result the knowledge and information which is at their disposal will be introduced and used in the process of policy development;

2   because of the participation of the above-mentioned organizations, the societal acceptance of the policy is furthered. Implementation and enforcement will therefore be less costly and easier to effect;

3   participation of many individuals, groups and organizations indicates that a great variety of interests and values are considered, which is favourable from a democratic point of view;

4   networks make it possible for governments to address societal needs and problems despite restricted capabilities. They improve the problem solving capacity and therefore the effectiveness of government.

Of course this discussion about the desirability of policy networks is strongly determined by values, which makes it hard to arrive at a consensus. We believe that the existence of networks cannot be denied. It is far better to face this fact and try to analyse how they work, looking for ways to improve them rather than trying to ignore or abolish them. Networks are here to stay and policy science must face the challenge. It is possible that policy networks are dysfunctional, but they are not dysfunctional by definition. A lot depends on the way they function, that is to say, on the quality of the interaction processes within networks.

Therefore, improvements in the way networks operate should start with a look at how actors interact. Only when it is clear that blocked interaction within a network is endemic and not due to a specific interaction problem, is changing the network an option. Network management is about improving the quality of interaction within policy networks. That brings us to the subject of the next section: what constitute effective interactions within networks?

Evaluating Interaction Processes

Interaction within networks is sometimes viewed as a way of increasing the effectiveness of policy or as a method of effective problem solving (Scharpf, 1978; Glasbergen, 1995). This means goal attainment is the criterion used to determine the success or failure of interactions within networks.

Using goal attainment and problem solving as criteria to judge interaction processes within networks is a fallacy: these criteria are appropriate on the *operational level*, where clearly formulated goals and problems are addressed. However, interactions within networks are *strategic*: goals are not given, but sought (cf. De Bruijn and Ten Heuvelhof, Chapter 7 of the present book). Goals and aspirations are put forward in this communication process, during which objectives are mutually adapted. It therefore makes no sense to use ex ante formulated goals or policies of one of the participants, even a governmental organization, as a yardstick.

Effectiveness and efficiency used as sole criteria for successful network management may degenerate into *instrumentalism*. Network interactions are then viewed as an opportunity to avoid or break the resistance of other actors to policy proposals by putting them aside or by mobilizing proponents of the measures under discussion. Network activation then becomes a strategic move to realize otherwise unattainable goals, and games and networks become instruments or strategies of steering organizations. Goals, interests and perceptions of others are considered complications of the process of goal attainment or problem solving. In fact such an approach is exemplary of the classical hierarchical governing style.

The normative objections to instrumentalism are evident: network management becomes manipulation in the negative sense: that is, altering or conditioning the alternatives for action by other actors either implicitly or under false pretences. But there are also practical objections: instrumentalism evokes resistance and conflict and may result in blocked interaction and damaged relations.

Towards a more effective evaluation criterion: ex post satisficing   Teisman (1992) and Klijn and Teisman (Chapter 6 in this volume) state that goal attainment is not an appropriate criterion for evaluating interactions. Instead they suggest the introduction of an *ex post satisficing criterion*: the extent to which game participants consider the interaction and its results satisfactory. If simplicity is the hallmark of truth, this criterion may be considered a lucky strike. It does justice to the interactive character of games involving a variety of actors with different, ambiguous and changing goals. Furthermore, this criterion integrates effectiveness and efficiency considerations in a more comprehensive evaluation. Participants include in their judgement the extent to which their goals and problem formulations are fulfilled and weigh this 'profit' against the interaction cost in terms of investments in time, energy and money. By making an inventory of the ex post judgements of participants, this evaluation offers a far more sophisticated image of the quality of interaction than is produced by evaluation based on the attainment of ex ante goals.

However, the ex post satisficing criterion has some shortcomings. First, there is the danger of ex post rationalizing and social pressure. How sure can we be that actors are expressing their true feelings about the interactions and its outcomes and are not simply trying to save face? They have invested in interaction, and, especially with regard to their constituency, which may have had to bear the cost of the endeavour, may not be able to freely express ex post doubts. They have to 'sell' their solution, also in the evaluation phase. However, this problem can in principle be solved by thorough research into the process, its outcomes and the way these results satisfy the different goals and interests of the various actors.

This is more difficult with the problem of aggregation: the weighing of the judgements of several actors. Can they simply be added up? Are all judgements of equal value, or are the judgements of those who bear the brunt of the cost more important? What if participants vary widely in their evaluations? What if the majority are satisfied, but not those to whom the former have shifted the cost of their joint action?

The third problem is the most serious. It is the issue of demarcation: whose judgements are included in the evaluation. A major danger of joint interaction in networks is that costs are shifted to actors outside the network. Focusing on joint interests, as Klijn and Teisman do in Chapter 6, means that the impact of joint actors on third parties risks neglect. This criticism is the focal point of opponents of the network approach. An important question is how external costs (and benefits!) should be included in evaluations.

Win-win situations: the sum of ex post satisficing judgements Ex post satisficing is related to the well-known criterion of 'win-win situations' which is sometimes proposed for judging the outcomes of networks. In fact we can say that win-win situations are the sum of the individual ex post satisficing judgements of participants. But what they are, exactly, is rarely indicated and the question as to how they should be measured is often not addressed. We may even assume that the concept is not so much a yardstick for evaluation as a management tool, a method for managers to persuade actors to participate in games and to adapt their aspirations during the interaction.

What exactly is a win-win situation? Does it refer to a real increase in benefits for those involved in interaction compared to situations in which they use 'go alone strategies'? Or does it also include outcomes that imply a lowering of aspirations and a preparedness of actors to settle for less? It may even be the case that network processes help actors accept losses because: (1) they see that others accept losses as well; (2) they committed themselves to procedures which led to these losses; (3) they expect future compensation, and/or (4) they can transfer costs to parts of their constituency without jeopardizing their own position. It is clear that use of the win-win situation is susceptible to the same problems as ex post satisficing: i.e. ex post rationalizing and the problems of aggregation and demarcation.

Process criteria A way to solve some of these problems is by using process criteria. The underlying idea is that if the process of interaction is prudent, unwanted external impacts will be less likely. Effective interaction is concerned not only with results, but also with the way these results are produced. Criteria such as reliability and prudence also belong to these process values (cf. Chapter 7).

To solve the problem of demarcation, it is important to add openness as a criterion. Openness refers to the presence of a variety of actors and ideas and the access of new ideas and actors to the interaction process (Chapter 5). If a process is relatively open, parties who have had a stake in the game have a chance to articulate their interests. In such a case, there are favourable conditions for a balanced weighing of interests and points of view.

Another important process criterion is that of democratic legitimacy. The involvement of democratically chosen bodies in network interaction processes, or adequate accountability to representative bodies of government officials who participate in networks, is an additional check on the promotion of the interests of under- and unrepresented parties in networks. Notice that the ex post satisficing criterion can be used here to measure the (quality of the) involvement of representatives in interaction processes.

In Chapter 9 De Bruijn and Ringeling state that a purely procedural evaluation of interaction is as one-sided as content evaluation. Good processes do not guarantee good results. This of course is true, just as a favourable outcome does not mean that it is realized in an acceptable way. Quite rightly they argue for a combined approach, although it is not clear what they consider a more content-oriented evaluation.

As an evaluation criterion for outcomes of processes in networks, we would suggest a combination of the ex post satisficing or win-win criteria and process criteria (the most important being openness). In this way effectiveness in multi-actor terms is coupled with legitimacy and access to the policy arena, ensuring that as many interests as possible are considered. It may be an important task for public actors to make sure that the policy arena remains open and that actors whose interests are at stake are involved. We will return to this point in the next section.

Evaluating network arrangements If interactions within networks are systematically evaluated as inadequate, we may assume that there is something wrong at the network level. Our impression is that causes of failure are far too easily sought at this level. From an instrumental perspective especially, it is very easy to blame the veto power of actors for hindering goal attainment. In doing so, we ignore the possibility that it is the goal itself or the way it is pursued that is the cause of the failure. Furthermore, we must be very cautious in suggesting adaptations on this level, as they may have impacts far beyond the solution of specific interaction problems. That is why De Bruijn and Ten Heuvelhof (Chapter 7) indicate that effectiveness and efficiency considerations with regard to a particular interaction should not dominate judgements on the institutional level. Hood (1991) and Hood and Jackson (1991) state that at this level robustness of institutions is important (compare Chapter 3). Administrative structures, which include networks, should be able to resist a crisis. If conflict in a game escalates, the network structure should not break down. Furthermore, networks should be able to recover from, for instance, damage caused by conflicts at the interaction level. In other words, networks should be able to adapt to new circumstances; and actors should be able to rely on network structures, especially in difficult periods (cf. Toonen et al., 1992).

Aside from their robustness, networks can support interaction processes in other ways as well. They help make strategic interaction possible. Institutional arrangements can contribute to openness and variety. In Chapter 9 Ringeling and De Bruijn stress the importance of the institutionalization of a variety of values within the network, because of the plurality of interests and goals that are at stake in specific interaction processes. Other provisions that facilitate interactions are the availability of administrators with negotiating capabilities and mediating skills, and the existence of institutions that can take up the role of arbitrator.

Evaluating Network Management

Now that we have discussed what we consider the underlying properties of 'effective' interactions and 'good' networks, we can address the issue of evaluating network management. Network management can be judged by the extent to which it enhances the conditions for 'favourable' interaction and the degree to which the network supports these processes. Based on the idea that networks are often characterized by cooperation problems caused by the lack of a dominant decision centre, network management is considered a success if it promotes cooperation between actors and prevents, bypasses or removes the blockages to that cooperation. This can be effected by taking advantage of the opportunities and avoiding the threats which can occur at game level and through actively influencing opportunities and threats at the level of the network and its environment. This general norm for assessing network management is developed below based on seven properties which are required for 'good' network management (cf. Klijn et al., 1995).

Achieving win-win situations   Instead of concentrating on one actor achieving their objective, network management needs to address itself to improving the starting position for all those concerned. This does not mean that everyone involved will achieve their objectives to the same extent. Often it will not be possible to give all the actors a feeling of winning. In such cases, a situation can be fostered which makes non-participation in interactions less attractive than participation (Dery, 1984; Teisman, 1992: 96). Good management contributes to the stimulation of interactions which will lead to such a situation, and to breaking through the deadlocks which hinder win-win situations.

Activating actors and resources   Interaction assumes that actors are willing to invest their resources in a joint process. They therefore need to realize the attractiveness of that interaction process. Network management should concentrate on promoting that willingness and stimulating enthusiasm.

Limiting interaction costs   The costs of interaction should be kept within reasonable limits. If interaction leads to endless squabbling or trench warfare it can cause participation in the interaction to result in a waste of resources and energy. It is necessary to prevent actors becoming disillusioned after an enthusiastic start. Interaction costs should be proportionate to the stake in the game. Network management should be aimed at restructuring, avoiding or ending interactions which lead to win–lose or lose–lose situations. In addition, good management of conflicts makes heavy demands on network management. Suppressing conflicts threatens the quality and transparency of the interaction. Regulation should prevent conflicts becoming dysfunctional and destructive (Termeer, 1993).

Procuring commitment   In addition to mobilizing actors and resources, network management needs to induce those involved to make a commitment to the joint undertaking. Without these 'voluntary ties', cooperation threatens to founder on the strategic uncertainties which play a role in collective action: the danger that the impact of actions will be shifted to others or that actors will pull out at crucial moments and leave others with the risks (Olson, 1965). By procuring a form of commitment to the collective action, this danger of withdrawal can be curbed. This commitment by the parties concerned can consist of informal agreements, or more formal arrangements, for example, entering into covenants or contracts or engaging the expertise of autonomous legal advisers (Teisman, 1992).

Political-administrative management   In network management particular attention needs to be focused on political commitment. The functioning of networks, indeed, is sometimes seen as posing a threat to the position of representative bodies such as municipal councils, provincial states and parliament (Hufen and Ringeling, 1990: 251). The existence of policy networks does not mean, however, that representative bodies are by definition excluded. On the contrary, they are often part of networks. For this reason, good political-administrative management is a part of network management. It is especially important to link up the various games in which representative bodies are involved with the games which are being played elsewhere in the network. The quality of political-administrative management is determined by the manager's 'feeling' for deciding what information is relevant and choosing the appropriate time to attempt political-administrative harmonization.

The quality and transparency of the interaction   Network management needs to do justice to the quality and transparency of the interaction within networks (Majone, 1986). After all, one of the dangers connected with the functioning of networks is that external effects are produced which are damaging in the long term both to those involved in the network and to those not represented. Furthermore, it is necessary to prevent a stranglehold consensus emerging within the network which results in 'groupthink' type situations in which criticism is not accepted and risks and the external impact of decisions are ignored, with all the concomitant repercussions (Janis, 1982; 't Hart, 1990).

Prudent use of network structuring   Network structuring can be judged by the extent to which it helps protect institutional arrangements from instrumental interventions. Only when there are indications that interactions within networks are systematically blocked as a result of the structural or cultural biases at the level of the network, can network structuring be considered. In that case interventions should, if possible, be incremental, because of the danger of destroying existing 'social capital'. Furthermore, institutional reform should procure institutional values such as robustness, openness, pluralism and facilitating capacities.

10.5 The Role of Public Actors in Networks

The approach presented in this book, which focuses on the options of governments in managing networks, may give the erroneous impression that this phenomenon is the exclusive domain of the public sector. Since government is just one of the actors in a network, network management is an activity that can involve public as well as private actors. However, it is this assumption ascribed to the network approach, that the government is 'an actor among actors', which receives most criticism. In this section we explore the scope of this position and its consequences for the status of public actors.

The Special Position of the Government

The network approach by no means presumes that governments are *like* other actors. Governments have certain resources at their disposal and work to achieve certain goals, which means that they often occupy a unique position that cannot be filled by others. Some of the resources which determine this unique role include: sizeable budgets and personnel, special powers, access to the mass media, a monopoly on the use of force and democratic legitimation. Access to these resources generally means that governments have considerable power. This is not an indication, however, that public actors are superior to other actors. At issue in the network approach is not the power difference between actors, but the notion that no one actor can define the strategic space of any other actor (though they can influence it).

Besides access to these specific resources, governments are also generally charged with special tasks. Based on the principle of the 'primacy of politics' which is rooted in the notion of the 'government as representing the people', they are supposed to serve the public interest. This public interest entails a number of functions that are typically 'governmental' in nature, for example, responsibility for the stability and security of the nation in order to protect its citizens against internal and external danger, and enabling the smooth functioning of society. Government is also responsible for the authoritative embodiment of values and for settling social conflicts. In addition, it is a producer of social goods and services, and must solve problems which are generally perceived as its responsibility. Finally, the government is guardian of a number of social and democratic values. These special tasks mean that public actors often have less strategic leeway than non-public actors, which makes government not only unique as an actor but interdependent as well.

In fact, in dealing with this interdependence, the government encounters certain limitations as a function of its uniqueness:

- The tasks of the government define to a great extent its interdependence and often condemn it to interactions with particular social and administrative partners which it is not at liberty to choose.
- In performing its duties, government is frequently not allowed to 'goal bargain'. In this respect, it often does not have the option of carrying out tasks through negotiation.
- This effect is reinforced because governments are bound, by their institutional setting, to the norms and rules they wish to impose on others: principles of good management, consideration for minorities and adversaries, working within the guidelines of democratic regulations, etc. Where other actors are able to operate with strategic ingenuity, governments are expected to show exemplary behaviour.
- Because of its public nature and the democratic monitoring to which governmental actions are subject, more demands are made on its strategic interactions. The actions of the public sector are scrutinized by the watchful eye of the media.
- More generally, government is not only expected to operate effectively and efficiently, its actions must also be legitimate: they must be 'backed' by politics, but there must also be social acceptance of public policy, if only to avoid the danger of political mobilization.

Strategic Options for Governmental Organizations

What is the implication of this unique status for the functioning of governments in network-like situations? First is the possibility that they choose not to join in networks and will want to impose their ideas and goals on other social actors. Seen from a more classical liberal democratic viewpoint, such an attitude is to be expected from public organizations. De Bruijn and Ringeling in Chapter 9 argue that governments, faced with the choice between effectiveness and legitimacy, would do well to choose the latter, since illegitimate actions are ultimately at the cost of effectiveness. The question is, to what extent is this strategic option realistic, given the often strong interdependencies between public actors on the one hand and private and semi-private actors on the other?

Second, governments may decide to perform their tasks within networks using various forms of public–private or public–public cooperation, since there is no conflict per se between effectiveness and legitimacy. Often, entering into dialogue with social organizations is considered quite legitimate. Reference can be made to the accommodation policy style, which in this century, in many fields and a variety of countries, has led to the creation of respectable consultative bodies to mediate between government and the social sector. We explicitly mention public–public cooperation, because it is entirely possible that the various public institutions, in performing their specialized tasks, come into contact with other governmental bodies in networks. But not every relationship with other social and administrative actors is acceptable or – given the existing culture – tolerable. A case in point is the fight against organized crime. Where intergovernmental relations are concerned, supervisory relationships can interfere with establishing alliances based on cooperation.

Third, government can, as network manager, try to facilitate interaction processes relating to certain problems or policy projects or, in the case of blockages and stagnation, get things going again through mediation and arbitration. The fact that government is supposed to protect the public interest, safeguard democratic values and be publicly accountable for its actions frequently makes it acceptable to others as a game manager or network builder. However, it is not always sensible for governmental organizations to let themselves be forced into that role, which suggests an impartiality often impossible to realize. The government frequently has a functional interest in interaction processes. The example of the Dutch Ministry of Housing, Physical Planning and the Environment was given earlier. The ministry functioned as project leader during the planning phase of the expansion of Schiphol Airport in the second half of the 1980s. This position made it very hard for the ministry to protect environmental interests at the same time. When public authorities who serve as mediators also try to actualize their own objectives, this can have serious consequences for their credibility precisely because the legitimacy they possess as mediators is based on their independent status.

Fourth, the government seems perfectly suited to the role of network builder given its responsibility for maintaining stability and security, and due to its special authority. Incidentally, this does not mean that it is in any position to arrive at an effective institutional design, since the necessary knowledge and information are not always available.

Finally, we should point out the danger of these four potential roles becoming muddled. This may occur for opportunistic reasons or if the government is not yet comfortable in a new role and, in the middle of an enterprise, reverts to old routines. Ten Heuvelhof (1993) mentions the risk of alternating between the policy styles of imposition and negotiation. We have already referred to the danger of pursuing an objective while acting as game manager. Network builder and game manager are not necessarily compatible either. Clearly, confusion of roles leads to misunderstandings with other actors, which could prove costly for the perceived reliability and legitimacy of the government.

The Role of Government Redefined

The special role of the government is often defended using the argument that public actors represent 'the public interest'. But what exactly does this mean? In principle, there are two possible answers. The first is that public actors must ensure that policy processes and political processes are carried out according to the rules of democracy. We agree with this notion. We think that public actors in networks are eminently suited to the task of ensuring a careful and equitable balance of interests. Therefore they should present themselves as network managers dedicated to the process. The norm of openness discussed earlier is an important touchstone in this regard. By opening up the procedure to interests affected by the policy process, the public actor enables the testing of policy proposals. It is the role of the public actor to find solutions able to withstand the test of criticism and which have as broad support as possible. This requires a government which actively participates in policy network processes and, alert to other interests, works towards tenable solutions.

Second, the term 'public interest' can refer to the content of policy processes. It can mean that the objectives of public bodies are superior to those of other actors. The argumentation is that public agencies, mandated by elections (i.e. the will of the people) are presented with a package of goals representing the general interest. The political science and public administration research of the last 50 years has, however, shown that the aggregation of individual preferences for governmental objectives by means of integral balancing of interests by elected bodies is problematic and that the functioning of democratic institutions is far from optimal. This will have consequences for our understanding of the concept of public interest: governmental goals cannot be unconditionally considered legitimate and superior to the goals of other actors. Therefore this view of the public interest needs adjustment. Goals of public actors are not by definition better than those of other actors. There is also the complication that within networks there is frequently a variety of public actors pursuing a variety of goals, raising the question of which of these actors represents the 'true' public interest. The objectives of public actors have to be tested in interaction processes, in which ideas are criticized and interests balanced.

In an effort to give meaning to the notion of public interest, we keep coming back to the importance of processual criteria such as openness and democratic procedures or to the importance of a package of goals created by a process of critical social testing. This is, in our opinion, where the challenge lies for a modern governmental organization that can no longer appeal to 'naturally bestowed authority', but which tries to achieve socially relevant results in situations of interdependence on other actors. The challenge is then, in interaction with those actors, to develop and realize policy that can engage social support, withstand the test of criticism and mobilize other actors to policy efforts. Public agencies fulfil a double role in that process. They must guide its course by for example seeing that under- and non-represented interests participate in the game, as well as contributing to the resolution of problems by trying to form a coalition committed to a particular solution. These roles have a conflictive relationship which requires a balancing act if the organizations are to successfully and simultaneously fulfil them.

The image of the role of governmental organizations in public administration presented in this discussion on network management is quite different from the notion of a retreating government currently popular in practice and theory. It is different in two respects. First, this image refines the notion of a government in retreat. The public organization which acts as network manager will assume a detached position in certain respects. This detachedness applies on the one hand to the functional objectives which can no longer be unconditionally embraced. In situations of mutual interdependence it is unthinkable that *one* actor exclusively determines the substance of collective solutions; it is unavoidable that other actors will have a role in determining policy content. On the other hand, when governments acknowledge this interdependence, other actors will necessarily be engaged in problem solving. The outcome will be delegation and the creation of more policy space for these actors to play a constructive part.

Second, the role of network manager means that public agencies will be actively involved in the interaction processes between actors, a role that is not at all consistent with the image of a strategically withdrawing public authority. In fact, by assuming the initiative for the arrangement and course of interaction processes, governments can take the offensive, promoting and helping to effect substantive solutions.

All this sets high standards for public organizations. Network management assumes a flexible government which is able to communicate with other (groups of) actors and, on the basis of the acquired information, is able to learn from the situations that arise, to mobilize the necessary innovative resources in order to make joint solutions possible.

10.6 Three Perspectives on Networks and Network Management

In an attempt to introduce some order into the variety of ideas on the subject, we suggest three perspectives on network management: an instrumental, an interactive and an institutional perspective. Although these approaches share the perception that governance takes place within networks and that these networks provide opportunities for governance, they differ in the interpretation of the consequences of networks for governance.

The three perspectives should be regarded as 'ideal types' in the sense that they do not appear in their 'pure' form in reality. Neither the work of scientists, nor the actions of practitioners will fit neatly within any of the categories. Therefore, where we classify authors in one of the categories we are aware of the fact that we do not do justice to them. Often the positions they take are more sophisticated and they combine elements of all three approaches. On the other hand, authors do not always give equal weight to these different elements, so classifying them on the basis of their dominant characteristics helps us understand the variation of ideas, concepts and positions with regard to network management by specifying the underlying assumptions.

First, there is the instrumental perspective. This is a refinement of the classical rational 'steering' approach, and an adaptation of that approach to the more complex network situation. The main line of argumentation is that the 'first generation' instruments of the 'classical' approach, the usual regulatory instruments, do not apply in a network situation because they are uniform and one-sided. In a network situation 'second generation' (more refined) instruments should be applied, like incentives, communicative instruments or covenants. The modern refined 'second generation' instrument perspective clearly emanates from the basic instrumental approach.

In this book De Bruijn and Ten Heuvelhof are clear representatives of this perspective. This is not surprising, as both authors developed the 'second generation instruments' approach. They define network management as 'creating conditions under which goal-oriented processes can take place' (Chapter 7 of this book).

Second, the interactive perspective stresses the multitude of actors, and particularly their interactions. Network management is not about attaining governmental goals, but about contributing to and providing conditions for the process of finding a common purpose. This perspective has clear European roots in that the work of the French sociologists Crozier and Friedberg is one of the main sources of inspiration. Chapter 6 by Klijn and Teisman on strategies and games, although it contains some elements of the institutional approach, is a conceptual and theoretical elaboration of this perspective too. Termeer and Koppenjan's chapter (Chapter 5), in which they discuss the opportunities for facilitating interaction processes fits within this perspective. O'Toole et al. in Chapter 8 also discuss interactions between actors, but they focus on networks as vehicles for problem solving, which is a more instrumental approach. Their contribution falls somewhere between the two perspectives.

Third, the institutional perspective emphasizes the role of institutions which shape the strategies and intentions of actors. Network management has to build upon these institutions. Proponents of this approach include the American neo-institutionalists like Ostrom (1990), who stresses the importance of using existing 'social capital' and March and Olsen, in addition to typical European structuralists like Rhodes and Scharpf and systems theory authors like Luhmann and Teubner. In this book, Chapter 4, by Schaap and

Van Twist, which deals with the closedness of networks, falls within this perspective.

Notice that the underlying dimensions of the typology, the roots of this division, apparently relate to the tripartite 'intellectual roots' of the network perspective – the policy, organization and political science roots – that Klijn distinguished in his survey in Chapter 2. The instrumental perspective has its roots in policy science and especially in approaches to policy instruments and implementation studies. The interactive perspective obviously relates to the 'process' approach in policy science and to some approaches in organization theory such as that of Crozier and Friedberg. The 'institutional' perspective is related to the British political science approaches of 'policy communities', to the European theory of neo-corporatism, and to the interorganizational theories. Below the three perspectives are elaborated more systematically.

The Instrumental Perspective

The 'instrumental' perspective is sometimes criticized for reintroducing the model of top-down steering by a single actor, the very denial of which forms the starting point of the network approach. How can one agree that there is no single dominant actor, but many and various actors with different goals, positions and strategies, yet focus on the steering instruments of one actor? The response to this criticism is essentially that 'not-white' does not automatically mean 'black'. As explained in the introductory chapter of this book the network approach can be located in the intermediate area between the extremes of monocentric monorational hierarchical steering on the one hand, and horizontal situations of complete autonomy of all actors on the other. The denial of the first extreme does not imply the acceptance of the latter.

Notice that the concept of 'steering actor' and 'goal-oriented influence' does not imply denial of the presence of other actors and other goals. This perspective differs from the classical steering approach because it accepts the inevitable presence of networks. It represents more or less the attitude of the *realpolitiker*, who understands that reality makes it impossible to attain his goals without compromise, but tries to make the best of it. This perspective represents a refinement of the classical steering approach rather than a radical break with it. However elaborate, refined and modern the perspective may be, it does stick to the fundamental assumption of one 'steering' actor who exercises goal-oriented influence on other actors – target groups. As in this approach, the instrumental-oriented network manager is trying to accomplish his own goals or to solve problems according to his own perceptions.

The instrumental perspective is primarily interested in the steering potential of one actor in this network, generally government, for two reasons. The first is the empirical argument that in public policy networks governmental actors apparently occupy a special position because of their specific public tasks, roles and powers. The second is the normative argument that government should play a special role due to its function in a democratic and legal state (compare Chapter 9).

With its focus on goal attainment, the instrumental perspective of network management interfaces well with the experience and ambitions of actors in the practice of administration. Moreover, this viewpoint is consistent with the normative notion of the role of government and the resulting steering ambitions. A weak point of the approach relates to the extent to which it addresses the limitations set on goal-oriented operations in networks. Its contribution is that through good network management, goals which the government would not have been able to realize on its own, are brought within range. But there are limits to these possibilities: the interests, objectives, perceptions and strategies of other actors and the institutional context in which they function. Furthermore, it can be stated that this perspective, more than the others, is vulnerable to the pitfall of instrumentalism: not enough attention is given to the interests and goals of others, which can result in the deterioration of relations between actors and the loss of commitment to a collective approach to problem solving.

The Interactive Perspective

In the interactive perspective the problem of collective action plays a central part. No single actor in the network is able to bring about a policy solution on their own. In contrast to the instrumental perspective, in this approach relations between actors are not defined in terms of controller and controlled, but in terms of a collection of actors who exercise mutual influence. The interaction forms the primary focus and object of interest in this perspective. The important theoretical concepts are actors, strategies, coalitions and games.

The concept of strategy means that actors attempt to influence the collective action. Strategies and the underlying goals are not fixed and unchangeable. Goals and strategies develop over time due to interactions and to the strategies and goals of other actors and due to learning processes in interaction. For the accomplishment of collective ends, the cooperation problem must be overcome. Goals and actions of actors should be mutually adjusted. This requires the efforts of entrepreneurs and the forming of coalitions. In order to arrive at a common decision or product it is necessary to form a 'winning' coalition. The stakes, rules, goals and strategies of other actors form the 'logic of the situation'. Based on this 'rationality' the actors adjust both their strategies and their goals. Too large a gap between individual and collective 'rationality' endangers the 'game'. Stagnation, the threat of lose-lose situations and destructive games may be the result. Network management is aimed at facilitating the process of interaction, including conflict reduction and conflict resolution.

The interactive perspective offers options for tackling problems which actors cannot solve alone and where conflicts of interest block collective performance. Furthermore, this perspective links up with important values such as those of a pluralistic, active society where government and society work together to resolve common problems. A weak point of the approach is the meagre attention given to the institutional aspects of policy networks.

Some objections can be made concerning the empirical validity of the interactive perspective. Its fundamental assumption is the absence of hierarchical ordering relations and the freedom of choice of actors, though some proponents of this approach include an analysis of the context of the game by looking at rules and the institutional embeddedness of games (Klijn, 1996). Nevertheless the strong emphasis on strategic behaviour and interactions tends to overlook the role of contextual factors and institutional influences. Although the interactive perspective does not state that all actors are equal, institutional factors like asymmetrical relations, dominating sets of rules, closedness, and exclusion, do not always get the attention they deserve. The communal interest of the parties working for a common goal is central to this approach. The consequences of interactions for actors outside the game or network have not received enough attention. These weak points restrict the empirical validity and practical applicability of the interactive perspective in administrative reality.

The Institutional Perspective

The institutional perspective emphasizes the role of institutions and institutionalization. In its approach to processes within networks it looks at the role of rules and organizational frameworks, which set the stage for strategy formulation and interactions. In this respect this perspective differs from the interactive approach. It also differs from the instrumental approach in that it is less interested in the attainment of specific goals. The perspective emphasizes the multi-purpose character of organizational arrangements and networks. Therefore, its attention is directed more at the impact of interactions on relations and the way institutional frames work.

Whereas an instrumental perspective will consciously seek to change organizational arrangements and an interactive perspective will disregard this option, an institutional perspective will put it into perspective. On the one hand any plans to consciously alter arrangements will be rejected, because of the limited possibilities and high costs. On the other hand, adapting institutions is not altogether impossible, according to proponents of this approach like Elinor Ostrom (Kiser and Ostrom, 1982; Ostrom, 1986). In other words, managing collective action in this view is about looking for the right incentive structures and the right set of rules. Because of the complexity and uncertainties surrounding processes of reorganization and their irreversibility, these attempts should be undertaken as prudently as possible. They should have an incremental character, in order to build on, rather than destroy, existing 'social capital'.

Furthermore, because this perspective examines network steering in its specific institutional context, it helps us gain insight into the conditions for management in networks. The picture presented of the potential for network management will be less optimistic than that of the other perspectives, because not all contextual factors can be manipulated.

This means that under certain conditions the chances for successful network management will be unfavourable, despite the efforts of a dedicated manager. The institutional perspective will help to specify the factors that contribute to its success or failure.

The criteria for good network management used in this approach are varied. Mention can be made of the degree of clarity and openness in the structure of the network, the contingency between network and social-administrative task domains around which they are organized and the representation of a variety of social values.

The advantage of the institutional approach is that it, more than the instrumental or interactive perspectives, offers points of departure for developing strategies focused on the structural and cultural features of the network. On the other hand, these features are manipulable only to a limited extent, which hinders the direct relevance of insights.

Review of the Three Perspectives

The three perspectives guide the judgements and actions of practitioners and policy scientists. They are implicit, use different assumptions and lead to different diagnoses and remedies of interaction situations in policy networks. In Table 10.2 the three perspectives are presented.

Table 10.2   *Three perspectives on network management*

	Instrumental perspective	Interactive perspective	Institutional perspective
Research focus	Improving steering conditions	Cooperation	Network arrangements and their impacts
Level of analysis	'Focal organization'	Interaction	Network
View of policy networks	Closed and pluriform object of steering	Horizontal interaction situation	Product and context of interaction and governance
Characterization of network management	Strategic use of steering strategies and treatment of dependency relations	Furtherance of co-operation and prevention and removal of blockages	Incremental adaptation of incentive structure and rules of structure and culture of policy networks
Criteria for evaluation and prescription	Effectiveness; problem solving	Satisfying policy, consensus and openness	Openness, robustness, facilitating interaction
Strong points	Applicability; consistent with steering ambitions of government	Realization of cooperation in pluralistic situations	Interest in role of institutions and institutionalization; cautions against easy structural solutions
Weak points	Limits to steering in connection with goal-orientedness; danger of instrumentalism	Too little attention to institutional aspects; danger of particularism	Limited manipulability of variables

Each of the perspectives has its strong points, but they are also biased. As mentioned before, they are ideal types, which do not exist in the real world. In practice, most approaches will combine elements of more than one perspective, which may mean that they are based on conflicting assumptions. It is therefore important to clarify the differences between the perspectives and their underlying assumptions. By distinguishing these perspectives the quality of analyses, evaluations and prescriptions can be improved. In the next section the strategies for network management dealt with earlier in this chapter are related to the three perspectives. From the point of view of, for instance, the instrumental perspective, different strategies will be used to influence points of intervention at both the game and network levels, than are used in the interactive or institutional approaches.

Strategies and Perspectives on Network Management

What can be said about the relation between these strategies and the three perspectives on network management? One characteristic of the instrumental perspective is that strategies are aimed at the realization of fixed goals or the solution of a well-defined problem. Cognitive strategies at the level of the game will be aimed at influencing the perceptions and goals of participants in one specific direction. This can be done by bargaining or persuasion. In its extreme form this style of network management can result in presenting selective or biased information, in order to try and manipulate the course of the game. This is what Scharpf (1978) calls 'negative coordination'.

Selective (de-)activation is a strategy directed at influencing the interactions between actors, which fits very well into an instrumental perspective. Only those actors who are indispensable for the attainment of certain goals or policy measures are invited to participate in interaction processes. Others are not invited and may even be excluded.

From an instrumental perspective strategies at the level of the network will be aimed at the internalization of certain norms and values in order to facilitate the adoption and implementation of certain policies. Attempts to restructure the network also fit within this scheme, and in this way it is possible to break the veto power of certain actors who are not committed to particular objectives. An example of such an instrumental endeavour is the discussion in the Netherlands about the duration of large-scale infrastructural projects. Because of the lengthy discussions about these projects, the Dutch economy is said to have an adverse competitive position compared to its neighbours. Therefore an attempt is being made to limit the legal options for local government to block these projects as well as restricting procedures for appeal by civilians.

From an interactive perspective strategies at the game level aimed at influencing ideas and perceptions of actors would increase the opportunities for common action, such as creating variety in order to find a common ground for joint decision making. Furthermore these strategies would certainly include attempts to collectively adjust strategies and goals. Social strategies would not necessarily be directed at selective (de-)activation, but at assuring commitment to joint action and the establishment of ad hoc arrangements to ensure and express this commitment. With regard to strategies at the network level, the interactive perspective is not very promising. Because of the policy freedom of actors in games, structural and cultural characteristics of networks are not considered crucial to the improvement of the quality of interaction.

The institutional perspective focuses on the long-term impact of game strategies on the network as a whole. Therefore it is not so committed to particular goals or policies, but instead stresses the importance of enhancing social and cognitive variety (compare Chapter 5). With regard to strategies at the network level, this perspective advocates resisting inclinations to change the network in order to achieve short-term goals or policies (compare Chapter 7). The closedness of networks and the self-referentiality of actors limit the possibilities for consciously adapting the network structure and culture. What is more, because of the unpredictable but probably irreversible impacts of these changes in the long run, they should be used with utmost prudence in other areas as well. Cognitive strategies on this level will include the development of a common language and facilitation of learning processes across the boundaries of coalitions, configurations and organizations (compare Sabatier, 1988). Strategies aimed at changing interactions will be directed at changing rules and incentive structures. All strategies will be directed at furthering conditions for cooperation. They will also be of an incremental nature: constitutional reform that does not destroy, but uses the existing 'social capital' within the current arrangement (Ostrom, 1990). Table 10.3 gives an overview of strategies and perspectives on management.

Table 10.3   *Strategies and perspectives on management*

	Instrumental perspective	Interactive perspective	Institutional perspective
Cognitive game strategies	Goal-oriented influencing perceptions	Mutual adaptation of perceptions and goals	Furtherance of cognitive variation
Social game strategies	Selective (de-)activation	Facilitating and arranging interactions	Furtherance of social variation
Cognitive network strategies	Internalization	Stressing policy freedom of actors	Furtherance of learning across boundaries
Social network strategies	Network adaptation for goal attainment/ problem solving	No perfect organization	Incremental adaptations; using existing social capital

10.7 Conclusions and Perspectives

The illusion prevalent in the heyday of the welfare state, that government would be able to 'steer' societal policy processes by means of integral planning methods, and the illusion of the state as the central governing authority in society, have given way to a more realistic view of government as one of many interdependent social actors influencing complex policy processes, i.e. the concept of a policy network. As stated in the introduction to this book the policy network concept was the scientific answer to the empirical observation of failing top-down hierarchical government control.

This book has contributed to the network approach by presenting the 'network' concept as a vehicle to improve public policy and governance rather than to explain its failures and limitations. The concept is not used in a negative anti-government sense but in a positive sense by exploring its potentials for public policy making and governance, and thus restoring trust and confidence in the abilities of the public sector. We believe the network concept indeed offers major opportunities for the management and governance of public policy processes. The realistic assumption that society cannot simply be controlled by government, and that public policy is much more complex, does not necessarily lead to the conclusion that policy is usually a mess and governance generally fails. Network management may well be complex, but it also offers new opportunities that go far beyond the limits of the alternatives: a relapse into traditional top-down steering and the strategic retreat of government from the societal domain. The central issue in this book, therefore, is the relevance of public policy networks for governance and public management.

Besides contributing to the discussion among policy scientists and practitioners on governance and public management, this book has also explored possible strategies for managing networks and critically considered their implications. In so doing we have clarified the concept of network management and hopefully contributed to the process of theory formation on policy networks as well as on governance and public management in (post)modern, complex societies.

The third contribution has been to bring some theoretical order to the great variety of ideas and models of networks and their management by developing three theoretical perspectives on network management: the instrumental, the interactive and the institutional approaches. Without pretending that this categorization is the final word on the subject, we claim that it offers an analytical vehicle for the further theoretical development of the field. The preceding discussion of the three perspectives in this concluding chapter has shed ample light on their analytical usefulness.

In recent years interest in the concept of 'policy networks' has spread among policy scientists and practitioners in the public and private sectors. We believe that the importance of thinking in terms of networks and network management will grow in the future. Societies are becoming more complex and the plurality of values is increasing, as well as their mutual interdependence. These trends are also apparent in countries previously under a centralized system. These social developments are supported by administrative trends. In many European nations a move towards small, active governments is taking place. These governments, more than in the past, will have to try and accomplish their tasks in tandem with other actors. New information technologies are increasing the visibility of the public sector and giving social actors the opportunity to influence policy with their knowledge. Developments such as European integration are causing a progressive administrative consolidation. Within the EU, the relative power positions of the administrative levels will shift, but there is no doubt that their mutual interactions will intensify with the extension of the European administrative layer. All these developments lead to the conclusion that interactions and arrangements supporting these interactions in the public sector will become more significant in the near future. The need for effective governance of these interactions, and therefore for new forms of public management such as network steering, will increase as well. There is, consequently, a lot of interest at present in the further development of theories on governance and public management and in the application of these theories in administrative practice.

In this book we have tried to show that, as a body of theoretical ideas, the network approach is quite well developed. And although, as usual, there are some differences between the various proponents of this approach, the general ideas are quite clear. Although the emphasis has been on theory and conceptual development, it must not be forgotten that, in the Netherlands as elsewhere, many explorative empirical studies have been conducted which served as the basis for theory development. Like real life, theories are never 'complete' or 'finished'. They develop through continuous discussion between policy scientists and practitioners where they are constantly refined, renewed and improved. An interesting question concerns the future of theoretical development of the network perspective. In principle all three perspectives which have been dealt with in Part III – the instrumental, interactive and institutional approaches – can be elaborated further. The question is whether refinement of the theory should continue along these three lines, based on the idea that the perspectives are best developed in mutual competition, or whether a synthesis should be sought. Although we believe that a combination of perspectives can work well, we do not think that all efforts at synthesis will necessarily be productive.

Combining the instrumental with the interactive perspective does not seem a very fruitful way to improve the network approach to governance and public management. In many ways these two perspectives make opposite assumptions about the potentials and modes of governance and the position of public actors. Furthermore, the institutional perspective is the least developed of the three concerning steering issues, which is the particular focus of our interest. Therefore the greatest theoretical and conceptual progress is achieved by combining the institutional perspective with one of the others which deals more explicitly with questions of governance. In so doing, the institutional perspective can add something vital to the other two. It focuses on the constraints and potentials of the institutional setting. More than the others, it addresses the nature of the influences of networks on interaction processes. As can be seen in the development of public administration in general, issues concerning institutions and institutionalization will undoubtedly dominate discussions on networks and network management.

These contributions to network management in the public sector and the consequences of networks for governmental steering are hardly definitive. The three perspectives sketched here indicate that the integration of scientific views which underlie the concept is limited and that there is still much to do. With regard to the management strategies elaborated, we still lack sufficient insight into their completeness, interconnection, implementability and functioning. Empirical research can help us in this. Furthermore, the significance of institutional aspects of policy networks and the role of the macro context have not received enough attention in these contributions until now. Also, little is known about the parameters of network management. This involves questions such as: in what contexts is the method applicable? In what circumstances is there a likelihood of success? When should network management be replaced by other steering methods such as hierarchical measures or self-regulation? Future research into the functioning of policy networks and network management should address these questions. On the basis of practical experience and theoretical results such as those discussed in this book, it can be stated that policy networks not only set limits on the steering potentials of government, but, by means of conscious and carefully applied network management, offer opportunities for confronting the many social and administrative problems in the domain of public administration.

Bibliography

Agranoff, R.I. (1986) *Intergovernmental Management. Human Services Problem-Solving in Six Metropolitan Areas*, State University of New York Press, Albany, NY.

Agranoff, R.I. (1990a) *Frameworks for Comparative Analysis of Intergovernmental Relations*, SPEA Occasional Paper no. 26, Indiana University.

Agranoff, R.I. (1990b) 'Responding to human crises: intergovernmental policy networks', in R.W. Gage and M.P. Mandell (eds), pp. 57–80.

Aiken, M. and Hage, J. (1968) 'Organizational interdependence and intra-organizational structure', *American Sociological Review*, 33(6) pp. 912–30.

Aldrich, H.A. (1979) *Organizations and Environments*, Prentice-Hall, Englewood Cliffs, NJ.

Aldrich, H.A. and Whetten, H.D.A. (1981) 'Organization-sets, action-sets and networks: making the most out of simplicity', in P.C. Nystrom and W.H. Starbuck (eds), pp. 385–408.

Allison, G.T. (1971) *Essence of Decision: Explaining the Cuban Missile Crisis*, Little, Brown, Boston, MA.

Allison, G.T. (1980) 'Public and private management: are they fundamentally alike in all unimportant aspects?', *OPM document*, 127–51–1, pp. 27–38. Reprinted in R.T. Golembievsky and F. Gibson (eds) (1983) *Readings in Public Administration*, Houghton Mifflin, Boston, MA. pp. 1–19.

Alt, J.E., Putnam, R.D. and Shepsle, K.A. (1988) 'The architecture of linkage'. Paper presented at the Workshop on Connected Games: Theory, Methodology, and Applications, Max-Planck-Institut für Gesellschaftsforschung, Cologne.

Arentsen, M.J., Klok, P.-J. and Schrama, G.J.I. (1994) *De milieuvergunning in bedrijf (fase 2): Een onderzoek naar het effect van de milieuvergunning op het milieugedrag in vier bedrijven*, Centrum voor Schone Technologie en Milieubeleid, Universiteit Twente, E.C.W. achtergrondstudie nr.21, Enschede.

Argyris, C. and Schön, D.A. (1978) *Organizational Learning: A Theory of Action Perspective*, Addison-Wesley, Reading, MA.

Auctoin, P. (1990) 'Administrative reforms in public management: paradigms, principles, paradoxes and pendulums', *Governance*, 3(2) pp. 115–37.

Axelrod, R. (1984) *The Evolution of Cooperation*, Basic Books, New York.

Bachrach, P. and Baratz, M.S. (1962) 'Two faces of power', *American Political Science Review*, 56(4) pp. 947–52.

Bardach, E. (1977) *The Implementation Game: What Happens after a Bill Becomes Law?*, MIT Press, Cambridge, MA.

Barret, S. and Fudge, C. (1981) *Policy and Action: Essays on the Implementation of Public Policy*, Methuen, London.

Barry, B. and Rae, D.W (1975) 'Political evaluation', in F.I. Greenstein and N.W. Polsby (eds), *Handbook of Political Science*, part 1, Addison-Wesley, Reading, MA. pp. 337–401.

Bekke, A.J.G.M. and de Vries, J. (eds) (1991) *Tussen politiek en klantenkring*, Vakgroep Bestuurskunde Rijksuniversiteit Leiden, Leiden.

Benson, J.K. (1978) 'The interorganizational network as a political economy', in L. Karpik (ed.), pp. 69–102.

Benson, J.K. (1982) 'A framework for policy analysis', in D.L. Rogers and D.A. Whetten (eds), pp. 137–76.

Berg, J.Th.J. (1991) 'Politieke wetenschap en de derde macht', *Acta Politica*, 26(3), pp. 257–68.

Berger, L. and Luckmann, T. (1966) *The Social Construction of Reality: A Treatise in the*

Sociology of Knowledge, Penguin Books, Harmondsworth, UK.

Beus, J.W. de and van Doorn, J.A.A. (eds) (1986) *De geconstrueerde samenleving: vormen en ge-volgen van classificerend beleid*, Boom, Meppel.

Blau, P.M. (1982) 'Structural sociology and network analysis: an overview', in P.V. Marsden and N. Lin (eds), pp. 273–80.

Bozeman, B. (1987) *All Organizations Are Public: Bridging Public and Private Organizational Theories*, Jossey-Bass, San Francisco, CA.

Bozeman, B. (ed.) (1993) *Public Management: The State of the Art*, Jossey-Bass, San Francisco, CA.

Braybrooke, D. and Lindblom, C.E. (1963) *A Strategy of Decision: Policy Evaluation as a Social Process*, Free Press, New York.

Bressers, J.Th.A., O'Toole Jr., L.J and Richardson, J. (1994) 'Networks as models of analysis: water policy in comparative perspective', *Environmental Politics*, 3(4), pp. 1–23.

Brown, L.D. (1983) *Managing Conflict at Organizational Interfaces*, Addison-Wesley, Reading, MA.

Bruijn, J.A., de (1990) *Economische Zaken en economische subsidies: een instrumentele en orga-nizatorische analyse van de toepassing van economische subsidies*, Vuga, Den Haag.

Bruijn, J.A., de and ten Heuvelhof, E.F. (1991) *Sturingsinstrumenten voor de overheid: over com-plexe netwerken en een tweede generatie sturingsinstrumenten*, Stenfert Kroese, Leiden.

Bruijn, J.A., de and ten Heuvelhof, E.F (1995) *Netwerkmanagement: strategieën, instrumenten, normen*, Lemma, Utrecht.

Bruijn, J.A., de, and Hufen, J.A.M. (1992) 'Instrumenten van overheidsbeleid', *Beleidswetenschap*, 6(1), pp. 69–93.

Burns, T.R. and Flam, H. (1987) *The Shaping of Social Organization: Social Rule System Theory with Application*, Sage, London.

Cangelosi, V.E. and Dill, W.R. (1965) 'Organizational learning: observations toward a theory', *Administrative Science Quarterly*, 10(2), pp. 175–203.

Cawson, A. (1985) 'Varieties of corporatism: the importance of the meso-level of interest inter-mediation', in A. Cawson (ed.), *Organized Interests and the State: Studies in Meso-Corporatism*, Sage, London. pp. 1–21.

Cawson, A. (1986) *Corporatism and Political Theory*, Basil Blackwell, Oxford.

Chandler, A. (1962) *Strategy and Structure: Chapters in the History of Industrial Enterprise*, MIT Press, Cambridge, MA.

Chandler, A.D., Jr. (1977) *The Visible Hand: The Managerial Revolution in American Business*, Harvard University Press, Cambridge, MA.

Cobb, R.W. and Elder, C.D. (1983) *Participation in American Politics: The Dynamics of Agenda-building*, Johns Hopkins University Press, Baltimore, MD. First published in 1972.

Cohen, I.J. (1989) *Structuration Theory: Anthony Giddens and the Constitution of Social Life*, St Martin's Press, Oxford.

Cohen, M.D., March, J.G and Olsen, J.P. (1972) 'A garbage can model of organizational choice', *Administrative Science Quarterly*, 17(1) pp. 1–25.

Cook, K.S. (1977) 'Exchange and power in networks of interorganizational relations', *The Sociological Quarterly*, 18(1) pp. 62–82.

Couwenberg, S.W. (1988) 'Besturen op afstand: particulier corporatisme als bestuursvorm', in J.G.A. van Mierlo and L.G. Gerrichhauzen (eds), *Het particulier initiatief in de Nederlandse verzorgingsmaatschappij: een bestuurskundige benadering*, De Tijdstroom, Lochem. pp. 20–50.

Crozier, M. and Friedberg, E. (1980) *Actors and Systems: The Politics of Collective Action*, University of Chicago Press, Chicago.

Dahl, R.A. (1970) *After the Revolution? Authority in a Good Society*, Yale University Press, New Haven, CT.

Damen, L.J.A. (1993) 'Publiek–private samenwerking en convenanten: een juridisch perpectief', in J.Th.A. Bressers et al. (eds), *Beleidsinstrumenten bestuurskundig beschouwd*, Van Gorcum, Assen. pp. 93–106.

Derksen, W. (1989) 'De werkelijkheid van de terugtred', in W. Derksen, Th.G. Drupsteen and

W.J. Witteveen (eds), *De terugtred van de regelgevers: meer regels, minder sturing?*, W.E.J. Tjeenk Willink, Zwolle. pp. 17–33.

Dery, D. (1984) *Problem Definition in Policy Analysis*, University Press of Kansas, Kansas.

Doelen, F.C.J. van der (1989) *Beleidsinstrumenten en energiebesparing: de toepassing en effectiviteit van voorlichting en subsidies, gericht op energiebesparing in de industrie van 1977 tot 1987*, Vakgroep bestuurskunde: Universiteit Twente, Enschede.

Doelen, F.C.J., van der (1993) *Instrumenten voor energiebesparing*, Vakgroep bestuurskunde: Universiteit Twente, Enschede.

Donaldson, G. and Lorsch, J.W. (1983) *Decision-making at the Top: The Shaping of Strategic Direction*, Basic Books, New York.

Dryzek, J.S., and Ripley, B. (1988) 'The ambition of policy design', *Policy Studies Review*, 7(4), pp. 705–19.

Dunn, W.N. (1981) *Public Policy Analysis: An Introduction*, Prentice-Hall, Englewood Cliffs, NJ.

Dunsire, A. (1993) 'Modes of governance', in J. Kooiman (ed.), pp. 21–35.

Easton, D. (1965) *A Systems Analysis of Political Life*, Wiley, New York.

Edelman, M. (1971) *The Symbolic Uses of Politics: Mass Arousal and Quiescence*, Markham Publishers, Chicago.

Edelman, M. (1977) *Political Language: Words that Succeed and Policies that Fail*, Academic Press, New York.

Eijk, C., van der and Kok, W.J.P. (1975) 'Nondecisions reconsidered', *Acta Politica*, 10(3) pp. 277–301.

Ellwein, T., Hesse, J.J., Mayntz, R. and Scharpf, F.W. (eds) (1987) *Jahrbuch zur Staats- und Verwaltungswissenschaft*, Nomos, Baden-Baden.

Elmore, R.F. (1979) 'Backward mapping: implementation research and policy decisions', *Political Science Quarterly*, 94(4) pp. 601–16.

Elster, J. (1986) Introduction, in J. Elster, *Rational Choice*, Basil Blackwell, Oxford.

Emerson, R.M. (1962) 'Power-dependence relations', *American Sociological Review*, 27, pp. 31–40.

Emery, F.E. and Trist, E.L. (1965) 'The causal texture of organizational environments', *Human Relations*, 18(1) pp. 21–32.

Erickson, B.H. (1982), 'Networks, ideologies and belief systems', in P.V. Marsden and N. Lin (eds), pp. 159–72.

Falcone, G. and Padovani, M. (1992) *Cosa nostra*, De Kern, Baarn.

Finer, S.E. (1970) *Comparative Government*, Allen Lane/The Penguin Press, London.

Fisher, R. and Ury, W. (1981) *Getting to Yes: Negotiating Agreement without Giving In*, Houghton Mifflin, Boston, MA.

Forester, J. (1989) *Planning in the Face of Power*, University of California Press, Berkeley.

Foucault, M. (1971) *L'ordre du discours*, Gallimard, Paris.

Foucault, M. (1976) *De orde van het vertoog*, Boom, Meppel.

Foucault, M. (1984) 'What is an author?' in P. Rabinow (ed.), *The Foucault Reader*, Pantheon Books, New York. pp. 101–20.

Fox, C.J. and Miller, H.T. (1996) *Post-modern Public Administration: Towards Discourse*, Sage, London.

Freeman, J.L. (1965) *The Political Process: Executive Bureau–Legislative Committee Relations*, Random House, New York.

Freeman, J.L. and Parris Steevens, J.P. (1987) 'A theoretical and conceptual re-examination of subsystem politics', *Public Policy and Administration*, 2(1) pp. 9–24.

Friend J.K., Power, J.M. and Yewlett, C.J.L. (1974) *Public Planning: The Inter-corporate Dimension*, Tavistock, London.

Gage, R.W. and Mandell, M.P. (eds) (1990) *Strategies for Managing Intergovernmental Policies and Networks*, Praeger, New York.

Gerrichhauzen, L.G. (1990) *Het woningcorporatiestelsel in beweging*, Delftse Universitaire Pers, Delft.

Giddens, A. (1979) *Central Problems in Social Theory*, Macmillan, London.

Giddens, A. (1984) *The Constitution of Society: Outline of the Theory of Structuration*, Macmillan, London.

Glasbergen P. (ed.) (1995) *Managing Environmental Disputes: Network Management as an Alternative*, Kluwer, Dordrecht.

Godfroy, A.J.A. (1981) *Netwerken van organizaties: strategieën, spelen, structuren*, Vuga, Den Haag.

Grant, W.P., Paterson, W. and Whitson, C. (1988) *Government and the Chemical Industry*, Clarendon Press, Oxford.

Guba, E.G. (ed.) (1990) *The Paradigm Dialog*, Sage, Newbury Park, CA.

Gunsteren, H.R. van (1976) *The Quest for Control*, John Wiley, London.

Hajer, M.A. (1989) 'Discours-coalities in politiek en beleid: de interpretatie van bestuurlijke heroriënteringen in de Amsterdamse gemeenteraad', *Beleidswetenschap*, 3(3) pp. 242–63.

Hall, P. (1993) 'Policy paradigms, social learning and the state', *Comparative Politics*, 25(3) pp. 275–96.

Hanf, K.I. (1978) Introduction, in K.I. Hanf and F.W. Scharpf (eds).

Hanf, K.I. (1993) 'Enforcing environmental laws: the social regulation of co-production', in M. Hill (ed.), *New Agendas in the Study of the Policy Process*, Harvester Wheatsheaf, New York. pp. 88–109.

Hanf, K.I. and O'Toole Jr., L.J. (1992) 'Revisiting old friends: networks, implementation structures and the management of interorganizational relations', *European Journal of Political Research*, 21(1–2) pp. 163–80.

Hanf, K.I. and Scharpf, F.W. (eds) (1978) *Interorganizational Policy Making: Limits to Coordination and Central Control*, Sage, London.

Hanf, K.I. and Toonen, Th.A.J. (eds) (1985) *Policy Implementation in Federal and Unitary Systems*, Nijhoff, Dordrecht.

Hanf, K.I., Hjern, B. and Porter, D. (1978) 'Local networks of manpower training in the Federal Republics of Germany and Sweden', in K.I. Hanf and F.W. Scharpf (eds), pp. 303–44.

Hardin, G. and Baden, J. (1977) *Managing the Commons*, Freeman, San Francisco.

Harmon, M.M. and Mayer, R.T. (1986) *Organization Theory for Public Administration*, Scott Foresman, New York.

Hart, P. 't (1990) *Groupthink in Government: A Study of Small Groups and Policy Failure*, Proefschrift Leiden, Leiden.

Heclo, H. (1978) 'Issue networks and the executive establishment', in A. King (ed.), *The New American Political System*, American Enterprise Institute for Public Policy Research, Washington, DC., pp. 87–124.

Heclo, H. and Wildavsky, A. (1974) *The Private Government of Public Money*, Macmillan, London.

Hedberg, B. (1981) 'How organizations learn and unlearn', in P.C. Nystrom and W.H. Starbuck (eds), pp. 3–27.

Heisler, M.O. (1974) 'Patterns of European politics: the European "Polity" model', in: M.O. Heisler (ed.), *Politics in Structure: Structures and Processes in Some Postindustrial Democracies*, David McKay, New York.

Heuvelhof, E.F., ten (1993) *Gedragsnormen voor overheden in horizontale structuren: het alterneren van eenzijdige en meerzijdige vormen van sturing bij de toepassing van het principe 'de vervuiler betaalt'*, Vuga, 's–Gravenhage.

Hirschman, A.O. (1970) *Exit, Voice and Loyalty: Responses to Decline in Firms, Organizations and States*, Harvard University Press, Cambridge, MA.

Hirst, P. (1990) *Representative Democracy and its Limits*, Polity Press, Cambridge.

Hirst, P. (1994) *Associative Democracy: New Forms of Economic and Social Governance*, Polity Press, Cambridge.

Hjern, B. and Porter, D.O. (1981) 'Implementation structures: a new unit for administrative analysis', *Organizational Studies*, 3, pp. 211–37.

Hood, C.C. (1983) *The Tools of Government*, Macmillan, London.

Hood, C.C. (1991) 'A public management for all seasons', *Public Administration*, 69(1) pp. 3–19.

Hood, C.C. and M. Jackson (1991) *Administrative Argument*, Dartmouth, Aldershot.

Hufen, J.A.M. and Ringeling, A.B. (eds) (1990) *Beleidsnetwerken: overheids-, semi-overheids- en particuliere organizaties in wisselwerking*, Vuga, Den Haag.

Hunt, J.W. (1972) *The Restless Organization*, Wiley, Sydney.

Hupe, P.L. (1993) 'The politics of implementation: individual, organizational and political co-production in social services delivery', in M. Hill (ed.), *New Agendas in the Study of the Policy Process*, Harvester Wheatsheaf, New York. pp. 130–51.

Janis, I.L. (1982) *Groupthink: Psychological Studies of Policy Decisions and Fiascoes*, Houghton Mifflin, Boston, MA.

Jenkins, K., Caines, K. and Jackson, A. (1987) *Improving Management in Government: The Next Steps*, HMSO, London.

Jordan, G. (1990a) 'Sub-governments, policy communities and networks: refilling the old bottles?', *Journal of Theoretical Politics*, 2(3) pp. 319–38.

Jordan, G. (1990b) 'Policy community realism versus "New" institutionalist ambiguity', *Political Studies*, 38(3) pp. 470–84.

Jordan, G. and Schubert, K. (1992) 'A preliminary ordering of policy network labels', *European Journal of Political Research*, 21(1–2) pp. 7–27.

Karpik, L. (ed.) (1978) *Organization and Environment*, Sage, London.

Kaufmann, F.X., Majone, G. and Ostrom, V. (eds) (1986) *Guidance, Control and Evaluation in the Public Sector: The Bielefeld Interdisciplinary Project*, Walter de Gruyter, Berlin.

Kelman, S. (1987) *Making Public Policy: A Hopeful View of American Government*, Basic Books, New York.

Kettl, D.F. (1988) *Government by Proxy*, Congressional Quarterly, Washington, DC.

Kickert, W.J.M. (1991) *Complexiteit, zelfsturing en dynamiek*, Samsom H.D. Tjeenk Willink, Alphen a/d Rijn.

Kickert, W.J.M. (ed.) (1993a), *Veranderingen in management en organisatie bij de rijksoverheid*, Samsom H.D. Tjeenk Willink, Alphen a/d Rijn.

Kickert, W.J.M. (1993b) 'Complexity, governance and dynamics: conceptual explorations of public network management', in J. Kooiman (ed.), pp. 191–204.

Kickert, W.J.M. (1993c) 'Autopoiesis and the science of (public) administration: essence, sense and nonsense', *Organization Studies*, 14 pp. 261–78.

Kickert, W.J.M., Aquina, H. and Korsten, A. (eds) (1985) *Planning binnen perken*, Kerckebosch, Zeist.

Kingdon, J.W. (1984) *Agendas, Alternatives and Public Policies*, Little, Brown, Boston, MA.

Kirlin, J.J. (1984) 'A political perspective', in T. Miller (ed.), *Public Sector Performance: a Conceptual Turning Point*, Johns Hopkins University Press, Baltimore, MD. pp.161–93.

Kiser, L. and Ostrom, V. (1982) 'The three worlds of action: A metatheoretical synthesis of institutional approaches', in E. Ostrom (ed.), *Strategies of Political Inquiry*, Sage, Beverly Hills, CA. pp. 197–222.

Klijn, E.H. (1993) 'Regels in beleidsnetwerken: de institutionele context van beleid', in O. van Heffen en M.J.W. van Twist (eds), *Beleid en wetenschap*, Samsom H.D. Tjeenk Willink, Alphen a/d Rijn., pp. 229–40.

Klijn, E.H. (1996) 'Analysing and managing policy processes in complex networks: a theoretical examination of the concept policy network and its problems', *Administration and Society*, 289(1) pp. 90–119.

Klijn, E.H. and Teisman, G.R. (1991) 'Effective policy making in a multi actor setting: Networks and steering', in R.J. in 't Veld et al., pp. 99–112.

Klijn, E.H. and Teisman, G.R. (1992) 'Besluitvorming in beleidsnetwerken: een theoretische beschouwing over het analyseren en verbeteren van beleidsprocessen in complexe beleidsstelsels', *Beleidswetenschap*, 6(1) pp. 32–51.

Klijn, E.H. and van der Pennen, T. (1992) 'Changes in local housing policy networks: re-establishing relations of housing authorities and housing associations' (Risbo paper B10). Paper presented at the international research conference 'European Cities: Growth and Decline', The Hague, April 13–16.

Klijn, E.H., Koppenjan, J.F.M. and Termeer, C.J.A.M. (1995) 'Managing networks in the public sector: a theoretical study of management strategies in policy networks', *Public Administration*, 73(3) pp. 437–54.

Koningsveld, H. and Mertens, J. (1986) *Communicatief en strategisch handelen: inleiding tot de handelingstheorie van Habermas*, Coutinhou, Muiderberg.

Kooiman, J. (ed.) (1993) *Modern Governance: New Government – Society Interactions*, Sage, London.

Kooiman, J. and Eliassen, K.A. (1987) *Managing Public Organizations: Lessons from Contemporary European Experience*, Sage, London.

Koppenjan, J.F.M. (1991) 'Falen en leren rond de paspoortaffaire: de hardleersheid van een ministerie geanalyseerd', *Beleid en maatschappij*, 18(1) pp. 20–30.

Koppenjan, J.F.M. (1993) *Management van de beleidsvorming: een studie naar de totstandkoming van beleid op het terrein van het binnenlands bestuur*, Vuga, 's-Gravenhage.

Koppenjan, J.F.M. and Hufen, J.A.M. (1991) 'Autopoiesis, learning and governmental steering', in R.J. in 't Veld et al., pp. 171–82.

Koppenjan, J.F.M., de Bruijn, J.A. and Kickert, W.J.M. (1993) *Netwerkmanagement in het openbaar bestuur*, Vuga, Den Haag.

Koppenjan, J.F.M., Ringeling, A.B. and te Velde, R.H.A. (eds) (1987) *Beleidsvorming in Nederland*, Vuga, 's-Gravenhage.

Kramer, R.M. (1981) *Voluntary Agencies in the Welfare State*, University of California Press, Berkeley.

Kuhn, T.S. (1962) *The Structure of Scientific Revolutions*, University of Chicago Press, Chicago.

Landau, M. (1969) 'Redundancy, rationality and the problem of duplication and overlap', *Public Administration Review*, 29(3) pp. 346–50.

Laumann, E.O. and Knoke, D. (1987) *The Organizational State: Social Choice in National Policy Domains*, University of Wisconsin Press, Wisconsin.

Laumann, E.O. and Pappi, F.U. (1976) *Networks of Collective Action: A Perspective on Community Influence System*, Academic Press, New York.

Lawrence, P.R. and Lorsch, J.W. (1967) *Organization and Environment: Managing Differentiation and Integration*, Harvard University Press, Cambridge, MA.

Lehmbruch, G. and Schmitter, P.C. (eds) (1982) *Patterns of Corporatist Policy-making*, Sage, London.

Lehning, P.B. (1991) *Beleid op niveau: over de architectuur van overheidsinterventie*, Boom, Meppel.

Levine, S. and White, P.E. (1961) 'Exchange as a conceptual framework for the study of interorganizational relationships', *Administrative Science Quarterly*, 5, pp. 583–601.

Levy, A. and Merry, U. (1986) *Organizational Transformation: Approaches, Strategies, Theories*, Praeger, New York.

Lindblom, C.E. (1965) *The Intelligence of Democracy: Decision Making through Mutual Adjustment*, Free Press, London.

Lindblom, C.E. (1979) 'Still muddling not yet through, *Public Administration Review*, 39,6, pp. 517–23.

Lindblom, C.E. and Cohen, D.K. (1979) *Usable Knowledge: Social Science and Social Problem Solving*, Yale University Press, New Haven, CT.

Lipsky, M. (1980) *Street-Level Bureaucracy: Dilemmas of the Individual in Public Services*, Russell Sage Foundation, New York.

Litwak, E. and Hylton, L.F. (1962) 'Interorganizational analysis: a hypothesis on co-ordinating agencies', *Administrative Science Quarterly*, 6(4) pp. 395–420.

Lorsch, J.W. (1975) 'Environment, organization and the individual', in A.R. Negandhi (ed.), pp. 77–89.

Loth, M.A. (1991) 'Schuld en solidariteit: over de collectivering van aansprakelijkheid', in A.M. Hol and M.A. Loth, *Dilemma's van aansprakelijkheid*, W.E.J. Tjeenk Willink, Zwolle. pp. 21–36.

Lowi, T.J. (1963) 'American business, public policy, case studies and political theory', *World Politics*, 16, pp. 677–715.

Luhmann, N. (1982) *The Differentiation of Society*, Columbia University Press, New York.

Luhmann, N. (1984) *Soziale Systeme: Grundriss einer allgemeinen Theorie*, Suhrkamp, Frankfurt am Main.

Luhmann, N. (1990) *Essays on Self-Reference*, Columbia University Press, New York.

Lynn, L.E. (1981) *Managing the Public's Business: The Job of the Government Executive*, Basic Books, New York.

Lynn, L.E., Jr. (1993) 'Policy achievement as a collective good: a strategic perspective on managing social programs', in B. Bozeman (ed.), pp. 108–33.

Majone, G. (1986) 'Mutual adjustment by debate and persuasion', in F.X. Kaufmann et al. (eds), pp. 445–58.

Mandell, M.P. (1990) 'Network management: strategic behavior in the public sector', in R.W. Gage and M.P. Mandell (eds), pp. 20–53.

Mandell, M.P. (1992) 'Managing interdependencies through program structures: a revised paradigm'. Paper presented at the European Consortium for Political Research, workshop, 'Management of Interorganizational Networks', Limerick, Ireland, March 30–April 4.

March, J.G. (1962) 'The business firm as a political coalition', *Journal of Politics*, 24, pp. 662–78.

March, J.G. (1978) 'Bounded rationality, ambiguity, and the engineering of choice', *The Bell Journal of Economics*, 9(2) pp. 587–608.

March, J.G. (ed.) (1988) *Decisions and Organizations*, Basil Blackwell, Oxford.

March, J.G. and Olsen, J.P. (1976a) 'Attention and the ambiguity of self interest', in J.G. March and J.P. Olsen (1976b), pp. 38–53.

March, J.G. and Olsen, J.P. (1976b) *Ambiguity and Choice in Organizations*, Universitetsforlaget, Bergen.

March, J.G. and Olsen, J.P. (1989) *Rediscovering Institutions: The Organizational Basis of Politics*, Free Press, New York.

Marin, B. and Mayntz, R. (eds) (1991) *Policy Networks: Empirical Evidence and Theoretical Considerations*, Westview Press, Boulder, CO.

Marsden, P.V. and Lin, N. (eds) (1982) *Social Structure and Network Analysis*, Sage, London.

Marsh, D. and Rhodes, R.A.W. (eds) (1992) *Policy Networks in British Government*, Clarendon Press, Oxford.

Mascarenhas, A. and Sienkiewicz, T. (1993) *Accounts and Audit of Pension Schemes*, Butterworths, London.

Mayntz, R. (1987) 'Political control and societal problems', in Th. Ellwein, J.J. Hesse, R. Mayntz and F.W. Scharpf (eds), *Yearbook of Government and Public Administration*, Nomos, Baden-Baden. pp. 81–98.

Mayntz, R. (1993) 'Governing failures and the problem of governability: some comments on a theoretical paradigm', in J. Kooiman (ed.), pp. 9–20.

Mayntz, R., et al. (1978) *Vollzugsprobleme der Umweltpolitik: empirische Untersuchung der Implementation von Gesetzen im Bereich der Luftreinhaltung und des Gewaesserschutzes*, Kohlhammer, Stuttgart.

Milward, H.B. and Wamsley, G.L. (1985) 'Policy subsystems, networks and the tools of public management', in K.I. Hanf and Th.A.J. Toonen, pp. 105–30.

Mintzberg, H. (1979) *The Structuring of Organizations*, Prentice-Hall, Englewood Cliffs, NJ.

Mitchell, J.C. (1969) 'The concepts and use of social networks', in J.C. Mitchell (ed.), *Social Networks in Urban Situations*, Manchester University Press, Manchester. pp. 1–50.

Moore, C.W. (1986) *The Mediation Process: Practical Strategies for Resolving Conflict*, Jossey-Bass, San Francisco, CA.

Morgan, G. (1986) *Images of Organizations*, Sage, London.

Negandhi, A.R. (ed.) (1975) *Interorganization Theory*, Kansas University Press, Kansas City.

Nelissen, N.J.M. (1992) *Besturen binnen verschuivende grenzen*, Kerkebosch, Zeist.

Nelissen, N.J.M. (1993) 'Over "net" werken in netwerken', in J.F.M. Koppenjan, J.A. de Bruijn and W.J.M. Kickert (eds), *Netwerkmanagement in het openbaar bestuur: over de mogelijkheden van overheidssturing in beleidsnetwerken*, Vuga, 's-Gravenhage. pp. 169–75.

Neumann, F. (1995) *The Incorporation of Environmental Elements in Strategic Decision-making Processes in Industry: Government–Corporate Interaction from a Business Perspective*, Humanitas, Rotterdam.

OECD (1990) *PUMA: Public Management Studies*, OECD, Paris.

OECD (1993) *Public Management: OECD Country Profiles*, OECD, Paris.

Olson, M. (1965) *The Logic of Collective Action: Public Goods and the Theory of Groups*, Harvard University Press, Cambridge, MA.

Osborne, D. and Gaebler, T. (1992) *Reinventing Government: How the Entrepreneurial Spirit is*

Transforming the Public Sector, Addison-Wesley, Reading, MA.

Ostrom, V. (1980) 'Hobbes, convenant and constitution', *Publius*, 10(4) pp. 83–100.

Ostrom, E. (1986) 'A method for institutional analysis', in F.X. Kaufmann, et al. (eds), pp. 459–79.

Ostrom, E. (1990) *Governing the Commons: The Evolution of Institutions for Collective Action*, Cambridge University Press, Cambridge.

O'Toole, L.J. (1986) 'Policy recommendations for multi-actor implementation: an assessment of the field', *Journal of Public Policy*, 6(2) pp. 181–210.

O'Toole, L.J. (1988) 'Strategies for intergovernmental management: implementing programs in interorganizational networks', *Journal of Public Administration*, 11(4) pp. 417–41.

O'Toole, L.J., Jr. (1995) 'Rational choice and policy implementation: implications for inter-organizational network management'. *American Review of Public Administration*, 25(1): 43–57.

O'Toole, L.J. and Montjoy, R.S. (1984) 'Interorganizational policy implementation', *Public Administration Review*, 44, pp. 491–503.

Outshoorn, J. (1986) 'The rules of the game: abortion politics in the Netherlands', in J. Lovenduski and J. Outshoorn (eds) *The New Politics of Abortion*, Sage, London. pp. 5–26.

Pêcheux, M. (1982) *Language, Semantics and Ideology: Stating the Obvious*, Macmillan, London.

Perry, J.L. and Rainey, H.G. (1988) 'The public–private distinction in organization theory', *Academy of Management Review*, 13(2) pp. 182–201.

Pfeffer, J. (1981) *Power in Organizations*, Pitman, Boston.

Pfeffer, J. and Novak, Ph. (1976) 'Joint ventures and interorganizational interdependence', *Administrative Science Quarterly*, 21(3) pp. 398–418.

Pollitt, C. (1990) *Managerialism and the Public Services: The Anglo-American Experience*, Basil Blackwell, Oxford.

Pollitt, C. (1993) *Managerialism and the Public Services: Cuts or Cultural Change in the 1990's?*, Basil Blackwell, Oxford.

Pool, J. (1990) *Sturing van strategische besluitvorming: mogelijkheden en grenzen*, VU Uitgeverij, Amsterdam.

Poulantzas, N. (1978) *l'État, le pouvoir, le socialisme*, PUF, Paris.

Pressman, J.L. and Wildavsky, A. (1983) *Implementation: How Great Expectations in Washington Are Dashed in Oakland*, University of California Press, Berkeley. First published 1973.

Provan, K.G. and Milward, H. Brinton (1991) 'Institutional-level norms and organizational involvement in a service-implementation network', *Journal of Public Administration Research and Theory*, 1(4) pp. 391–417.

Rainey, H.G. (1991) *Understanding and Managing Public Organizations*, Jossey-Bass, San Francisco, CA.

Rapport Externe Commissie Ministeriële verantwoordelijkheid (voorz. Scheltema) *Steekhoudend ministerschap*, Tweede Kamer, 1992–1993, 21427, nr. 40–1.

Rein, M. and Schön, D.A. (1986) 'Frame-reflective policy discourse', *Beleidsanalyse*, 15(4) pp. 4–18.

Rein, M. and Schön, D.A. (1992) 'Reframing policy discourse', in F. Fischer and J. Forester (eds), *The Argumentative Turn in Policy Analysis and Planning*, Duke University Press, Durham, NC. pp. 145–66.

Rhodes, R.A.W. (1980) 'Analysing intergovernmental relations', *European Journal of Political Research*, 8(3) pp. 289–322.

Rhodes, R.A.W. (1981) *Control and Power in Central and Local Relations*, Gower, Farnborough.

Rhodes, R.A.W. (1988) *Beyond Westminster and Whitehall: The Sub-central Governments of Britain*, Unwin Hyman, London.

Rhodes, R.A.W. (1990) 'Policy networks: a British perspective', *Journal of Theoretical Politics*, 2(3) pp. 293–317.

Rhodes, R.A.W. (1997) *Understanding Governance*, Open University Press, Buckingham.

Rhodes, R.A.W. and Marsh, D. (1992) 'New directions in the study of policy networks', *European Journal of Political Research*, 21(1–2) pp. 181–205.

Richardson, J.J. (ed.) (1982) *Policy Styles in Western Europe*, Allen and Unwin, London.

Richardson, J.J. and Jordan, A.G. (1979) *Governing under Pressure: The Policy Process in a Post-Parliamentary Democracy*, Martin Robertson, Oxford.

Ringeling, A.B. (1983) *Instrumenten van overheidsbeleid*, Samson, Alphen a/d Rijn.

Ringeling, A.B. (1993) *Het imago van de overheid*, Vuga, 's-Gravenhage.

Ringeling, A.B. and Koppenjan, J.F.M. (1988) *De besluitvorming rond het nieuwe paspoort*, Tweede Kamer zitting, 20.559, no. 11.

Ripley, R.B. and Franklin, G. (1987) *Congress, the Bureaucracy and Public Policy*, Dorsey, Homewood, IL. First published 1976.

Robbins, S.P. (1980) *The Administrative Process*, Prentice-Hall, Englewood Cliffs, NJ.

Rogers, D.L. and Mulford, C.L. (1982) 'Consequences', in D.L. Rogers and D.A. Whetten (eds) pp. 32–54.

Rogers, D.L. and Whetten, D.A. (eds) (1982) *Interorganizational Coordination: Theory, Research, and Implementation*, Iowa State University Press, Ames.

Sabatier, P.A. (1986) 'Top-down and bottom-up approaches to implementation research', *Journal of Public Policy*, 6(1) pp. 21–48.

Sabatier, P.A. (1988) 'An advocacy coalition framework of policy change and the role of policy oriented learning therein', *Policy Sciences*, 21, pp. 129–68.

Sabatier, P.A. and Hanf, K.I. (1985) 'Strategic interaction, learning and policy evolution: a synthetic model', in K.I. Hanf and Th.A.J. Toonen (eds) pp. 301–34.

Sabatier, P.A. and Jenkins-Smith, H.C. (1993) *Policy Change and Learning: An Advocacy Coalition Approach*, Westview Press, Boulder, CO.

Scharpf, F.W. (1978) 'Interorganizational policy studies: issues, concepts and perspectives', in K.I. Hanf and F.W. Scharpf (eds) pp. 345–70.

Scharpf, F.W. (1989) 'Decision rules, decision styles and policy choices', *Journal of Theoretical Politics*, 1(2) pp. 149–76.

Scharpf, F.W. (1990) 'Games real actors could play: the problem of mutual predictability', *Rationality and Society*, 2(4) pp. 471–94.

Scharpf, F.W. (1991) 'Games real actors could play: the challenge of complexity', *Journal of Theoretical Politics*, 3(3) pp. 277–304.

Scharpf, F.W. (ed.) (1993) *Games in Hierarchies and Networks: Analytical and Empirical Approaches to the Study of Governmental Institutions*, Westview Press, Boulder, CO.

Scharpf, F.W., Reissert, B. and Schnabel, F. (1976) *Politikverflechtung: Theorie und Empirie des kooperativen Föderalismus in der Bundesrepublik*, Scriptor, Kronberg.

Scharpf, F.W., Reissert, B. and Schnabel, F. (1978) 'Policy effectiveness and conflict avoidance in intergovernmental policy formation', in K.I. Hanf and F.W. Scharpf (eds) pp. 57–114.

Schattschneider, E.E. (1960) *The Semisovereign People: A Realist's View of Democracy in America*, Holt, Rinehart and Winston, New York.

Schmitter, P.C. and Lehmbruch, G. (eds) (1979) *Trends toward Corporatist Intermediation*, Sage, London.

Schuyt, C.J.M. (1985) 'Sturing en het recht', in M.A.P. Bovens and W.J. Witteveen, pp. 113–25.

Simon, H.A. (1957) *Administrative Behaviour: A Study of Decision-making Processes in Administrative Organization*, Macmillan, New York.

Smith, M.J. (1992) 'The agricultural policy community: maintaining a close relationship', in D. Marsh and J.A.W. Rhodes (eds), pp. 27–50.

Soet, M.C., de (1990) 'Omgaan met milieuconflicten in de besluitvorming: de consensusbenadering voor win/win-uitkomsten', *Milieu*, 5(1) pp. 8–13.

Stever, J.A. (1988) *The End of Public Administration: Problems of the Profession in the Post-progressive Era*, Transnational Publishers, Dobbs Ferry, NY.

Stillman, R.J. (1991) *Preface to Public Administration: A Search for Themes and Direction*, St Martin's Press, New York.

Stoker, R.P. (1991) *Reluctant Partners: Implementing Federal Policy*, University of Pittsburgh Press, Pittsburgh, PA.

Stones, R. (1992) 'Labour and international finance, 1964–1976', in: D. Marsh and R.A.W. Rhodes (eds), pp. 200–48.

Streeck, W. and Schmitter, P.C. (eds) (1985) *Private Interest Government: Beyond Market and State*, Sage, London.

Stuurman, S. (1985) *De labyrinthische staat: over politiek, ideologie en moderniteit*, SUA, Amsterdam.

Susskind, L. and Cruikshank, J. (1987) *Breaking the Impasse: Consensual Approaches to Resolving Public Disputes*, Basic Books, New York.

Tak, Th. van der (1988) *Vergunning verleend: een bestuurskundige studie naar vergunningen op grond van de Wet inzake de luchtverontreiniging en de Wet algemene bepalingen milieuhygiëne*, Eburon, Delft.

Taylor, M. (1987) *The Possibility of Cooperation*, Cambridge University Press, Cambridge.

Teisman, G.R. (1992) *Complexe besluitvorming: een pluricentrisch perspectief op besluitvorming over ruimtelijke investeringen*, Vuga, 's-Gravenhage.

Termeer, C.J.A.M. (1993) *Dynamiek en inertie rondom mestbeleid: een studie naar verandering-sprocessen in het varkenshouderijnetwerk*, Vuga, 's-Gravenhage.

Teubner, G. (1982) 'Reflexives Recht: Entwicklungsmodelle des Rechts in vergleichender Perspektive', *Archiv für Rechts- und Sozialphilosophie*, 68(1) pp. 13–59.

Thompson, J.D. (1967) *Organizations in Action*, McGraw-Hill, New York.

Thompson, G.J., Frances, R., Levacic and Mitchell, J. (eds) (1991) *Markets, Hierarchies and Networks*, Sage, London.

Toonen, Th.A.J. (1981) 'Gemeentelijke invloed in een vervlochten bestuur', *Beleid en maatschap-pij*, 8(11) pp. 334–341.

Toonen, Th.A.J. (1987) *Denken over binnenlands bestuur*, Vuga, Den Haag.

Toonen, Th.A.J. and Ten Heuvelhof, E.F. (1993) *Democratiseren door convenanten*, Rijksuniversiteit Leiden/Erasmus Universiteit Rotterdam, Leiden.

Toonen, Th.A.J., Raadschelders, J.C.N. and Hendriks, F. (1992) *Meso-bestuur in Europees per-spectief: de Randstadprovincies uit de pas?*, Vakgroep bestuurskunde: Rijksuniversiteit Leiden, Leiden.

Truman, D. (1964) *The Governmental Process*, Knopf, New York.

Tsebelis, G. (1990) *Nested Games: Rational Choice in Comparative Politics*, University of California Press, Berkeley.

Turk, H. (1970) 'Interorganizational networks in urban society: initial perspectives and com-parative research', *American Sociological Review*, 35(1) pp. 1–18.

Twist, M.J.W., van (1991) *Organizeuren: configuratiepraatjes en autopoëzie*, RISBO, Rotterdam.

Twist, M.J.W., van and Termeer, C.J.A.M. (1991) 'Introduction to configuration approach: a process theory for societal steering,' in R.J. In 't Veld et al. (eds), pp.19–30.

Varela, F.G., Maturana, H.R. and Uribe, R. (1974) 'Autopoiesis, the organization of living sys-tems, its characterization and a model', *Biosystems*, 6(5) pp. 187–96.

Veld, R.J., in 't (1989) *De verguisde staat*, Vuga, 's-Gravenhage.

Veld, R.J., in 't, Schaap, L., Termeer, C.J.A.M. and van Twist, M.J.W. (eds) (1991) *Autopoiesis and Configuration Theory: New Approaches to Societal Steering*, Kluwer, Dordrecht.

Veld, R.J., in 't, Schaap, L. Termeer, C.J.A.M. and van Twist, M.J.W. (1992) *Recommendations for a Process Standard concerning the Environmental and Feasibility Analysis as Laid Out in the Dutch Covenant on Packaging*, Erasmus Universiteit, Rotterdam.

Voogt, A.A. (1991) 'Managing of social cognitive configurations in a multiple context', in R.J. in 't Veld et al. (eds), pp. 67–79.

Waarden, F., van (1992) 'Dimensions and types of policy networks', *European Journal of Political Research*, 21(1–2) pp. 29–52.

Wamsley, G.L. (1985) 'Policy subsystems as a unit of analysis in implementation studies: a strug-gle for theoretical synthesis', in K.I. Hanf and Th.A.J. Toonen (eds), pp. 71–96.

Wamsley, G.L. (1990) *Refounding Public Administration*, Sage, Newbury Park, CA.

Warren, R.L., Burgunder, A.F., Newton, J.W., and Rose, S.M. (1975) 'The interaction of com-munity decision organizations: some conceptual considerations and empirical findings', in A.R. Negandhi (ed.), pp. 167–181.

Wassenberg, A. (ed.) (1980) *Netwerken: organizatie en strategie*, Boom, Meppel.

Wassenberg, A. (1984) 'Netwerken binnenste buiten', in A.J.G.M. Bekke and U. Rosenthal (eds), pp. 199–213.

Weick, K.E. (1979) *The Social Psychology of Organizing*, Random House, New York.

Wildavsky, A. and Tenenbaum, E. (1981) *The Politics of Mistrust: Estimating American Oil and Gas Resources*, Sage, Beverly Hills, CA.

Wilks, S. and M. Wright (1987) *Comparative Government Industry Relations*, Clarendon Press, Oxford.

Williamson, O.E. (1985) *The Economic Institutions of Capitalism*, The Free Press, New York.

Williamson, P.J. (1989) *Corporatism in Perspective*, Sage, London.

Wright, D.S. (1983) 'Managing the intergovernmental scene: the changing dramas of federalism, intergovernmental relations and intergovernmental management', in W.B. Eddy (ed.) *Handbook of Organization Management*, Marcel Dekker, New York. pp. 417–54.

Wright, M.W. (1988) 'Policy community, policy network and comparative industrial policies', *Political Studies*, 36(4) pp. 593–612.

Wouden, H.C., van der (1990) *De Dynamiek van Beleid: Onbetaalde Arbeid en Theorieën over Beleid*, ICG Printing, Dordrecht.

Author Index

Subject Index